Prospects for pragmatism

Frank Ramsey on Red Pike in the Lake District in 1925.
(Courtesy of Mrs Lettice Ramsey)

Prospects
for pragmatism

ESSAYS IN MEMORY OF
F. P. RAMSEY

Edited by D. H. MELLOR

CAMBRIDGE UNIVERSITY PRESS

Cambridge
London New York New Rochelle
Melbourne Sydney

Published by the Press Syndicate of the University of Cambridge
The Pitt Building, Trumpington Street, Cambridge CB2 1RP
32 East 57th Street, New York, NY 10022, USA
296 Beaconsfield Parade, Middle Park, Melbourne 3206, Australia

First published 1980

Phototypeset in V.I.P. Bembo by
Western Printing Services Ltd, Bristol

Printed and Bound in Great Britain
at The Pitman Press, Bath

British Library Cataloguing in Publication Data
Prospects for pragmatism.

1. Pragmatism – Addresses, essays, lectures
I. Ramsey, F. P. II. Mellor, David Hugh
144'.3   B832   80–49881

ISBN 0 521 22548 5

Contents

v

Preface

The occasion of this volume is the fiftieth anniversary of the death of F. P. Ramsey in 1930 at the age of twenty-six. All the essays in it have been produced for the occasion by writers who have been influenced by Ramsey's work. This seemed an apt way to mark the tragically early death of the finest of even that remarkable generation of Cambridge thinkers. Hagiolatry, however, has not been our object, nor has hagiography. We have not all set out to defend Ramsey, nor primarily indeed to write about his work. We have written about it because that is usually still the best way to debate the issues that concern us.

We have not tried to match the range of Ramsey's thought. In particular, mathematics and economics have been left out, despite the current interest in his work on those subjects. We confine ourselves to philosophical questions which Ramsey himself addressed; philosophy being, as his friend and editor R. B. Braithwaite put it, Ramsey's vocation if not his profession. So there is at least a professional unity to the volume; but the unity of Ramsey's philosophy gives it, I hope, more than that. His philosophical work was of a piece in more than originality and depth. He called himself a pragmatist, and he developed that outlook in various fields of philosophy. The outlook still flourishes, although it is not of course uncontentious, nor is it always conscious. 'Pragmatism' is a crude label for subtle and far reaching doctrines, and I do not mean to exaggerate the unanimity of thinkers to whose work it can usefully be applied. But the philosophical disposition it indicates – roughly, to focus philosophy on the believing, wanting self and its consequent behaviour – is sufficiently widespread, and affects enough important issues, to be worth ascribing. And from time to time it is worth asking where and how far we can hope to gratify this disposition, what the prospects for pragmatism are. Our essays should help to answer that question for the present, while being, we hope, also of individual interest. I dare say, though, that we have improved pragmatism's prospects less than Ramsey would have wished, or would himself have done, if only he had lived.

Cambridge   D. H. M.
November 1979

Introduction

Ramsey's pragmatism centres on belief: its nature, its laws, its degrees and its objects. So therefore does this volume. Each essay tackles a problem posed by one or other of these aspects of belief.

The central question about belief is how it relates to truth. Ramsey's answer is clearly affected by his assuming that, whereas belief comes by degrees, truth does not. Haack thinks this is probably true but less obvious than Ramsey supposed. Her essay canvasses linguistic, metaphysical and methodological arguments for degrees of truth and finds them wanting. She observes that Ramsey's own theory of truth does not commit him to bivalence but that, even without it, he would have good reason to reject truth values other than 'true' and 'false'.

From degrees we turn to types of truth, the idea devised to deal with antinomies in semantics and set theory. Ramsey's type theory couples Frege's theory of concepts with Russell's treatment of classes as logical fictions, and Chihara thinks this coupling has been underrated. He shows how its Fregean foundations save it from familiar objections to Russell's theory and give a better rationale for its type restrictions. He defends the Frege–Russell–Ramsey analysis of number both against its competitors and against the common opinion that analysis is futile and that a formally adequate *ersatz* arithmetic is good enough.

Ramsey's redundancy theory of truth, of all types, has been much misunderstood. It is not that truth presents no problem, merely no separate problem, since to think a belief true is just to be aware of sharing it. A redundancy theory's real problem is to say what a belief is without relying in turn on the concept of truth. It must, in particular, give the content of a belief without appeal to the mean-

ix

ing of sentences, understood as truth conditions. And if a theory of belief can do that, it should, as Loar puts it, itself "serve nicely as the foundation of the theory of meaning and of truth conditions". In search of this semantic prize, Loar sets out to construct a theory satisfying these and other Ramseyan requirements for beliefs: namely, to be interlinguistically ascribable, and to be defined by their causal relations to perception and behaviour rather than as relations to propositions, Fregean senses and the like.

Skorupski is less impressed by Ramsey's account of belief, especially the *Tractatus*-like "picture" theory of how we represent its objects. This, Skorupski thinks, only works for *de re* thoughts, and for those its problematic "mental tokens" are superfluous: Wallace's refinement of Russell's relational account will do. Such an account, he argues, also goes better with Ramsey's own view of belief as a disposition to act.

But that view too has problems. The dispositions that fix respectively the contents and the degrees of our beliefs need apparently to be governed by psychological laws of logic and subjective probability. But how then can we be illogical, as we often seem to be? And how can we criticise error, for example in our general beliefs and in our probabilistic decision making? To answer this question for general beliefs, Hookway exploits Ramsey's suggestion that a disposition, *e.g.* to judge *F*s to be *G*s, also needs linguistic expression to make it open to logical criticism. The problem of criticising degrees of belief, Hookway thinks, is that while they affect decisions, only the content of belief figures in inference conceived as a succession of Ramseyan pictures. He concludes that a more complex idea of inference is needed to explain how we monitor and assess our decisions.

One way of explaining this may be to admit "second order" degrees of belief, *i.e.* degrees of beliefs about our beliefs. This is not an idea Ramsey considered, and it has been widely suspected of incoherence or triviality. Skyrms defends it against these charges, and goes on to show how it can be used in determining how new data should affect our first order beliefs. He maintains that it shows in particular why conditionalising them is usually right, and also explains the pathological cases in which doing that is wrong.

In the following essay, I use the same idea to give a Ramseyan account of being aware of believing something, namely as believing one believes it. A dispositional theory of belief needs some such account of conscious belief in any case, and I argue that it explains in particular why the use of language needs this sort of consciousness. This account also enables me to rebut recent attacks on subjective probability as measuring how strong our beliefs actually are, as well as how strong they should be. I conclude by dealing with some difficulties raised by necessary propositions having to have subjective probabilities of 1.

Blackburn takes us from degree of belief to chance. Chance for Ramsey is an inductively sound degree of belief in, say, a coin landing heads, not the factual content of an extra belief about the toss. Similarly a law, that all Fs are G, states for Ramsey only that the habit of inferring G from any instance of F is reliable, not an extra general fact over and above the facts that this F is G, that F is G, *etc*. Blackburn sees these views as extending to law and chance Hume's treatment of cause and value as "projections" of our attitudes rather than as extra facts in the world. Such "projectivist" views, Blackburn thinks, have been unfairly dismissed – and hailed – as merely subjective. Of chance in particular he argues that the subjective theory of conditionalisation does not suffice to accommodate induction, whereas Ramsey's projectivist view does. It can, Blackburn maintains, accommodate all our realist talk about probability without having to make chances into mysterious facts, incompatible with determinism and somehow capable of causing and explaining events.

Ramsey invoked reliability in accounting for knowledge as well as for law. It is, he said, true belief got by a reliable process. Grandy rehearses the many *prima facie* advantages this has over the traditional justification requirement: no regress, immunity to Gettier counter-examples, application to mathematics, and ability to explain the scope of Goldman's causal theory. It is not, however, easy to make suitable sense of a process being reliable, especially a sense sufficient for the reliability of our knowledge of laws. We end up, Grandy thinks, either denying that we know the conjunction of all the things we know, or giving up on knowledge altogether. He prefers the latter option, regarding the idea of absolute knowledge as a conceptual hangover, like absolute space. The difference being that we so far lack a good theory of relative reliability with which to replace it.

Apart from the reliability of our knowledge of them, laws pose another problem for Ramsey, the traditional one of distinguishing them from accidentally true generalisations. Cohen thinks Ramsey's two attempts to make good this distinction differ less than he supposed. The second attempt relied on Peirce's idea of the true scientific system as what inquiry would come to in the end. This, Cohen argues, reduces to his first idea of laws as what would follow from the simplest axiomatisation of everything. Neither attempt explains what Cohen takes to be the real mark of laws, namely their supporting "ampliative" counterfactuals, *i.e.* ones whose antecedents posit more things than in reality there are. None of the familiar truth-functionalist accounts of law does this, nor do possible world accounts of counterfactuals, since they themselves need laws to order their worlds. The real difference, Cohen concludes, is epistemological. Laws support ampliative counterfactuals because they in turn are supported by eliminative induction, which tests them by varying general conditions, not just instances. Accidental generalisations, on the other hand, being supported by merely enumerative induction, can support only non-ampliative counterfactuals.

We turn finally from laws to theories, and the significance of a theory's "Ramsey sentence", which replaces its theoretical predicates with existentially quantified variables. Giedymin distinguishes Duhem's instrumentalism, which takes a theory's descriptive content to reduce to its observable consequences, from Poincaré's conventionalism, which stresses the structural element in theoretical knowledge. He thinks Poincaré was influenced in this by Hamilton, whose geometrical optics was a model of the Ramsey sentence approach. Hamilton axiomatised the common content of contemporary wave and particle theories of light without pronouncing on its nature. But unlike Ramsey, Hamilton took his theory's content to include its structure, which he supposed to reveal a real structure in the world, even though its noumenal nature remained hidden. This is the aspect of Hamilton's thought developed by Poincaré, albeit stripped of its Kantian rationale; and Giedymin sees in it also a vague anticipation of recent attempts to improve the Ramsey sentence account of scientific theory.

Readers of Ramsey will observe how little of his thought we have touched on in the essays I have thus briefly described. There is much more even to Ramsey's philosophy than his theories of the nature and contents of belief, besides what is in his economics and mathematics. But we have, I hope, done enough to illustrate how philosophically profitable the study of Ramsey's work still is. It will not, I predict, become less so in the next fifty years.

D. H. M.

1 Is truth flat or bumpy?

SUSAN HAACK

> . . . if we believe pq to the extent of $\frac{1}{3}$ and $p\bar{q}$ to the extent of $\frac{1}{3}$, we are bound in consistency to believe $\bar{p}$ also to the degree of $\frac{1}{3}$. . . . but we cannot say that if pq is $\frac{1}{3}$ true and $p\bar{q}$ $\frac{1}{3}$ true, $\bar{p}$ also must be $\frac{1}{3}$ true, for such a statement would be sheer nonsense (Ramsey 1978: 89).

My concern, in this paper, is not the claim that belief comes in degrees, but the claim that truth does not.

I think that here, as so often, Ramsey's intuitions are rather shrewd. But the issues involved are much more complex than his somewhat perfunctory dismissal of the idea of degrees of truth suggests. In the first place, the question of whether truth comes in degrees may be tackled from a linguistic, a metaphysical, or a methodological point of view; and this raises further questions about which of these approaches takes priority (*e.g.* should one reject a metaphysical theory because it requires one to override linguistic evidence, or because it obstructs the operation of a smooth and simple logical representation?). And where Ramsey himself is concerned, the question arises of what the connection is between the redundancy theory and the rejection of degrees of truth.

I shall try to say something – though often it will have to be something less than conclusive – about each of these questions. I'll take linguistic, metaphysical, and methodological considerations in turn, and then, in the final section, I shall be in a position to suggest some conclusions about whether Ramsey's view is justified.

I Linguistic considerations

Zadeh: 'true' as a fuzzy predicate. Zadeh first (1965) introduces the idea of a *fuzzy* set, *i.e.* a set to which objects may belong to any

Thanks are due to the following people for helpful comments on an earlier draft: Michael Carroll, Ivor Grattan-Guinness, Mark Helme, David Holdcroft, Douglas Odegard, Graham Priest, Jane Robertson, Lofti Zadeh, and members of the philosophy department at the University of Cape Town; to Peter Geach, for comments on the "mountain in fog" analogy; and to Rob Gill, for 'too true'.

degree between full membership and complete exclusion. (Classical set theory is thus a special case of fuzzy set theory.) A predicate which determines a fuzzy, rather than a classical, set, is a *fuzzy predicate*. 'Tall', 'old' and 'beautiful', for instance, are said to be fuzzy predicates; 'square', '6 feet tall', '76 years old', are presumably not fuzzy.

Fuzzy set theory can be used to give an interpretation of Łukasiewicz's indenumerably many-valued logic. *Fuzzy logic* proper is a further development, motivated by the additional claim that the metalinguistic predicates 'true' and 'false' are themselves fuzzy, which leads Zadeh to introduce *fuzzy truth values*, fuzzy subsets of the set of values of the base logic (Zadeh 1975; Zadeh and Bellman 1977; for critical discussion, *cf.* Haack 1978: 162–9; and 1979). Since a fuzzy predicate is one which determines a set in which there are degrees of membership, it can be said to stand for a property that comes in degrees. So if 'true' is a fuzzy predicate, truth comes in degrees.

Zadeh's claim that 'true' and 'false' are fuzzy predicates is supported, in part, by an appeal to linguistic evidence: that certain adverbial modifiers which apply to fuzzy predicates like 'tall' and which indicate the degree to which the predicate applies (*e.g.* 'very', 'not very', 'quite', 'more or less', 'slightly', 'rather', 'somewhat') also apply to 'true' and 'false'. I shall argue that Zadeh is wrong about this.

There are, however, difficulties about assessing his claim because of the heterogeneity of the predicates classed as 'fuzzy'. One might, for instance, usefully distinguish predicates where there is a corresponding numerical scale (*e.g.* 'tall', 'old', 'heavy') from those where there is not (*e.g.* 'beautiful', 'clever'); again, one might distinguish within the former category those predicates for which the locution '*n* units *F*' is acceptable (*e.g.* 'tall', 'old') and those for which it is not (*e.g.* 'heavy', 'cold'); and one might observe that in the first of these categories there are asymmetries between a predicate and its opposite (*e.g* '6 feet tall' but *'4 feet short' – I use the asterisk to mark unacceptable locutions) which might have significance for the relation between 'true' and 'false', should these be supposed to belong to this category. And these, I fear, are no more than rather coarse, preliminary classifications.

I shall try to avoid these complications by the following strategy: first, I shall argue that there are many adverbial modifiers which apply to 'tall' and not to 'true', that there are several which apply to 'true' and not to 'tall', and that the behaviour of 'quite' and 'very', which, as Zadeh claims, apply both to 'true' and to 'tall', is not such as to support the view that 'true' is a fuzzy predicate. Then I shall investigate whether this argument can be extrapolated to show that 'true' is not like 'heavy' or 'beautiful' either, before concluding that the linguistic evidence does not show 'true' to be relevantly similar to Zadeh's paradigms of fuzzy predicates.

There is another complication caused by the fact that some predicates take certain modifiers which other predicates do not, for reasons which are, I assume, irrelevant to the sorts of issue I have in mind. For example, we have 'highly intelligent' but *'highly tall', presumably because of the semantic connections between 'high' and 'tall' (*cf.* *'pretty beautiful'). I shall try to avoid placing any of the weight of the argument on modifiers whose behaviour in the relevant cases is affected by this sort of consideration.

Of the following modifiers of 'tall' (I'll call them "degree" modifiers): 'extremely', 'rather', 'fairly', 'pretty', 'relatively', 'unusually', none applies to 'true'. And of the following modifiers of 'true' (I'll call them "success" modifiers): 'absolutely', 'perfectly', 'wholly', 'almost', none applies to 'tall'.

This leaves 'quite' and 'very', which, I agree, apply to 'true' as well as 'tall'. But these two modifiers behave differently with the different predicates. When 'quite' modifies 'tall', it is roughly equivalent to 'fairly' or 'rather'. But 'quite' also modifies nonfuzzy predicates, such as 'ready', and in such uses 'quite F' does not approximate to 'rather (fairly) F', but to 'absolutely (perfectly) F' and, indeed, to 'F'; 'quite ready' is roughly equivalent to 'perfectly ready', and hence to 'ready'. Furthermore, when 'quite' modifies a nonfuzzy predicate, 'not quite F' is acceptable, whereas when 'quite' modifies a fuzzy predicate, 'not quite F' is not acceptable (*'not quite tall', unless, that is, one reads it with heavy stress, as 'not *quite* tall, ENORMOUS'; contrast 'not quite tall enough to be a policeman'). There are two distinct uses of 'quite':

(a) applying to fuzzy predicates; roughly equivalent to 'fairly' or 'rather'; *'not quite F', and;

(b) applying to nonfuzzy predicates; roughly equivalent to 'absolutely' or 'perfectly'; 'not quite F' acceptable. (*Webster's Dictionary* gives both uses; the *Oxford English Dictionary*, more conservatively, only (b). *Cf.* Bolinger 1972: 106 on affinities of 'quite' with 'altogether', 'entirely', *etc.*) In sense (a), 'quite' is a degree modifier; in sense (b), a success modifier. The behaviour of 'quite' with 'true' is clearly on the pattern of (b) rather than (a):

quite true $\neq$ *fairly true $\neq$ *rather true,

but

quite true $\simeq$ absolutely true $\simeq$ perfectly true $\simeq$ true. And 'not quite true' is perfectly acceptable. Similarly with 'false'.

What about 'very true'? According to Zadeh, 'very' is an intensifier; if $x \varepsilon F$ to degree n, $x \varepsilon$ *very* F to degree n^2. And Zadeh thinks that, just as 'very tall' is roughly equivalent to 'extremely tall', 'very true' indicates possession of a high degree of truth. But since *'extremely true', 'very true' can't mean *that*. Furthermore, when 'very' modifies a fuzzy predicate, 'not very F' is acceptable; but *'not very true'. And whereas 'very short' is the opposite of 'very tall', *'very false' is not the opposite of 'very true'. I suggest that 'very true', like 'quite true', is roughly equivalent to 'true', but with something of the pragmatic flavour of 'true, and furthermore, important'. Compare 'true enough', which suggests, not that 'p' is true to a sufficient extent (for . . . ?), but that the speaker concedes that p, but considers q more important to the issue at hand.

Those who feel that I have been cavalier in my gloss on 'very true' may ponder the sense of the idiom 'too true' (would Zadeh say that this means that $p \varepsilon True$ to degree > 1?); I dare say even they would wish to be cavalier about that! ('Too false', interestingly, can be "excessive" in the way that 'too tall' is, but 'too true' is not.)

The arguments I have offered why 'true' does not behave like 'tall' also apply, *mutatis mutandis*, to show that 'true' does not behave like 'heavy'. They cannot, however, be so straightforwardly extrapolated to contrast 'true' with 'beautiful'. 'Beautiful', like 'tall' and 'heavy' and unlike 'true', takes degree modifiers like 'extremely', 'rather', *etc.*, but it also, like 'true' and unlike 'tall' and 'heavy', takes success modifiers like 'absolutely', 'perfectly', *etc.* I think this is because 'beautiful' belongs in a category different from 'tall' and 'heavy', *and* from 'true', a category about which I shall have something more to say below (p. 7).

Despite these differences between 'tall' and 'heavy', on the one hand, and 'beautiful', on the other, it seems clear, at any rate, that the linguistic evidence does not support the claim that the behaviour of 'true' with degree modifiers shows it to be a fuzzy predicate.

Unger: 'true' as a limit predicate. Unger (1975: 47–91, 272–319) distinguishes between "limit" (or "absolute") terms, "degree" (or "relative") terms, and terms which are neither. The category of limit terms plays an important part in Unger's overall strategy, which is to argue for a radical scepticism. Typically, he argues, limit terms fail to apply to anything in the world – they represent ideals that are never achieved. And according to Unger, both 'certain' and 'true' are limit terms, and consequently fail to apply; neither certainty nor truth is attainable.

On Unger's account, a *limit* term is supposed to represent the limit approached to the extent to which some *degree* term is absent; *e.g.*, corresponding to the limit term 'flat' we have the degree term 'bumpy', and 'x is flat' is roughly equivalent to 'x is absolutely (perfectly) flat', and to 'x is not bumpy to any degree'. Both degree terms and limit terms take "modifiers of degree", but these modifiers have different senses in the two cases. With such a modifier attached to a degree term we have, *e.g.*, 'x is pretty bumpy' meaning 'x is bumpy to quite a high degree'; whereas with such a modifier attached to a limit term we have, *e.g.*, 'x is pretty flat' meaning 'x is quite close to being absolutely flat', which furthermore, implies that x is not absolutely flat. Whereas with a degree term 'very' has an intensifying effect – something very bumpy is bumpier than something just bumpy – with a limit term 'very' has a moderating effect – something very flat falls short of being absolutely flat, being only nearly flat. Both degree terms and limit terms have comparative and superlative forms, but once again these forms have different senses in the two cases. In the case of a degree term, we have, *e.g.*, 'x is bumpier than y' meaning 'x is bumpy to a higher degree than y'; whereas in the case of a limit term, we have 'x is flatter than y' meaning 'Either x is (absolutely) flat and y is (at best) close to being flat, or x is closer to being flat than y is.' If F is neither a limit term nor a degree term, it does not take modifiers of degree, nor have comparative or superlative forms.

Unger holds that the linguistic evidence shows 'true' to be a limit term. At one point he suggests that the associated degree term is 'accurate'. Usually, however, he explains "'p' is true' as "'p' is in agreement with the whole truth about everything', and suggests that the associated degree term (of which, presumably, 'true' marks the upper rather than the lower limit) is 'agrees with the whole truth about everything'. Unger believes that 'true' has comparative and superlative forms, with the sense typical of such forms for limit terms. He glosses 'what A said is truer than what B said' as 'Either what A said is true and what B said is not, or what A said is closer to being true than what B said.'

But 'false', according to Unger, belongs to a different category from 'true'. It is neither a limit term nor a degree term; it doesn't take modifiers of degree, and it doesn't have a comparative form either. The asymmetry is supposed to arise because ''p' is false' means ''p' is inconsistent with the whole truth about the world', and inconsistency with the whole truth, unlike agreement with the whole truth, is not a limit one can approach.

I think Unger is right to hold that 'true' is not a degree predicate. But the claims he makes over and above this are confused. This confusion can be brought into sharp relief by considering the behaviour of 'true' with the modifier 'very'. 'Very true', Unger correctly observes, does not indicate possession of a high degree of truth, but is roughly equivalent to 'absolutely true', and hence to 'true'. But on Unger's own theory, if 'true' were a limit term, 'very true' should mean 'very close to being (absolutely) true', and, so far from being equivalent to 'true', should imply 'not true'. So 'true' isn't a limit term, since 'very' doesn't have with it the characteristic moderating effect it is supposed to have with limit terms; it isn't a degree term, since 'very' doesn't have with it the characteristic intensifying effect it is supposed to have with degree terms; and yet it can't be neither a limit term nor a degree term, since in that case 'very' shouldn't apply to it at all! I conclude that there is something amiss with the distinction between limit and degree terms.

Unger's trichotomy must be replaced with something more sophisticated. Consider, as a step towards achieving this, the contrast between 'tall', which takes degree modifiers but not success modifiers, and 'bald' which takes both (*e.g.,* 'very', 'rather', 'pretty', 'extremely', 'somewhat', and 'quite' in sense (a), and, on the other hand, 'completely', 'absolutely', 'perfectly', 'totally', 'entirely', 'almost', 'nearly', and 'quite' in sense (b)). In the case of 'bald', I should say we have two senses or uses, in one of which 'bald' is a degree predicate, but in the other of which it indicates an extreme of the same property; I shall call it a "degree/extreme" predicate.

Now while 'bumpy', like 'tall', is a degree predicate, 'flat' like, *e.g.,* 'full', 'empty', 'pure' and, I suspect, 'certain', is a degree/extreme predicate. (So, I conjecture, is 'beautiful', which explains the anomalies of its behaviour by comparison with 'tall' and 'heavy'.)

But 'true' is, anyway, *not* like 'flat'; it can't be a degree/extreme term, for the adverbs of degree that apply to 'flat' and 'bald' do not apply to it, except for 'quite' and 'very', which, however, behave differently with 'true'. (And so, if I am right about 'beautiful', we can now tie up a loose end from p. 4; 'true' does not behave with adverbial modifiers like 'beautiful', any more than it does like 'tall' or 'heavy'.)

Achievement predicates. What seems to be needed is a category of predicates which, unlike degree and degree/extreme terms, don't take modifiers of degree, and, unlike degree terms, do take success modifiers. For 'true' doesn't take 'extremely', *etc.*, and does take 'absolutely', *etc.* Another predicate which seems to behave in this way is 'ready', which doesn't take 'extremely', 'rather', 'fairly', 'pretty' (or even 'very'), but does take 'completely', 'quite', in sense (b), and 'almost', 'nearly', 'pretty nearly', *etc.,* these last all implying 'not ready'. Interestingly, the analysis of comparatives that Unger offers for his "limit terms" seems rather suitable for 'ready', where 'x is readier than y' is roughly equivalent to 'x is more nearly ready than y'.

I'll call predicates which don't take degree modifiers but do take success modifiers "achievement predicates". What other predicates, besides 'true' and 'ready', belong in this category? For example: predicates formed from predicates of degree by the formula 'F enough to be a G' (as, 'tall enough to be a policeman'); 'shut'; 'dead'; 'overwhelmed'; 'justified'. 'Open' and 'closed' compare interestingly with 'shut'; they seem to take the modifiers typical of achievement predicates in their literal sense, as of doors and windows, but to take degree modifiers when used metaphorically, as of societies, faces, or minds. 'Finished' and 'complete' compare interestingly with 'ready'; they take the modifiers characteristic of achievement predicates when used in a narrow sense, but also take degree modifiers when used in a broader sense, equivalent to, respectively, 'polished' or 'comprehensive'.

'True' also takes a number of other modifiers, so far ignored, which call for some comment. Among these are: 'wholly', 'substantially', 'largely', 'mostly' (or 'for the most part'), 'partly' (or 'in part'), 'essentially' (or 'in essence'), 'not completely', 'not entirely', and 'not altogether', which seem to say something about the *extent* to which a statement is true; 'approximately', 'not exactly', 'not strictly', 'strictly speaking' and 'more or less', which seem to say something about a statement's *accuracy*; and 'undeniably', 'admittedly', 'allegedly', 'supposedly' and 'apparently', which seem to indicate the speaker's or some other person's attitude towards the statement in question.

One can make sense of modifiers in the first group, without needing to admit degrees of truth, by understanding them to indicate how much of a statement is true, along the lines of:

'*p*' is wholly true – all of '*p*' is true

'*p*' is largely (mostly, substantially) true – a large part of '*p*' is true

'*p*' is partly true – part of '*p*' is true

'*p*' is true in essence – the essential part of '*p*' is true.

(This, of course, requires sense to be made of the notion of part of a statement being true, which is relatively straightforward in the case of conjunctive statements, more problematic in other cases. The sensitivity of this notion to notational changes, such as the replacement of '*p* & *q*' by '*r*', is at the root of the difficulties in Popper's theory of verisimilitude; *cf.* p. 14 below.) Such locutions as 'there is some truth in . . .' and 'no less true . . .' have obvious affinities with 'largely true', *etc*. It is also worth noticing that the modifiers in this group (with the odd exception of 'substantially') work in a similar way with other adjectives appraising statements, theses, proposals, *etc.*, such as 'critical', 'favourable', 'original', 'derivative', and 'justified'.

One can make sense of the second group of modifiers as indicating that some statement other than, but related in a certain way to, the one referred to, is true, along the lines of: ' "He is 6 feet tall" is approximately true' – ' "He is approximately 6 feet tall" is true.'

And one can understand the third group as expressing the speaker's attitude, as in 'It is apparently true that *p*' *i.e.*, 'It seems that *p*', or someone else's, as in 'It is supposedly true that *p*', *i.e.*, 'Some people suppose that *p*.'

What, now, of 'probably true'? 'Probable', of course, takes modifiers of degree ('highly', 'rather', and 'quite' in sense (a), for instance), and does not take success modifiers. But the fact that probability comes in degrees certainly does not require us to suppose that the locution 'It is probably true that . . .' shows that truth comes in degrees. (Ramsey, significantly, holds that probability, which he identifies with degree of belief, is precisely *un*like truth in being a matter of degree.) 'Probably' is like 'allegedly', *etc.*, in that it modifies the whole statement in which it occurs, rather than the adjective it happens to precede. 'He is probably short like his parents' amounts to the same as 'Probably he is short like his parents', and doesn't say anything about the way in which, nor the degree to which, he is short. (Contrast 'He is very short, like his parents'.) Similarly, 'It is probably true that *p*' amounts to the same as 'Probably, it is true that *p*', and doesn't say anything about the way in which, nor the degree to which, '*p*' is true.

The significance of the linguistic evidence. Thus far, I have been considering what sort of a predicate 'true' is in current English, and arguing that there is evidence to support Ramsey's claim that it is nonsense to speak of degrees of truth.

But it is important not to overestimate the significance of this evidence. The problem isn't just that the evidence I have considered is very restricted (largely to the adjective 'true' rather than the noun 'truth', for instance, and then only to the behaviour of a relatively small range of adverbs with it), nor, even, that it is parochial (though it is a good question how much of what I have said goes for languages other than English). What is most troubling is this: it is possible that, should some theory according to which truth comes in degrees come to be widely accepted, usage might well change so as to allow 'true' to take degree modifiers (indeed, the usage of some proponents of Zadeh's enterprise *has* already changed in this way). The most that follows from my linguistic arguments is that a theory which introduces degrees of truth will require linguistic innovation, that it will be a piece of *revisionary metaphysics*. But the mere fact that it is revisionary is no objection to a metaphysical theory (*cf.* Haack 1979a). The issue will be, rather, whether any convincing arguments can be given for the proposed conceptual innovation: this is the concern of the next section.

II Metaphysical considerations

Some theories of truth, *e.g.* those in which truth is defined in terms of some property or relation which can itself come in degrees, are more congenial than others to the idea of degrees of truth. If one defines truth as, say, "copying reality" then, since there can presumably be better and worse copies, truth could, though it needn't, come in degrees. The qualification, 'though it needn't', is important; it remains open to insist that a certain standard of copying is required before a proposition counts as true, but that all propositions meeting the minimum standard qualify equally as simply true. It is because he doesn't see this that Lakoff (1975) assumes that the fact that some object-language predicates come in degrees requires that we admit degrees of truth; Zadeh, by contrast, realises that one could insist on a cut-off point, a degree of tallness such that 'x is tall' is (plain) true if x is tall to degree $\geq n$, and false otherwise. The properties expressed by some object-language predicates come in degrees; it doesn't follow that truth does too.

Tarski (1931; 1944) excludes degrees of truth; a wff is true iff it is satisfied by all sequences of objects, and since a closed formula is satisfied either by all sequences or by none, it is either plain true or plain false. However, a definition like Tarski's, but in which satisfaction came in degrees, could allow degrees of truth. (Similarly, the T-schema ('p' is true iff p') rules out non-bivalent definitions of truth provided the metalinguistic 'iff' is taken to be itself classical.)

Some writers, however, notably Bradley, have made the strong claim that the correct metaphysical theory actually *requires* the admission of degrees of truth; and it is to Bradley's argument that I now turn.

Bradley's arguments for partial truth

There are, one may say, two main views of error, the absolute and the relative. According to the former view there are perfect truths, and on the other side there are sheer errors . . . This absolute view I reject . . . Ultimately, there are, I am convinced, no absolute truths, and on the other side there are no mere errors . . . All truths and all errors in my view may be called relative, and the difference in the end between them is a matter of degree (Bradley 1914: 252).

Bradley's position is radical; he holds both, (a), that truth comes in degrees and, (b), that absolute truth, the maximum degree of truth, is unattainable. (a), of course, could be held without (b) (this is Zadeh's position, that truth comes in all degrees up to and including the maximum, complete truth), or (b) without (a) (this is Unger's position, that truth is absolute, but unattainable).

Bradley's arguments for his radical view are to the effect that a theory of truth can only be given by means of a theory of reality, and that the correct, wholistic theory of reality entails that all truths are only partial. He thus associates *wholism* with the *relative* view of truth, and *pluralism* – which allows that reality is divisible into facts in virtue of correspondence to which judgements can be perfectly true – with the *absolute* view. His arguments are all variations on the theme that truth is a relation between judgements and reality which, because of the radically disparate characters of the intended relata – the essentially fragmentary character of judgements and the essentially unitary character of reality – can never hold better than imperfectly. (There is, one might say, an incompatibility between the partners which prevents the consummation of their indefinitely protracted engagement in marriage!) The exact nature of the supposed discrepancy is not so clear. There are traces of three arguments:

(1) There cannot be the appropriate relation between judgements and reality because a judgement is itself part of reality.
(2) Judgements necessarily have a certain structure, and thus divide a reality which is essentially undivided.

But these arguments are inconsistent with one another, for, if judgements are part of reality and are essentially structured, reality, after all, has a structure. So I shall concentrate on the third argument:

(3) All judgements are implicitly conditional, and the implicit conditions of a judgement can never be sufficiently specified to make the judgement absolutely true.

Bradley writes:

all truths are in varying degrees erroneous. The fault of every judgement may be said to consist in the taking its subject too narrowly or absolutely. The whole of the conditions are not stated. And hence, according to the way in which you choose to fill in the conditions . . . the assertion and its opposite are either of them true (1914: 257).

More accurately, then, the argument may be restated like this: all judgements are less than fully specific, so that (a) their truth is a matter of degree; one can make a judgement successively *more* specific, but never *fully* specific, and so long as the conditions are not fully specified, there are conditions in which the judgement is false as well as conditions in which it is true, so that (b) complete truth is unattainable. Take 'Grass is green', for instance – Bradley would no doubt point out that *dry* grass is not green, and then that 'Adequately watered grass is green', is still not fully specific, since adequately watered grass suffering from rust disease is not green . . . and so on.

This argument is open to question at (at least) two points: it is not clear that all judgements require further specification before they are completely true, and, even in the case of judgements where this *is* needed, it is not clear why the process of specifying the conditions cannot be completed.

(i) It might reasonably be argued that, unlike general judgements, judgements about particulars do not require specification of allegedly implicit conditions. Bradley, however would insist that judgements ostensibly about particulars are really about universals (1893: 71–4; *cf.* Quine on the elimination of singular terms, 1960: §§ 37–8). But, even if this were granted, there are other kinds of judgement to which one might appeal; Bradley himself discusses a relevant example:

'It is possible to produce sparks by striking flint' is . . . offered as an instance of an unconditional truth. But the opposite of this . . . is also true. The thing . . . is possible or not possible according to the conditions, and the conditions are not sufficiently expressed in the judgement (1914: 233).

He is presumably suggesting that this judgement is true in some conditions (*e.g.* if the flint is dry and there is oxygen present) and false in others (*e.g.* if the flint is wet or there is no oxygen present). But this is surely to miss the point of the choice of a modal example, which is, presumably, that if there are *any* conditions in which one produces sparks by striking flint, then it *is* possible to produce sparks by striking flint. (The same kind of argument could be given with respect to quantified judgements.) Not all judgements are implicitly conditional.

(ii) Bradley offers no argument, but just asserts, that implicitly conditional statements can never be fully specified. His fallibilism naturally leads him to doubt that we could ever know what all relevant conditions are, but it scarcely follows that they are unstatable. This is where Bradley's holism comes in; the idea seems to be that because of the essential interconnectedness of reality the conditions which would make the judgement wholly true would have to be unrestrictedly comprehensive (not *e.g.* just about the grass and its immediate environment), so that there is no limit to what conditions could be relevant. (If this is right, holism is not a premiss of the argument that truth comes in degrees, which depends, rather, on Bradley's theory of judgement, but only of the argument that absolute truth is unattainable.) But even if one accepted all the metaphysical assumptions here, it wouldn't follow that there is no way to state the conditions so as to yield a judgement that was perfectly true, *e.g.*, as 'In certain (*or*, in appropriate) conditions, grass is green.' ('In appropriate conditions . . .' might reasonably be thought rather special, in that the resulting judgement is arguably *trivially* true. 'In certain conditions . . .' does not have this drawback.)

It might be thought that there is a more direct refutation available of the thesis that truth is unattainable: if no judgement is completely true, the judgement that no judgement is completely true is not completely true, so Bradley's thesis is self-defeating. But this attempted refutation isn't quite successful, for Bradley allows that some judgements are truer than others, and his thesis could be saved if interpreted to claim only that the thesis of the unattainability of truth is more true than rival theories of truth. (This will, admittedly, require sense to be made of 'truer', which will not, since the limit is supposed to be unattainable in principle, be a trivial matter.)

In summary: Bradley's metaphysical argument requires two premises, that all judgements are implicitly conditional, and that the relevant conditions are not completely specifiable, which are open to question even if one accepts Bradley's theories of judgement and reality. It is far from being a conclusive argument for the relative view of truth.

Approaching the truth. Bradley speaks of successive approximations to the truth, of judgements getting more true as they are more fully specified. This idea has important affinities with Popper's theory of verisimilitude (*cf.* Holdcroft forthcoming). But there are also important differences. Bradley's idea is of *partially true and partially false* judgements getting *progressively truer,* but *never reaching absolute truth;* Popper's is of *false* theories getting *progressively nearer* to, and perhaps *eventually achieving absolute* (Tarskian) *truth.*

So some writers, like Popper, deny that truth comes in degrees, but allow that some falsehoods are *closer to being true, nearer the truth,* than others. Among those who favour this idea, besides Popper (1963; 1972) is Peirce, who defined truth as the opinion that would eventually be agreed on by users of the scientific method (1877; *cf.* Haack 1976). Quine, however, criticising Peirce's idea of truth as the limit of the application of the scientific method, expresses scepticism about the whole idea of approximation to the truth.

On the face of it, there is a good deal to be said for the idea. If some sentences are more nearly true than others, there is an alternative explanation of the linguistic phenomena that have been thought to lend plausibility to the idea of degrees of truth; *e.g.*, the fact that *'pretty true' acquires a different significance in view of the acceptability of 'pretty nearly true'. (Other achievement predicates allow for degrees of nearness to *F*ness, as in 'pretty nearly ready', 'not nearly tall enough to be a policeman', *etc.*) So it is worth looking at Quine's objections.

Quine is understandably unhappy about Peirce's reliance on a supposed "canon of scientific method", and on the idea of the progress of science as an infinite process. (However, it is notable that, in an attempt to account for the role of dispositional idioms within an extensional notation, Quine himself appeals (1973) to a hypothetical "completed science".) But, more pertinently, Quine is unhappy with Peirce's use of the notion of limit:

> There is a faulty use of numerical analogy in speaking of a limit of theories, since the notion of limit depends on that of 'nearer than', which is defined for numbers and not for theories (1960: 23).

But the idea of nearness to the truth does not, as this suggests, require a numerical scale, but only an ordering (*cf.* Russell 1919: 114–16). Compare 'tall enough to be a policeman', where there is a numerical scale, and 'ready', where there is only an ordering. What is required for nearness to the truth to make sense is that there be some suitable ordering of the items (propositions, theories or whatever) which are supposed to be nearer or further from the truth.

What I have just said should not be taken as involving any commitment to the details of Popper's theory of verisimilitude, in which there are, of course, well-known difficulties (see, *e.g.*, Miller 1974; Tichý 1974; but *cf.* Mortensen 1978). It is perhaps worth my offering a brief comment on the character of those difficulties. They typically arise from the fact that relations of verisimilitude between theories are not constant under apparently trivial restatements. This character they share with a number of related problems, *e.g.*, variability of degree of confirmation as a result of logically equivalent restatement of hypotheses. So the problem with verisimilitude is not an isolated one; and this lends some plausibility to the conjecture that the trouble may lie, not in the concepts of confirmation or verisimilitude themselves, but in the assumption that they should be constant under restatement preserving logical equivalence. Quine's faith in the adequacy of an extensional language for science obliges him to lay the blame elsewhere.

My discussion of modifiers such as 'mostly', 'largely', *etc.*, has affinities with the idea that the theory of verisimilitude is trying to capture, that one theory is nearer the truth than another if more of it is true. I suspect that 'mostly', *et al.*, motivate one ordering and 'strictly', *et al.*, another; but this, in view of the intuition that one theory may be more comprehensive but less accurate than another, and that in such a case the first theory is in one way nearer and in another further from the truth than the second, need not be alarming. (Popper's analogy, of theories approaching the truth to mountaineers climbing a mountain shrouded in fog, can be appropriately extrapolated: different mountaineers may be at the same distance from the summit but from different directions.)

I have not, of course, been able to offer anything like an exhaustive survey of all possible truth-theories and their consequences with respect to degrees of truth. Even if I had, there would be the further problem that, while some might regard the fact that a certain theory excludes degrees of truth as an argument against degrees of truth, others might regard it as an argument against that theory. ("Adequacy conditions" would only postpone this difficulty, since they too stand in need of justification.) For now, however, I shall turn to methodological considerations, on the assumption that no conclusive metaphysical argument for degrees of truth has, so far, been found.

III Methodological considerations (truth and consequences)

In the absence of convincing metaphysical arguments for degrees of truth, it becomes pertinent to inquire whether there are any important methodological advantages, in terms of smoothness of logical theory, in admitting them. (But plausible metaphysical arguments, if we had found them, would, I think, override methodological considerations.)

If truth comes in degrees, need the *Principle of Bivalence* (every wff, sentence, or whatever, is either true or else false: hereafter PB) fail? Well, not every sentence will be either *plain* true or else plain false;

but if all degrees above 50% counted as degrees of truth, and all degrees below 50% as degrees of falsehood, say, then every sentence would be either true (to some degree) or false (to some degree). PB may still fail even if truth does not come in degrees, for although in that case every sentence will be either true or not true, it remains possible to hold that some sentences are *not true and not false either*. In Kripke (1975), for example, truth is only partially defined and some sentences have no truth-value, so that PB fails; but Kripke does not allow degrees of truth. So admission of degrees of truth is neither necessary nor sufficient for the failure of PB.

The *Law of Excluded Middle* ($p \lor -p$; hereafter LEM) is distinct from PB; in particular, it is possible to retain LEM while rejecting PB, as in van Fraassen's supervaluations, where wffs may be true, false or truth-valueless, but LEM, like all classical tautologies, is always assigned 'true', since it would be assigned that value whether its components were true or false (van Fraassen 1969; *cf.* Haack 1974: 64–71). Though Zadeh rejects LEM, Kamp, who also accepts degrees of truth, does not, but proposes to use van Fraassen's supervaluations in the logic of vagueness so as to preserve LEM (Kamp 1975). And LEM may fail for other reasons than the admission of degrees of truth, as in some quantum logics (*e.g.* Reichenbach 1944). So admission of degrees of truth is neither necessary nor sufficient for the failure of LEM either.

Some writers have hoped to interpret many-valued logics by means of degrees of truth; Reichenbach, for example, wants to interpret the values of his many-valued logic as representing degrees of truth, which he identifies with probabilities (notice how radically this is at odds with the sentiments expressed by Ramsey in the quotation at the beginning of this paper). But this is certainly not the only way to interpret a many-valued logic; Łukasiewicz, for example, interprets his third value as "indeterminate", and intends it to apply to future contingent statements (see his 1920). So degrees of truth are not necessary for the interpretation of many-valued logic. It might seem at least that the admission of degrees of truth is sufficient to motivate a many-valued logic; but even this is not so clear in view of the fact that in Zadeh's fuzzy logic, though there are certainly more than two truth-values (*viz*, a countable set of fuzzy subsets of the indenumerably many values of the base logic), the operations of the system are not truth functions of these values, since a compound wff may fail to have a fuzzy truth value even though its components have fuzzy truth values, so that it is not certain that the system is properly called 'many-valued' in the conventional sense.

I have expressed more sympathy with the idea of nearness to the truth than with the idea of degrees of truth; so it is worth observing that it is possible to interpret Post's many-valued logic as a calculus of partial truth in the sense in which ' 'p' is partly true' $\simeq$ 'part of 'p' is true' (see Post 1921; and Haack 1974: 62–4).

The admission of degrees of truth would obviously have an effect on the definition of logical consequence. But it need not be such as to require degrees of consequence; it is open to us to define, *e.g.*, $A \vdash B$ as 'in all interpretations the degree of truth of $B \geq$ the degree of truth of A'. (*Cf.* Maydole 1975; Priest 1979 for applications of this idea to the Sorites paradox.)

I conclude that the admission of degrees of truth is not required simply because of reservations about PB or LEM, nor to make sense of many-valued logic.

IV Ramsey

According to Ramsey, 'It is true that p' just means that p, and 'It is false that p' that not p. More complicated cases, in which the propositions said to be true are only referred to and not actually presented, are to be dealt with by means of propositional quantifiers: *e.g.*, 'Everything he says is true' means that for all p, if he asserts p, then p. The question I want to ask is whether this theory requires, or, more weakly, allows Ramsey to deny that truth comes in degrees.

Since on Ramsey's theory truth is not defined in terms of any property or relation of propositions, this question can't be tackled by investigating whether the property or relation in terms of which truth is defined admits of degrees. But this itself suggests an answer to my question: since, according to Ramsey, to say that it is true that p is not to ascribe any property to 'p', but simply to assert that p, *a fortiori* 'true' does not stand for a property that 'p' may possess in greater or lesser degree.

Another way to see what is essentially the same point is this: given that he holds that 'It is true that p' means that p, it is natural that Ramsey should say that 'It is ⅓ true that p' means nothing at all, for there seems to be no way of modifying the right-hand side of

Ramsey's definition to give a sense to the modified left-hand side. Contrast other adverbial modifiers of 'true', such as 'It is necessarily true that p', which Ramsey could comfortably accommodate as meaning that, necessarily, p. (Interestingly, the redundancy theory suggests an account which gives priority to Quine's somewhat neglected second grade of modal involvement; see Quine 1953; and *cf.* Grover, *et al.*, 1975: 72.) Ramsey could handle 'allegedly', 'probably', *etc.,* similarly.

One could put the point, rather simple-mindedly, like this: one could expect Ramsey to allow a sense to modifiers of 'true' which can plausibly be paraphrased by means of modifiers of the contained sentence, *i.e.,* such that 'it is Mly true that p' $\simeq$ 'M'ly p'. This, for Ramsey, is the connection between linguistic phenomena and metaphysical theory.

So it is not hard to see why Ramsey should have rejected degrees of truth; nevertheless, it might be suggested, it is not so clear that the redundancy theory absolutely rules them out. To explain the objection, I must return briefly to the distinction between LEM and PB. If 'It is true that p' just means that p, and 'It is false that p' just means that not p, then 'Either it is true that p or it is false that p' just means that either p or not p; *i.e.,* on the redundancy theory the distinction between LEM and PB collapses. (I am inclined to regard this as a consideration against the redundancy theory.) However, it now becomes clear that, though the redundancy theory must equate LEM and PB, it need not be committed to either; it remains open to deny that for all p, either p or not p, and hence that, for all p, it is either true or false that p (*cf.* Haack 1978: 127–34). But this only shows that Ramsey's theory is compatible with a formal semantics allowing intermediate truth values. And I think the arguments given earlier indicate that Ramsey would have quite good reasons for refusing to interpret such intermediate values as representing degrees of truth.

The arguments of this paper have not been exhaustive. So far as they go, though, they indicate that the linguistic evidence is against degrees of truth, and that there are no compelling metaphysical or methodological considerations in their favour. It begins to look as if Ramsey was right to reject them.

University of Warwick

REFERENCES

Bolinger, D. 1972. *Degree Words*, Mouton.
Bradley, F. H. 1893. *Appearance and Reality*, George Allen (page references to 2nd edition, 1908).
Bradley, F. H. 1914. *Essays on Truth and Reality*, Oxford UP.
Fine, K. 1975. Vagueness, truth and logic, *Synthese* **30**, 265–300.
van Fraassen, B. C., 1969. Presuppositions, supervaluations and free logic, in *The Logical Way of Doing Things*, ed. Lambert, K., Yale UP, 67–91.
Grover, D., Belnap, N. D. Jr, and Camp, J. 1975. A prosentential theory of truth, *Philosophical Studies* **27**, 73–125.
Haack, S. 1974. *Deviant Logic*, Cambridge UP.
Haack, S. 1976. The Pragmatist theory of truth, *British Journal for the Philosophy of Science* **27**, 231–49.
Haack, S. 1978. *Philosophy of Logics*, Cambridge UP.
Haack, S. 1979. Do we need "fuzzy logic"?, *International Journal of Man-Machine Studies* **11**.
Haack, S. 1979a. Descriptive *versus* revisionary metaphysics, *Philosophical Studies*, **35**.
Holdcroft, D. (forthcoming). Bradley and the impossibility of truth, *History and Philosophy of Logic* 2.
Kamp, J. A. W. 1975. Two theories about adjectives, in Keenan, E. L., ed., *Formal Semantics of Natural Language*, Cambridge UP, 123–55.
Kripke, S. 1975. Outline of a theory of truth, *Journal of Philosophy* **72**, 690–716.
Lakoff, G. 1975. Hedges: a study in meaning criteria and the logic of fuzzy concepts, in Hockney, D. J. *et al.*, eds., *Contemporary Research in Philosophical Logic and Linguistic Semantics*, Reidel, 221–71.
Łukasiewicz, J. 1920. On 3-valued logic, in *Polish Logic*, ed. McCall, S., Oxford UP, 1967, 16–18.
Maydole, R. E. 1975. Paradoxes and many-valued set theory, *Journal of Philosophical Logic* **4**, 269–91.
Miller, D. W. 1974. Popper's qualitative theory of verisimilitude, *British Journal for the Philosophy of Science* **25**, 166–77.
Mortensen, C. 1978. 'A theorem on verisimilitude', *Bulletin of the Section of Logic*, **7**, 34–43.
Peirce, C. S. 1877. The fixation of belief, *Popular Science Monthly* **12**, 1–15; and in Weiner, P. P., ed., *Charles S. Peirce, Selected Writings*, Dover, 1958.
Popper, K. R. 1963. *Conjectures and Refutations*, Routledge and Kegan Paul.
Popper, K. R. 1972. *Objective Knowledge*, Oxford UP.
Post, E. 1921. Introduction to the general theory of elementary propositions, *American Journal of Mathematics* **3**, and in Heijenhoort, J. van, ed., *From Frege to Gödel*, Harvard UP, 1967.
Priest, G. G. 1979. A note on the Sorites paradox, *Australasian Journal of Philosophy* **57**, 74–5.

Quine, W. V. O. 1953. Three grades of modal involvement, *Proceedings of the XIth International Congress of Philosophy*, **14**, North Holland; and in *Ways of Paradox*, Random House, 1966, 158–76.

Quine, W. V. O. 1960. *Word and Object*, Wiley.

Quine, W. V. O. 1973. *The Roots of Reference*, Open Court.

Ramsey, F. P. 1978. *Foundations*, ed. D. H. Mellor. London. Routledge and Kegan Paul.

Reichenbach, H. 1935. *Wahrscheinlichkeit*, Leiden; *The Theory of Probability*, California UP, 1949.

Reichenbach, H. 1944. *Philosophic Foundations of Quantum Mechanics*, California UP.

Russell, B. 1919. *Introduction to Mathematical Philosophy*, Allen and Unwin.

Tarski, A. 1931. The concept of truth in formalised languages, in *Logic, Semantics and Metamathematics*, ed. Woodger, J., Oxford UP, 1956, 152–278.

Tarski, A. 1944. The semantic conception of truth, *Philosophy and Phenomenological Research* **4**, 341–76; and in Feigl, H. and Sellars, W., eds., *Readings in Philosophical Analysis*, Appleton Century Crofts, 1949, 52–84.

Tichý, P. 1974. On Popper's definitions of verisimilitude, *British Journal for the Philosophy of Science* **25**, 155–60.

Unger, P. 1975. *Ignorance*, Oxford UP.

Zadeh, L. A. 1965. Fuzzy sets, *Information and Control* **8**, 338–53.

Zadeh, L. A. 1975. Fuzzy logic and approximate reasoning, *Sythese* **30**, 407–28.

Zadeh, L. A. and Bellman, R. A. 1977. Local and fuzzy logics, in *Modern Uses of Multiple-Valued Logic*, ed. Epstein, G. and Dunn, J. M., Reidel, 105–65.

2 Ramsey's theory of types: suggestions for a return to Fregean sources

CHARLES S. CHIHARA

F. P. Ramsey's frequently cited paper 'The foundations of mathematics' contains a number of suggestions for revising the theory of types of *Principia Mathematica (PM)*. Of these, perhaps the best known is his proposal to eliminate the "ramified" part of Russell's hierarchy of propositional functions in order to obviate the need for the controversial *Axiom of Reducibility*.[1] But the details

This paper was written while I was on sabbatical leave with financial support from the University of California Humanities Research Fellowship Program. I am grateful for this support and for the constructive criticisms and suggestions I received from George Bealer, Bill Craig, Philip Kitcher, Michael Resnik, and Phyllis Rooney. Versions of this paper were read at Reed College and at the Montreal meeting of the Society for Exact Philosophy.

[1] For a discussion of Russell's ramified theory of types and the Axiom of Reducibility, see (Chihara 1973: chapter 1). The more general aspects of Ramsey's views on the theory of types are examined in (Wang 1974: 114–20). Recently, R. O. Gandy has claimed (1977: 176–7) that the usual things said about Ramsey's paper have missed the main point, which supposedly is made in the following quotation from the paper: 'The possibility of indefinable classes and relations in extensions is an essential part of the extensional attitude of modern mathematics . . . that it is neglected in *Principia Mathematica* is the first of the three great defects in that work. The mistake is made not by having a primitive proposition asserting that all classes are definable, but by giving a definition of class which applies only to definable classes, so that all mathematical propositions about some or all classes are misinterpreted.' Interestingly, Russell acknowledged this "defect" (1931: 477). However, I am inclined to think that all three of these logicians have been unfair to *PM*. Where is the justification for Ramsey's claim that the definition of class in *PM* applies only to definable class? To put it differently, is there any reason to suppose that the set theory of *PM* is a theory of definable classes (*i.e.* is applicable only to definable classes)? Here's a reason for thinking otherwise: the set theory of *PM* is equivalent to standard versions of simple type theory, and no one supposes that simple type theory is a theory of definable classes. I suspect that these logicians have been misled by the predicate/attribute ambiguity contained in Russell's use of the term 'propositional function' (Chihara 1973: 24–8).

Finally, something should be said about the notation used in this paper. Lower case Roman letters are used as object (individual) symbols; upper case Roman letters are used as object (individual) symbols; upper case Roman letters are used, sometimes in combination with the lower case letters and the circumflex, as 1st level (order) concept (propositional function) symbols; lower case Greek letters are used as class, set, or totality symbols; and of Ramsey's suggested theory of types have been largely ignored, primarily, I suspect, for the following reasons: First of all, the Wittgensteinian *(Tractatus)* foundations of Ramsey's theory have been widely regarded, especially by philosophers, as undermined by subsequent criticisms such as those of the later Wittgenstein. Secondly, the question of the truth or acceptability of logicism became a dead issue some time ago for most logicians and philosophers of mathematics, and, as a result, there has not been much interest in pursuing Ramsey's search for "tautologous" axioms of logic which would suffice for the derivation of classical mathematics. Thirdly, most of the dominant figures in the area of foundations of mathematics during the relevant period were either mathematicians or philosophers possessing a very mathematical outlook. So the tendency was to overlook features of foundational work that were not mathematically significant. Since the main set-theoretical improvements suggested by Ramsey were thought to be incorporated into standard simple type theories – which were being thoroughly studied – it is not surprising that there was little interest in the details of the theory. But what has not been generally noticed is that the basic structure of the Ramseyan system suggests a coupling of Gottlob Frege's theory of concepts with Bertrand Russell's "no-class" theory. Like Frege's hierarchy of concepts, the propositional functions of Ramsey's system form a simple type structure; but the set-theoretical antinomies are avoided by the Russellian device of regarding classes as "logical fictions".[2] The resulting theory has, I believe, many interesting features which warrant further study and development. In this paper, I intend to explore some of these features, especially in connection with the Frege–Russell programme of providing a logical analysis of our intuitive arithmetic. In particular, I shall suggest a line of development from Frege's original programme, through Russell's advances, to Ramsey's suggestions, in terms of which the resulting system and analysis of arithmetic will be defended against some recent criticisms by Paul Benacerraf, Willard Quine, Mark Steiner, and Robert Hambourger.

upper case Greek letters are used as 2nd level (order) concept (propositional function) symbols.

I should also add that the term 'concept' will be used in this paper so as to include *relations*, thus allowing Fregean concepts to correspond to Russellian propositional functions of two or more variables.

[2] For more on the Russellian "no-class" theory and its relevance to the paradoxes, see (Chihara 1973: 13–18).

But first of all, it may be wondered why I bring in Frege at all. After all, in his article, Ramsey was really concerned with revising the Russellian system of types: he certainly was not advocating replacing that system with the Fregean one. What is striking, however, is that Frege's hierarchy of concepts has just the sort of simple type structure Ramsey was advocating. Of course, Frege did not explicitly develop a system encompassing infinitely many levels of concepts, as would be needed if it were to replace the Russellian ramified hierarchy in the way Ramsey suggested; but an extrapolation from Frege's system will engender such a system.[3] And there are several significant advantages, which I shall describe below, to developing Ramsey's suggestions in terms of the Fregean system instead of the sort of simplified Russellian hierarchy generally described in the literature.

Frege's concepts are extensional, unlike Russell's propositional functions (Frege 1964: xxxix). For example, if first-level concepts $F\hat{x}$ and $G\hat{x}$ have exactly the same objects falling under them, then $F\hat{x}$ is identical to $G\hat{x}$.[4] Now, in Frege's system, there is no primitive identity relation for first-level concepts, so we would have to make use of some sort of device to express this extensionality property. This can be done, for example, by using the Russellian method of defining identity, yielding the following *Axiom of Extensionality*:

$$(F)(G)((x)(Fx \longleftrightarrow Gx) \rightarrow (\Phi)(\Phi F \longleftrightarrow \Phi G)).$$

Now this extensionality feature makes Fregean concepts much closer to sets than are Russellian propositional functions. As a result, the translation (or transformation) of sentences about sets into sentences of the logical language (which, after all, provides the essentials of the "no-class" theory) can be significantly simplified

---

[3] One of my students, Phyllis Rooney, has carried out such an extrapolation; and she has shown that the deductive system of the higher order predicate calculus of (Church 1972) is derivable from, essentially, the *Grundgesetze* system (only very minor changes being required). Of course, the possibility of developing Frege's levels of concepts beyond the third level is well-known. Thus, Michael Dummett describes the Fregean hierarchy as a "potentially infinite one" (1973: 48); and Michael Resnik explicitly formulates Frege's system of concepts as a simple type theory (1965: 330). For a more detailed description of the Fregean system of concepts, see (Dummett 1973: chapter 3).

[4] Of course, Frege would not have put it this way. Since Frege maintained that identity is a relation that can be asserted to obtain between objects only, he was compelled to characterise the extensionality of concepts in a roundabout way by saying, for example, that "coinciding in extension is necessary and sufficient criterion for the holding between concepts of the relation corresponding to identity for objects" (Frege 1964; xliv; see also Frege 1952: 80).

by adopting the Fregean hierarchy. For example, whereas in *PM*

[1] $a \, \varepsilon \, \hat{x}Fx$

is an abbreviation for

[2] $(\exists G)((x)(Fx \longleftrightarrow G!x) \, \& \, G!a),$

in the system *FRR*, obtained, essentially, by replacing the Russellian hierarchy with the Fregean, we can regard [1] as an abbreviation for the much simpler

[3] $Fa.$

Indeed, the transformations required in *FRR* are so simple that many of the complications involving scope that plagued the original Russellian system can be avoided.[5]

Also, *FRR* is immune from Rudolf Carnap's objection to the translation rules of Russell's "no-class" theory. Assuming that the property of being *human* is different from, but is co-extensive with, the property of being a *featherless biped* – which we can express in our notation:

[a] $H\hat{x} \neq F\hat{x}$
[b] $(x)(Hx \longleftrightarrow Fx)$

– and that $H\hat{x}$ and $F\hat{x}$ are what Russell called 'properties', *i.e.* predicative propositional functions, we can infer sentences which the "no-class" theory of *PM* translates into:

[c] $\hat{y}Hy = H\hat{x}$

and

[d] $\hat{y}Hy \neq H\hat{x}.$

Although [c] and [d] are not, strictly speaking, contradictions (they are not abbreviations of sentences of *PM* that contradict one another), Carnap argues that such examples show that Russell's "no-class" transformations are defective in so far as they fail to yield class expressions which "can be manipulated as if they were names of entities" (1958: 149). Needless to say, one cannot use this example to generate an objection against *FRR*, for the set consisting of [a] and [b] is simply inconsistent with the *Axiom of Extensionality*

---

[5] Gödel indicates the nature of the scope problem in (1964a: 212). The formal details of the transformational rules and, indeed, of the system *FRR*, itself, will be published separately.

alluded to earlier. To put the basic point another way, one cannot generate the Carnapian objection in the system *FRR*, for one cannot construct different Fregean first-level concepts that are co-extensive.

Another advantage of *FRR* arises from the fact that Frege's concepts are simpler than Russell's propositional functions: first-level concepts can be regarded as functions from the totality of objects to the truth values, whereas order 1 propositional functions map individuals to propositions (and only indirectly to truth values). Essentially, then, propositional functions involve the added complication of requiring totalities of propositions as values, which engenders a more complicated semantical structure for the Russellian system than is found in the Fregean (Church 1974).

Closely connected with the above is the fact that the extensionality of Fregean concepts shields *FRR* from the typically Quinean objection to Russell's "no-class" theory, which consists in arguing that the reduction of classes to propositional functions is of dubious value since we are given no criterion of identity for propositional functions, when we do have such a criterion for classes.

Finally, the philosophical basis of the Fregean hierarchy, although by no means as sound and firm as I would like, is less confused and more cleanly worked out than that of the Russellian (Chihara 1973: 19–39).

The system I have been discussing may not appear worth developing for reasons quite different from the one answered above. After all, do we not already have precise and well-developed versions of simple type theory which capture everything of value in *FRR*? As Quine has noted, once classes have been introduced in *PM*, propositional functions are hardly mentioned again (1966: 22). So would it not be better to introduce 'ε' in the beginning as a primitive symbol, thereby avoiding the added complications introduced by "no-class" versions of type theory?

Certainly, if one's interest in logical systems is mainly mathematical – if what one thinks really counts about such a system is its set theory – then there would be reasons for being unenthusiastic about developing *FRR*. But, in general, philosophers have wider interests and deeper concerns than that (cf. Cocchiarella 1974). Both Frege and the team of Russell and Whitehead constructed their systems with much more in mind than the development of classical mathematics from a basic set of axioms: their systems were to be used in the analysis of human thought – not just mathematical thought (Church 1974). Frege's theory of predication, for example, contains principles that involve much more than pure mathematics. So unless the Fregean theory is, itself, not worth studying and exploiting, there is surely a value in seeing how mathematics can be developed within its framework. Furthermore, there is the historical question of how Frege could have met the challenge of the paradoxes without abandoning too much of his basic theory of predication. Clearly, jettisoning classes (*i.e.* value ranges of concepts) from the ontology of the *Grundgesetze* would eliminate the infamous *Axiom V*, which Frege saw to be the source of Russell's contradiction (1964: 127). Of course, some axiom must be substituted for the paradox producer to allow the generation of mathematics; but *PM* points the way to what is needed. Adding an *Axiom of Infinity* will allow the construction of arithmetic, and only the *Axiom of Choice* will be needed to obtain the mathematics of *PM* (Wang 1974: 111–12). Thus, the fundamental laws of *FRR* need not be very different from Frege's original system, and the actual development of mathematics could follow the details of *PM* very closely.[6]

Another way of seeing the relevance of *FRR* for Fregean studies is to view the post-paradox situation in terms of the Fregean ontology of concepts and value ranges. Since the system of concepts is (essentially) already sufficient to generate the classical mathematics of *PM*, and since the assumption of value ranges expressed by *Axiom V* got the system into trouble, why not simply drop value ranges entirely and use a "no-class" system? The result would be the sort of system sketched above.[7]

---

[6] *FRR* could be criticised, as was *PM*, on the grounds that its axioms (especially the Axiom of Infinity) are not all "self-evident truths"; but if, as was suggested earlier, we no longer concern ourselves with defending the logicist's epistemological thesis of the analyticity of arithmetic, such criticisms need not be worrysome. Furthermore, as will be seen later, there is an interpretation of *FRR* under which the Axiom of Infinity does seem to be such a self-evident truth.

[7] In (Hinst 1975), it is also suggested that Frege could have "founded arithmetic" on a system without courses-of-values (or extensions of concepts). However, Hinst only addresses himself to the question of whether Frege could have expressed in his system the fundamental arithmetical notions without appealing to courses-of-values. He seems not to have considered how the required theorems could have been derived in such a system. Thus, in discussing the question of why Frege did not take such a route, Hinst does not even consider the problem of how Fregean proofs of the fundamental laws of arithmetic could be given without *Axiom V*.

Frege, himself, must have found the idea of trying to get by without extensions of concepts attractive. Thus, he wrote: 'The difficulties which are bound up with the use of

There is another feature that makes "no-class" versions of type theory preferable to the set-theoretical ones. Critics of type theory have frequently pointed to the absurdity of infinitely many null sets. Quine articulates this objection clearly:

One especially unnatural and awkward effect of the type theory is the infinite reduplication of each logically definable class. There is no longer one universal class V to which everything belongs, for the theory of types demands that the members of a class be alike in type. . . . This reduplication is particularly strange in the case of the null class. One feels that classes should differ only with respect to their members, and this is obviously not true of the various null classes (1938: 131).

There *is* something absurd about different empty sets. What distinguishes the null set of type 1 from the null set of type 2? After all, they are both empty. Evidently, the former has no members of type 0, whereas the latter has no members of type 1. This reminds me of the old joke about the person in a cafe who asks for coffee without cream and is told, 'Sorry, we don't have any cream, but we can give you coffee without milk instead.'

Notice that this objection does not apply to the "no-class" versions we have been considering. In *FRR*, there are no empty classes, strictly speaking: a sentence about the empty class of level 1 is just short-hand for a sentence about a concept (function) mapping all objects to the truth value *False*. And there is no difficulty in distinguishing a function which maps all objects to False from one which maps all first-level concepts to False – here there is no temptation to say that such functions must be identical.

Another, closely related, objection to standard simple type theories appeals to our intuition concerning the natural numbers that "it is difficult to believe in the infinite reduplication of the natural numbers, and everything constructed from them, to which the theory [of types] is committed" (Moss 1972: 233). But in *FRR*, again *strictly speaking*, there is no infinite reduplication of the natural numbers: it is only the structure of the natural number system and the logical conditions for the truth of the appropriate cardinality statements that is reduplicated – something that is not at all counter-intuitive.

classes vanish if we only deal with objects, concepts, and relations, and this is possible in the fundamental part of Logic. The class, namely, is something derived, whereas in the concept – as I understand the word – we have something primitive. Accordingly, also, the laws of classes are less primitive than those of concepts, and it is not suitable to found Logic on the laws of classes' (Jourdain, 1912: 251).

Finally, the "no-class" system I have been discussing gives promise of providing a kind of rationale for its type restrictions which standard simple type theories have lacked. The formal restrictions on meaningfulness (or well-formedness) which characterise such set theories have seemed *ad hoc* and motivated by little more than the goal of cutting down the *Abstraction Axiom* to paradox-avoiding size. This is why Quine could drop these restrictions with such equanimity in motivating his shift from type theory to the "zig-zag" system of (1938). Whatever one may think of Frege's reasoning regarding the type-theoretical structure of his ontology of concepts, it cannot be denied that the structure was specified and supported by argumentation *before* the contradictions in his system were discovered: Frege certainly did not devise his type theory *ad hoc* to free his logical system from the paradoxes.[8]

Continuing the progression of objections I have been taking up, I should now like to consider the more extreme position of those who view all type-theoretical theories – "no-class" and set-theoretical alike, as well as the "zig-zag" modifications of Quine – as aberrant systems contributing nothing of significant value to the analysis of mathematical concepts and reasoning.[9] Such critics, who are inclined to opt for the iterative concept of set of the Zermelo-type systems, would regard *FRR* as just one more in the long line of mathematical monstrosities constructed by philosophers. In answer to such critics, it should be noted that type-theoretical systems offer a framework for presenting the Frege–Cantor–Russell analysis of our intuitive cardinality theories (including the theory of natural numbers); in contrast, the usual Zermelo-type set theories require cardinal numbers of a quite different sort. I shall argue that the Frege–Russell analysis of cardinal number more closely and straightforwardly fits certain of our intuitions and intuitive theories than does its standard competitor, the von Neumann. Still, it might be wondered what value there is to analys-

[8] It is pointed out in (Hinst 1975: 43) that the type-theoretical structure of Frege's system results from the forbidding of isolated concept names, and is thus founded on the distinction between names and predicates. I do not wish to leave the reader with the impression that I regard the Fregean justifications of his system of types as completely convincing (see Chihara 1973: 35–8) or that I believe the Fregean theory of concepts to be free from difficulties (*cf.* Resnik 1965). Still, there is a certain plausibility to the justifications; and I believe that the well-known difficulties can be overcome by making suitable adjustments in the overall view.

[9] I follow Fraenkel and Bar-Hillel in classifying the Quinean systems as "type-theoretical" (1958: chapter 3).

ing the natural numbers along the lines laid down by Frege and Russell, especially since so many have been persuaded by Paul Benacerraf's article (1965) that the conditions of adequacy of an explication of natural number are such that *"any purpose* we may have in giving an account of the notion of number" [italics mine] will be equally well (or badly) served by any of the well-known accounts of natural number (and indeed by infinitely many other possible accounts). According to Benacerraf, "any system of objects, whether sets or not, that forms a recursive progression must be adequate" (1965: 69). If Benacerraf's view is accepted, then the Frege–Russell analysis of the natural numbers is not to be preferred to the von Neumann, no matter what purpose we may have in giving our account of number. On this point, Benacerraf is quite explicit: 'Frege chose as the number 3 the extension of the concept 'equivalent with some 3-membered set' . . . Although an appealing notion, there seems to be little to recommend it over, say [the von Neumann]' (1965: 58).

But is Benacerraf correct? Well, what reasons does he give to support his claim? It is difficult to say. There seems to be nothing in the paper that can be plausibly reconstructed into anything like a convincing argument for such a strong claim. However, there are some indications in the article of how he came to his view. In a footnote (p. 51), one finds a quotation from (Quine 1960) in which a very similar position is taken: 'The condition upon all acceptable explications of number . . . can be put . . . any progression – *i.e.*, any infinite series each of whose members had only finitely many precursors – will do nicely.' In this quotation, Quine goes on to explain why he differs from Russell, who had placed a further condition on acceptable explications. Since Benacerraf sides, partially, with Russell on this issue, we may come to see how the strong position under examination was arrived at by reviewing this three-way dispute.

In (Russell 1920), the point is made that "every progression verifies Peano's five axioms". But Russell rejected the view that the axioms give an adequate basis for arithmetic on the grounds that "we want our numbers to be such as can be used for counting common objects, and this requires that our numbers should have a *definite* meaning, not merely that they should have certain formal properties" (1920: 10). Quine sees this argument as based on a mistake, claiming that any progression will satisfy the additional requirement cited by Russell. Benacerraf, however, denies that Russell's additional requirement can be met by just any progression: he argues that the order relation of the progression must be recursive (1965: 52–3). Having thus arrived at an additional requirement, Benacerraf seems to have felt satisfied with his search for a sufficient set of conditions for the adequacy of an account of number: 'I trust . . . that the preceding contains *all the elements of a correct account*' [italics mine]. Evidently, he simply could not conceive of any additional requirements.

Perhaps, then, we should reconsider the sort of considerations that guided Frege to his account of number. In the *Grundlagen,* Frege set forth his analysis of cardinality in the course of outlining his programme of showing that the "truths of arithmetic" are analytic. To make his programme plausible, Frege felt the need to give analyses of common-variety arithmetical assertions. Thus he attempted to specify the "sense of a proposition in which a number word occurs" (1953: 73). For Frege's case for logicism to be convincing, it must be plausible that the "definitions" provided in that work result from a successful analysis of our (intuitive) concepts and that the theorems of Frege's system actually include all the true propositions of ordinary arithmetic: it is not enough to provide an effective 1–1 mapping, f, from the set of arithmetic truths to a set of sentences of Frege's formal system such that for every arithmetic truth Φ, $f(\Phi)$ is a theorem, especially if Φ and $f(\Phi)$ differ significantly in sense or meaning. In other words, Frege's programme – at least as it is set out in his *Grundlagen* – seems to require some sort of logical or set-theoretical *analysis* of our actual intuitive arithmetical concepts, which can be judged to be superior to available rival analyses, and not the mere construction of substitute concepts which function only vaguely like our pre-analytic ones. Given such aims – or similar ones[10] – we can seriously doubt that just *any* analysis specifying a recursive progression as the natural numbers will serve as well (or badly) as any other.

Thus, consider the following: I shall specify some effectively calculable functions, each with a domain equal to the set of von Neumann natural numbers and a range which is some subset of the domain. Let $P(n)$ = the nth prime von Neumann natural number; let $f(n)$ = the von Neumann number corresponding to the nth digit

[10] Consider, for example, the aim of analyzing our intuitive arithmetical notions as part of a "theory of understanding" (Putnam 1978: Part III).

to the right of the decimal point in the decimal expansion of pi; and let $a(n)$ = the von Neumann number corresponding to $P(n)$ raised to the power $f(n)$. Finally, let B be the sequence

$$a(0), \ a(1), \ a(2), \ \ldots$$

Now Benacerraf would have us believe that B would serve as our natural number sequence, in a set-theoretical analysis of our intuitive theory of natural numbers, as well as any other recursive progression. But surely that is implausible. Had Frege put forward such an analysis, would anyone have taken him seriously? (Try to specify, set-theoretically, even the *immediate-successor* relationship for such a system.)

I do not wish to suggest that the aim of providing a workable analysis of our arithmetical concepts is all that clear or that Frege himself was clear about them in setting forth his definitions; but still, it should be evident that one can require one's analyses of number to satisfy much more than the properties set forth in standard mathematical developments from Peano's axioms. For example, one can evaluate proposed analyses on the basis of how well our intuitive ideas are preserved or approximated, and of how well we can make sense of both our arithmetical notions and operations. Then, in terms of such criteria, one can make a case for maintaining that our intuitive ideas of number are such that the natural numbers are just special cases of the cardinal numbers. This was done by Frege in the *Grundlagen* by analysing ordinary situations in which 'How many?' questions are raised. Typically, cardinal numbers are cited in answer to such questions. This led to Frege's analysis of simple cardinality statements, such as 'There are five apples on the table'. It should be recalled that the definition of 'natural number' is given in the *Grundlagen* only after an analysis of such cardinality statements is completed and 'cardinal number' is defined. Now once the totality of cardinal numbers is specified, it is hard to see how just any recursive progression will do as the set of natural numbers (*i.e.* the finite cardinal numbers).[11] So if the adequacy of an analysis of the natural number notion is judged by reference to its "closeness of fit" with intuitive notions, it is by no means obvious that Benacerraf's claim should be accepted. Not

---

[11] It is noteworthy that Benacerraf essentially restricts his discussion of numbers to the natural numbers – as if one's analysis of the natural number is, or should be, independent of one's analysis of the cardinal numbers.

only have we been given no good argument by Benacerraf for accepting his claim regarding competing analyses of our notion of number, we now see that there are at least some positive grounds for questioning the claim: it can be plausibly maintained that not all recursive progressions fit our intuitions about cardinality and the natural numbers equally well (or badly).

I have suggested that the Fregean analysis of cardinality is, in certain respects, a much more intuitively natural and straight-forward development than the usual von Neumann set theoretical account given these days. Some of my reasons for making this suggestion can be brought out by the following example. Consider:

(1) John has Sue as his legal wife

(or equivalently 'John has a legal wife, *viz*. Sue'), where legality is understood to be specified by the Californian legal system. Now it is natural to hold that if (1) is true, there must be some special relationship R which John has to Sue. Well what properties would we expect R to have? Surely at least these:

(2) For every person x and y, xRy iff x has y as his legal wife;

and, since no one can be legally married to more than one person,

(3) It is not possible for there to be persons x, y, and z such that xRy and xRz and $y \neq z$.

Now compare the statement

(1') α has 3 as a cardinal number

(or equivalently 'α has a cardinal number, *viz*. 3'). Again, it is natural to think that (1') is true if there is some special relationship S that α has to 3. Let us now draw some comparisons between the Fregean and the von Neumann approaches to cardinality. Both can be regarded as undertaking set-theoretical analyses: the respective domains from which the referents of number terms are to be selected consist of sets; and the relationship of *being a cardinal number of a set* is to be defined set-theoretically, *i.e.* S is to be specified set-theoretically in such a way that the following will hold:

(2') For all totalities x and y, xSy iff x has cardinal number y.

Of course, a non-circular analysis must not make use of the notion of cardinal number in its specification of the relation S. Fortunately, a variety of other conditions can be specified which a satisfactory set-theoretical definition of S would have to satisfy and which do not make use of the notion of cardinal number. For example,

(3') It is not possible for there to be totalities x, y and z such that xSy and xSz and $y \neq z$;

and

(4′) For all totalities x, y, and z, if xSy and x is equinumerous with z, then zSy.

(We would expect any satisfactory set-theoretical analysis of S to enable us to conclude (3′) and (4′)). Now with what relationship S does the Fregean analysis supply us? Essentially: *is equinumerous with all and only the members of*. Notice that, apart from some basic logical notions, this relationship involves only the concept of *equinumerosity* – a concept which, one could plausibly argue, is intrinsic to the notion of cardinality. But now compare the relationship we are given by the von Neumann analysis, *viz. the relationship x and y have to one another when y is an initial ordinal number and x is equinumerous with y*. In effect, the von Neumann development of cardinal numbers requires a detour through ordinal number theory – a detour involving some sophisticated set-theoretical notions in addition to complicated logical reasoning. Compared to the much simpler and straightforward Fregean relationship, the von Neumann, although quite elegant (from the mathematical point of view), seems artificial and unnatural by comparison: it is hard to believe that our intuitive notion of cardinal number corresponds to such a relationship.

Another aspect of our intuitive notion of cardinality seems to favour the Frege–Russell development. It is quite natural to infer from the fact that A is some well-defined set that there is some definite number of elements of A – we may not know how many, but it seems obvious that we can speak of "the number of things that belong to A". Thus, in arguing for the view that there is only one reasonable way of extending the notion of number from the finite case to the infinite, Kurt Gödel asserted that "whatever 'number' as applied to infinite sets may mean, we certainly want it to have the property that *the number of objects belonging to some class does not change if, leaving the objects the same, one changes in any way whatever their properties or mutual relations*" (1964b: 258 italics mine). Gödel also makes use of the premiss (which he also takes to be obvious) that if any set A is transformed into a set completely indistinguishable from a set B, then A and B have the same number of elements. (Notice: it is assumed as obvious that A and B each has some definite number of elements – the only question is whether they have the same or a different number.) Now if our intuitive notion of number has this feature, *i.e.* if the apparent obviousness of the statement that every set has a cardinal number is not an illusion produced, say, by a bad induction from finite cases, then the Frege–Russell development again seems to provide a more natural and plausible fit than the von Neumann. For within the former, it is both trivial and straightforward to infer from the fact that A is a well-defined set, that A has a cardinal number; whereas within the latter, the reasoning required to justify the inference is so intricate (involving such mathematically sophisticated axioms as Choice and Replacement) that it is hard to see how anyone could consider the inference *obviously* valid.

The point of all of this – I hasten to add – is not to argue that the Fregean analysis is completely adequate or even that it is definitely better overall than the von Neumann.[12] Rather, I wish to argue against closing off certain avenues of investigation. I see no *a priori* reasons for thinking that the above two competing analyses must yield equally satisfactory accounts of arithmetic – indeed, I don't see how such a conclusion can be drawn in the absence of a detailed investigation into the matter. Hence, I see no need to turn our backs on the pioneering work of Frege and Russell on cardinal numbers. Since their views do provide useful and enlightening insights into at least some of our intuitive practices and beliefs that are not provided by available alternative accounts, a system such as *FRR*, which permits this kind of analysis, has distinct advantages.

Benacerraf's position is obviously quite similar to Quine's view of the situation. Quine, too, has claimed that the chief competitors of the Fregean account of number, Zermelo's and von Neumann's, as well as countless other alternatives, are "equally correct" (1969: 43). But this is an especially strange position for Quine to take since he has also denied that the various alternative set theories that have been developed in this century are equally correct. For Quine, mathematical theories are not different in nature from empirical theories, and we should no more treat alternative set theories as equally compatible "with the facts" than we should alternative empirical theories. The fact that the Continuum Hypothesis is independent of the standard axioms of set theory does not mean, for

[12] The logicist's definition of 'natural number' involves the *ancestral relation*, which (one could argue) is too logically complex to be part of the ordinary man's conceptual repertoire (*cf.* Bostock 1974: 199f). A detailed discussion of this issue would be out of place here; but perhaps the following points should be made: (1) the complexity introduced by the ancestral is due to the need to convert an implicit inductive definition ('0, $s0$, $ss0$, . . .') into an explicit one; (2) the other set-theoretical analyses of the natural number sequence are open to much the same objection in so far as implicit inductive definitions are made explicit by the Dedekind–Frege method.

Quine, that the question of the truth or falsity of the hypothesis loses its meaning. Quine is a Realist. Set-theoretical statements have truth values, whether or not we can *determine* which values they have. Furthermore, the considerations that ought to move us to accept or reject a set-theoretical statement (or a set theory for that matter) are ultimately, for Quine, pragmatic.

Each man is given a scientific heritage plus a continuing barrage of sensory stimulation; and the considerations which guide him in warping his scientific heritage to fit his continuing sensory promptings are, where rational, pragmatic (1961: 46).

What sort of pragmatic considerations are relevant to evaluating rival theories? For Quine, practically anything can count. He tells us that the acceptance of an ontological position, a set theory, or even a theoretical hypothesis of natural science is "as much a pragmatic matter as one's adoption of . . . a new system of bookkeeping" (1966: 125). Thus, Quine's special brand of Pragmatism implies that Reason could very well demand the acceptance of one sort of set theory to the exclusion of the available alternatives.[13] But, as I noted earlier, the Frege–Russell account of number cannot even be given within Zermelo-type set theories; conversely, the von Neumann cardinals cannot be constructed within simple type theories (Quine 1963: 284; Fraenkel 1966: 61–3). So if pragmatic considerations were to demand the acceptance of simple type theory, then they would, in effect, require the rejection of the von Neumann account. Similarly, if the Quinean constraints on rationality were to lead to the acceptance of Zermelo–Fraenkel set theory, then it should also lead to the rejection of the Frege–Russell account. So how can Quine say that these various incompatible accounts are all "equally correct"?

It should now be clear that the implications of accepting either Benacerraf's or Quine's position regarding competing accounts of number flow into rather deep philosophical waters. We see that such claims require a type of justification that involves far-reaching considerations of the nature of confirmation and justification, of logic and language, and of mathematics and science – something that is all too often overlooked by those who are certain that Benacerraf and Quine are obviously right.

Another reason has recently been given for discounting the significance of the Frege–Russell analysis. Mark Steiner has argued

[13] These doctrines are examined in (Chihara 1973: chapter 3). References to many of the relevant works of Quine will also be found there.

that any account of number according to which natural numbers are identified with, or taken to be, sets or concepts is misguided. Contrary to those, such as Quine, who have hailed the Fregean theory as accomplishing a theoretically important "ontological reduction", in so far as it allows us to replace the postulation of a special realm of abstract entities with constructions from the set-theoretical ontology presupposed by classical mathematics, Steiner claims that "none of the infinite ways of reducing number theory to set theory is justified" (1975: 92). He argues that such a reduction "presupposes that we can divorce ontological from epistemological questions, that one can achieve ontological without epistemological gain, indeed at epistemological loss. This seems to be an absurdity" (1975: 75). Basically, Steiner regards the attempted "reduction" as one in which an epistemologically secure theory (number theory) is, in some sense, *replaced* by a much shakier one (set theory).

We are in the situation of the data-processing director of a large firm who is offered a proposal by IBM to exchange his small CDC computer for a more elaborate one. On paper, the trade looks good: the flowchart of the IBM includes that of the CDC, so that in theory the former could do the work of the latter and more. The catch: the IBM machine is prone to break down, to slow down, to err. Even if we assume that the director must rent the IBM because it is flowcharted to solve problems beyond the range of the CDC, *must* he then throw out the latter? (1975: 75)

Of course not, says Steiner. Analogously, it is argued, it would be absurd to give up the certainty and security of number theory just for the gain of ontological simplicity promised by the Frege–Russell reduction.

This argument has, perhaps, an initial plausibility; but it does not stand up to scrutiny. Indeed, it is difficult even to state the argument in anything like a precise way. At first glance, Steiner seems to be claiming, as a premiss of the argument, that one simply cannot achieve any reduction at the cost of a loss of certainty ("epistemological loss"). But Steiner seems to take it back later when he allows that there are "bona-fide reductions" of a weak but more certain theory to a stronger but less certain theory; and he gives, as a particular example of such, the reduction of the Boyle–Charles laws to the molecular kinetic theory of gases (1975: 86).[14] He allows the rationality of such a reduction on the grounds that it makes certain theoretical improvements, *e.g.* it provides an increase in explana-

---

[14] This was pointed out to me by Douglas Winblad.

tory power in so far as it explains why the original theory fails to be universally true. Evidently, Steiner is using the premiss that a reduction involving a loss of certainty is rational only so long as the reduction engenders theoretical gains that outweigh the epistemological loss. But how are we to compare the theoretical gains against the epistemological losses resulting from the logicist's reduction? By what criterion or method are we to make the necessary "weighing"? Steiner never tells us! This is surprising since his position requires an argument to the effect that the epistemological losses clearly outweigh any theoretical gains accruing from the reduction; and it is hard to see how such an argument can even get off the ground without some way of comparing the gains and losses, *i.e.* without some method of doing the weighing. It hardly needs adding that Steiner never provides this required argument. Indeed, he does not even tell the reader how *he* determined that the theoretical gains of the reduction are outweighed by the epistemological losses or how *he* decided what those gains are. That there are such gains cannot seriously be doubted. There is, for example, the systematisation and unification of theory achieved by the reduction, the value of which is easy to comprehend not only on general methodological grounds, but also because the reduction allows for: (1) an increase in explanatory power (the empirical applicability of number theory as well as the rationale of such concrete procedural activities as counting and grouping are explainable by means of the reducing theory); and (2) an overall simplification of laws (formal features of the computational laws of numbers – natural numbers, rational numbers, real numbers, complex numbers, cardinal numbers, and ordinal numbers – can all be derived from the basic logical laws of the reducing theory). But I am far from clear at this time as to how one can determine, with any degree of precision and any real confidence, that such-and-such is *all* that one gains from the reduction.

Let us turn to the epistemological loss that purportedly results from the ontological reduction. But first, it might be helpful to describe in more detail the view Steiner is criticising. The logicist's ontological reduction is supposed to enable us to "get by without numbers". But what, specifically, is "getting by without numbers"? Steiner tells us: it is "reinterpreting as referring to particular classes, the terms purporting to denote numbers; reconstructing as true of classes, predicates taken to be true of certain numbers;

redefining as ranging over classes, variables understood to range over numbers". He then goes on to say: 'Since we "need" sets anyhow for other mathematical purposes, the possibility of such a reinterpretation, Quine holds, is grounds enough to support an ontic conclusion: that numbers are to be "eliminated", "dropped" from the universe' (1975: 73). Although the view under attack is attributed to Quine, the attribution should by no means be restricted to him. Indeed, Russell's view of the situation is not very different (1920: 18). And under one reading of the *Grundgesetze*, Frege's position is compatible with the view. In any case, Steiner clearly did not wish to restrict his target to Quine alone; for the conclusion of his argument is more inclusive:

even if we accept the Fregean point of view, such that a priori there is nothing wrong with identifying numbers with "something else", from a different category, it does not follow that any such identification must be successful. If our critique of Quine holds good, it shows that the entire view that we have a right to "reinterpret" number theory needs examination. It shows that it is misleading to say 'Anything can play the role of 3.' For in my view, none of the infinite ways of reducing number theory to set theory is justified (1975: 92).

We saw earlier that Steiner's critique is based on the premiss that the sort of reduction we have been describing results in a loss of certainty. But what, according to Steiner, generates this loss? Evidently, it has something to do with the *impredicativity* of the reducing theory. Now impredicativity has been thought to be the source of the paradoxes of logic and set theory that beset early foundationalists (Chihara 1973: chapter 1). But Steiner does not seem to want to rest his argument on any analysis of the paradoxes. At least, he does not explicitly bring in the paradoxes to support his case. Evidently, Steiner believes that there is something intrinsic to impredicativity which makes such theories epistemologically suspect. 'Once we assume that a mathematician does not know any number theory,' he says (1975: 80), 'that person really ought to worry, because he might have reason to suspect an impredicative theory of inconsistency.' Notice the strange twist in the reasoning: why should a mathematician worry just because "he might have reason" to suspect some theory of his of inconsistency? Ordinarily, I don't start to worry about some theory I have accepted until I have reason to suspect it either of falsity or of lack of support – I don't start worrying just at the thought that I *might* have reason to suspect it. Besides, could one not say of practically any significant theory (impredicative or not) that one *might* have reason to suspect it of inconsistency?

But why should we assume, in determining the "epistemological loss" accruing to the logicist from his reduction, that he knows no number theory? Some insight into Steiner's thoughts on this matter may be obtained from a consideration of the particular view of the natural numbers he is trying to establish in his book. Roughly (to be somewhat question-begging), the view is that no system of objects other than the natural numbers themselves can, even in principle, be identified with the system of natural numbers. He argues that numbers "cannot be interpreted outside number theory" on the grounds that no more basic science is available to do the interpret-ing (1975: 92). Evidently, Steiner also thinks the natural numbers cannot be identified with the finite cardinals – a subdomain of cardinal number theory.) For Steiner, arithmetic is an "autonomous science" having as subject matter the natural numbers, which "are objects in the same sense that molecules are objects" (1975: 87).

Further insights into Steiner's position can be obtained by way of contrast. Recall that the present-day theory of natural numbers was not developed overnight by a few great minds. It has its origins in the use of number symbols which, so far as we know, goes back to primitive times. Our methods of addition, subtraction, multiplica-tion, and division are the results of hundreds of years of struggle and effort. And the early development of number theory was intimately connected with, and not kept separate from, developments in other areas of mathematics, the empirical sciences, and even philosophy (think of the Pythagoreans and their interpretation of number). It was only in the latter part of the nineteenth century that, essentially, present-day versions of axiomatisations of the natural number sys-tem were given; and rigorous logical formalisations of the theory are twentieth century achievements. Now, according to the Fregean interpretation of these developments, the theory of natural numbers is (or can be taken to be) a theory about logical objects, whereas Steiner interprets the theory as being about certain abstract objects different from sets, concepts, functions, or, it would seem, any sort of entity treated by a theory distinct from number theory. And he suggests that if we accept Frege's interpretation, we must renounce all our knowledge of the theory of natural numbers. But why?

Consider the following (somewhat fanciful) example. In 1662, the Boyle–Charles Law was established. Letting P_i and V_i be the pressure and volume of a gas at temperature T_i (expressed in degrees absolute), $i = 1, 2$, the law asserts the following to hold (approximately):

$$\frac{P_1 V_1}{T_1} = \frac{P_2 V_2}{T_2}.$$

At that time, we shall suppose, this law was understood in terms of the Caloric Theory of Heat, according to which heat is a fluid, possessing volume, that flows into a body when it is heated and flows out of the body when it is cooled. Many centuries later, another theory of heat was proposed which explained heat and pressure as due to the kinetic motion and collision of atoms and molecules. Thus, a controversy arose between those who favoured the *caloric interpretation* of the Boyle–Charles Law and those who advocated the *kinetic interpretation*. The caloric defenders argued that the kinetic interpretation presupposed the abandonment of our knowledge of the gas law – a substantial epistemological loss! The kinetic theorists rejected this argument, claiming that their view did not require giving up any laws already established, but only involved a reinterpretation of some of these laws. Such a reinterpretation was justified, it was argued, since it resulted in a more uniform and far-reaching theory, which better systematised our scientific knowledge and provided a theoretical framework for linking the well-known properties of gases with such diverse phenomena as black-body radiation, Brownian motion, cloud-chamber tracks, and measurements of the electric charge of electrons. Furthermore, a simplification of ontology – an ontological reduction – would be achieved, since there would no longer be any need to postulate the existence of a special fluid to account for the properties of heat.

Clearly, the defenders of the caloric interpretation have a weak argument; for there is little reason to think that the testing and confirmation which established the validity of the gas law rested on the caloric interpretation. But are there any compelling reasons for thinking that the testing and confirmation of our arithmetical laws depended on the acceptance of the metaphysical interpretation Steiner advocates? It seems to me highly doubtful that there are. And if there are, Steiner certainly does not supply them.

Throughout his critique of the logicist's reduction, Steiner seems to assume that the certainty that accrues to our numerical theories is due to our acceptance of a particular ontological interpretation of arithmetic. But, as we have seen, such an assumption is highly questionable. It is not even clear that many people do accept the ontological interpretation Steiner advocates. In any case, one could argue, with at least as much plausibility, that the certainty of number theory is due to a myriad of facts of experience, including countless successful applications we have made of intuitive (unformalised, unaxiomatised) arithmetic in everyday, as well as in scientific and mathematical, contexts – experiences that are not essentially tied to any one interpretation of the formal systems of arithmetic.

Philip Kitcher has raised a different, but closely related, objection to Steiner's doctrine that the logicist's reduction would deprive us of arithmetical knowledge. Kitcher argues that even if Steiner were right in claiming that our evidence for the truth of the axioms of arithmetic consisted in a grasp of the intended interpretation of Peano's axioms, it would still not follow that this evidence would have to be abandoned when the logicist's reduction is accepted for, "we may continue to justify arithmetical claims by means of this grasp, and arithmetic will be no less certain than before. The only difference will be that we now claim that the elements of this model are sets" (1978: 122). Thus, Kitcher argues, even though the reduction gives us a proof of the Peano axioms from the axioms of set theory, we should not suppose that our confidence in the truth of Peano arithmetic would then have to rest on the proof and on the principles of set theory used in the proof:

there are many cases in which we happily accept a proof while continuing to base our beliefs on the evidence that was previously available . . . as the history of mathematics shows, mathematicians are often prepared to concede that a new rigorous proof is inferior as justification than old, intuitive evidence. Bolzano and Cauchy, for example, recognized explicitly that loose geometrical arguments provide much better evidence for theorems about continuous functions than the long arithmetical derivations they hoped to produce (1978: 122–3).

One final Steinerian argument against the logicist's reduction should be mentioned. After urging that we ought to "segregate error-prone from error-free theories, in order best to know where to search for revision, should revision become necessary", Steiner argues:

whenever we need arithmetical facts, either for their own sake, or for some ulterior motive, the counsel of rationality is to use undiluted arithmetic where undiluted arithmetic alone will do . . . arithmetic need not rest, by and large, on any other mathematical science, and therefore it ought not. Why settle in arithmetic for the certainty that set theory can supply, just because we must thus settle in analysis or ordinal number theory? (1975: 85)

In this argument, there is a sort of unstated premiss (or presupposition) which is closely related to the assumption of the preceding argument. In the previous argument, it was assumed that the logicist of the sort I have been defending here was precluded from knowing any number theory; in this argument, it seems to be assumed that the logicist is precluded by his reduction from doing certain things: (1) from segregating error-prone from error-free theories; and (2) from using undiluted arithmetic where undiluted arithmetic alone will do. Here again, Steiner seems to place an enormous faith in the unique efficacy of his own ontological interpretation of arithmetic. Earlier, we noted the belief that the rejection of this interpretation entailed the abandonment of all numerical knowledge. Now we find an equally remarkable (and unjustified) belief on the part of Steiner.

Why is the logicist precluded from segregating his mathematical theories according to some criterion of certainty (subjective or objective)? Surely, the Fregean (no less than Steiner) can distinguish a proof in, say, first-order Peano arithmetic from a proof using principles of analysis or set theory. For example, it is well-known, among mathematicians, that certain proofs of the fundamental theorem of algebra are not algebraic in nature but use principles of analysis. If ordinary mathematicians, many of whom may have no special acquaintance with that branch of logic known as proof theory, can distinguish proofs according to the principles used, why cannot the sophisticated logicians who advocate the reduction? Clearly, the reduction of the scientific ontology sketched earlier would not preclude the physicist from distinguishing a scientific explanation using, essentially, only the Boyle–Charles Law from one using a whole array of principles from the kinetic theory. Why then cannot the Fregean place more confidence in certain simple proofs in first-order arithmetic than in other proofs of arithmetical theorems using powerful cardinality axioms of set theory? I see no reason for thinking that his reduction makes him blind to such distinctions.

One final objection to the Frege–Russell account of number will be taken up briefly here. In (Hambourger 1977), it is claimed that the numeral '1' is what is called, in Kripkean possible world semantical theory, a 'rigid designator', *i.e.* one and the same entity is designated by '1' in each possible world. The argument for this claim is based on the plausible intuition that the statement

[*] The number of John's children in W_1 is identical to the number of John's children in W_2

(where W_1 and W_2 are possible worlds) is true iff 'the number of John's children' has the same referent in W_1 as it does in W_2. The idea is that if '1' were not a rigid designator, we could have a situation in which [*] is true, in so far as John has exactly one child in both W_1 and W_2, even though what 'the number of John's children' refers to in W_1 differs from what it refers to in W_2 (contradicting the above intuition). The conclusion that '1' is a rigid designator spells trouble for the Frege–Russell account of number, since the set of all units sets of objects, *i.e.* the number *one* according to that account, in one possible world need not be the same as the set of all unit sets of the objects in another (Hambourger 1977: 413–14).

Now I suspect that Frege would not have been terribly bothered by such an argument, based as it is on a conception of modality that is quite foreign to his own (Frege 1967: 13). And it seems not unlikely that Frege would have simply rejected, as lacking in clear sense, such statements as [*], which contain purported references to specific (non-actual) possible worlds.[15] However, suppose it is allowed that [*] could be literally true – we can suppose here that the set-theoretical model presented in the Kripkean semantical theory is more than a mere model or metaphorical development of some intuitive ideas and that it, instead, provides a literal account of "Reality". A view of this sort is to be found in (Lewis 1973: 84–5) where it is said:

I believe that there are possible worlds other than the one we happen to

---

[15] Kripke, himself, warns us not to take his possible worlds model too seriously: 'we do not begin with worlds (which are supposed somehow to be real, and whose qualities, but not whose objects, are perceptible to us), and then ask criteria of transworld identification; on the contrary, we begin with objects which we *have*, and can identify, in the actual world. We can then ask whether certain things might have been true of the objects' (1972: 157).

inhabit . . . When I profess realism about possible worlds, I mean to be taken literally. Possible words are what they are, and not some other thing.

Now is the Frege-Russell account of cardinality, as presented within the framework of *FRR*, open to the Hambourger objection? Let us consider the semantical underpinnings of [*] suggested by the Kripkean model. It would seem that the extension of the concept of *being a child of John's* is a function of possible worlds: what falls under the concept in W_1 need not be the same as what falls under it in W_2, so the concept can, so to speak, shift its extension from world to world. More specifically, letting U be the union of the domains of the possible worlds, a concept is a function mapping each member of the totality of possible worlds to some subset of U (Kripke 1971: 66–7). And when a concept P takes some possible world W as its argument, its value is a set, the intersection of which with the domain of W can be regarded as *the extension P has in W*. Now given the existence of such Kripkean concepts, there seems to be nothing to prevent us from specifying another sort of concept that is not a function of possible worlds at all, but that simply separates out of U some subtotality. Thus, corresponding to the Kripkean concept of *being a child of John's*, we can specify the concept of *being a child of John's in W_1*, which has as its extension the very extension the former concept has in W_1. The latter concept, in effect, gathers together those possible objects of U that are children of John's in W_1. From the Fregean point of view, according to which concepts are functions having a subset of [T,F] as its value range, the concept of *being a child of John's in W_1* would be a function whose domain is U and which takes the value T only for those possible objects that belong to the extension the Kripkean concept of *being a child of John's* has in W_1. Looked at set-theoretically, there seems to be no reason why there shouldn't exist such a Fregean concept, given the existence of the concepts postulated in the Kripkean semantical theory. Analogously, there should be functions, each with a value range that is a subset of [T,F] and a doman $= U^n$ (where U^n is the nth Cartesian product of U with itself), corresponding to the n-ary relations postulated in the semantical model. Let us call these Fregean concepts, which can be so specified in terms of the Kripkean concepts, 'possible worlds concepts'. Then, taking U as the domain of objects, and the possible worlds concepts as the first level concepts of the Fregean hierarchy of concepts, we can specify an interpretation of *FRR* in terms of which pretty much the standard Frege–Russell analysis of cardinality can be given and which is immune from the Hambourger objection. Since within this framework, '1' would not denote anything, it would not denote different sets in different possible worlds; and since possible worlds concepts do not, so to speak, shift their extensions from world to world, if [*] were true, the cardinality of *being a child of John's in* W_1 would correspond to the same totality of first level concepts as would the cardinality of *being a child of John's in* W_2.

This interpretation of *FRR* has an interesting "spin off". The Axiom of Infinity, given the more standard interpretations, has always seemed to lack the quality of self-evidence that logicists since Frege have wanted their axioms to possess (Russell 1920: 202–5). But, under the above interpretation, that has changed: the axiom is obviously true and in some sense necessarily so.

So much for objections. I have not attempted to meet all that I can think of. And no doubt, there are some others I should have addressed. But one can spend only so much time answering critics. I think enough has been said to motivate further work on *FRR*. *Type theory is not dead*! And if my intuitions are right, we have not heard the last of Ramsey's theory of types.

University of California, Berkeley

REFERENCES

Benacerraf, Paul. 1965. What numbers can be. *Philosophical Review* **74**, 47–73.
Bostock, David. 1974. *Logic and Arithmetic*. Oxford.
Carnap, Rudolf. 1958. *Meaning and Necessity*, 2nd ed., 2nd imp. Chicago.
Chihara, Charles. 1973. *Ontology and the Vicious-Circle Principle*. Ithaca and London.
Church, Alonzo. 1972. Axioms for functional calculi of higher order. In *Logic & Art, Essays in Honor of Nelson Goodman*, ed. R. Rudner & I. Scheffler, pp. 197–213. Indianapolis.
Church, Alonzo. 1974. Russellian simple type theory. *Proceedings and Addresses of The American Philosophical Association* **47**, 21–33.
Cocchiarella, Nino. 1974. Formal ontology and the foundations of mathematics. In *Bertrand Russell's Philosophy*, ed. George Nakhnikian, pp. 29–46. New York.
Dummett, Michael. 1973. *Frege: Philosophy of Language*. Worcester and London.

Fraenkel, A. A. 1966. *Abstract Set Theory*, 3rd ed. Amsterdam.

Fraenkel, A. A. and Bar-Hillel, Y. 1958. *Foundations of Set Theory*. Amsterdam.

Frege, Gottlob. 1952. [Extracts from] a review of Husserl's *Philosophie der Arithmetic*. In *Translations from the Philosophical Writings of Gottlob Frege*, ed. P. Geach & M. Black, pp. 79–85. Oxford.

Frege, Gottlob. 1953. *The Foundations of Arithmetic*, trans. J. L. Austin. Oxford.

Frege, Gottlob. 1964. *The Basic Laws of Arithmetic*, intro. and trans. M. Furth. Berkeley and Los Angeles.

Frege, Gottlob. 1967. *Begriffsschrift*. In *From Frege to Gödel, A Source Book in Mathematical Logic, 1879–1931*. pp. 1–82. Cambridge, Mass.

Gandy, R. O. 1977. The simple theory of types. In *Logic Colloquium* **76**, ed. R. Gandy & M. Hyland, pp. 173–81. Amsterdam.

Gödel, Kurt. 1964a. Russell's mathematical logic. In *Philosophy of Mathematics: Selected Readings*, ed. P. Benacerraf & H. Putnam, pp. 211–32. Englewood Cliffs, New Jersey.

Gödel, Kurt. 1964b. What is Cantor's continuum problem? In *Philosophy of Mathematics: Selected Readings*, ed. P. Benacerraf & H. Putnam, pp. 258–73. Englewood Cliffs, New Jersey.

Hambourger, Robert. 1977. A difficulty with the Frege–Russell definition of number. *Journal of Philosophy* **74**, 409–14.

Hinst, Peter. 1975. Hatte Frege ohne Wertverlaufsfunktion auskommen können? In *Frege und die Moderne Grundlagenforschung*, ed. C. Thiel, pp. 33–51. Meisenheim am Glan.

Jourdain, Philip. 1912. The development of the theories of mathematical logic and the principles of mathematics. *The Quarterly Journal of Pure and Applied Mathematics* **43**, 219–314.

Kitcher, Philip. 1978. The plight of the Platonist. *Noûs* **12**, 119–36.

Kripke, Saul. 1971. Semantical considerations on modal logic. In *Reference and Modality*, ed. L. Linsky, pp. 62–72. Oxford.

Kripke, Saul. 1972. Naming and necessity. In *Semantics of Natural Language*, ed. D. Davidson & G. Harman, pp. 137–239. Dordrecht.

Lewis, David. 1973. *Counterfactuals*. Cambridge, Mass.

Moss, J. M. B. 1972. Some B. Russell sprouts (1903–1908). In *Conference in Mathematical Logic – London '70*, pp. 211–50. Berlin.

Putnam, Hilary. 1978. *Meaning and the Moral Sciences*. London, Henley and Boston.

Quine, W. V. O. 1938. On the theory of types. *Journal of Symbolic Logic* **3**, 125–39.

Quine, W. V. O. 1951. *Mathematical Logic*, revised ed. Cambridge, Mass.

Quine, W. V. O. 1960. *Word and Object*. Cambridge, Mass.

Quine, W. V. O. 1961. Two dogmas of empiricism. In *From a Logical Point of View*, 2nd ed. Cambridge, Mass.

Quine, W. V. O. 1963. *Set Theory and Its Logic*. Cambridge, Mass.

Quine, W. V. O. 1966. Carnap and logical truth. In *The Ways of Paradox and Other Essays*. New York.

Quine, W. V. O. 1969. Ontological relativity. In *Ontological Relativity and Other Essays*. New York and London.

Ramsey, F. P. 1925. The foundations of mathematics. In his *Foundations*, ed. D. H. Mellor, pp. 152–212. 1978. London.

Resnik, Michael. 1965. Frege's theory of incomplete entities. *Philosophy of Science* **32**, 329–41.

Russell, Bertrand. 1920. *Introduction to Mathematical Philosophy*. London.

Russell, Bertrand. 1931. Review of Frank Ramsey's *The Foundations of Mathematics and other Logic Essays*. *Mind* **41**, 476–82.

Steiner, Mark. 1975. *Mathematical Knowledge*. Ithaca and London.

Wang, Hao. 1974. *From Mathematics to Philosophy*. London.

3   Ramsey's theory of belief and truth

BRIAN LOAR

Ramsey's outstanding 1927 paper, 'Facts and propositions', is perhaps best known for its redundancy theory of truth. But that theory can be seen to be, in Ramsey's scheme, ancillary to the far more important foundational concern of the theory of belief or judgement – that is, the analysis of ascriptions of the form 'x believes (judges) that . . .' When Ramsey's theory is seen in that context, it takes on a quite different aspect than when viewed alone: to explicate completely what it is for something to be true turns out to require a substantive theory of belief, the conditions of which, as we shall see, may be represented as part of the meaning of 'true'. This is contrary to an established view of Ramsey as holding the analysis of 'true' to require no elaborate philosophical constructions.

While in what follows I shall be concerned to show that the connections between a redundancy theory of truth and other more substantive and complex theories of truth can be quite different from what they are often supposed to be, that is not ultimately the main point. For, with Ramsey, it seems to me that the fundamental question concerns the theory of belief; and the theory of belief that he sketched in 'Facts and propositions' is the sort of theory that, if it could be spelled out, would serve nicely as the foundation of the theory of meaning and truth conditions. In the last part of this paper I shall indicate a way of filling out Ramsey's sketch.

Ramsey's conception of the general nature of belief has quite dropped from view in subsequent theorising, largely, I think, because of difficulties in its account of the logical form of belief sentences. It would be of major importance to the theory of meaning and of mental representation if such a conception were still viable despite the long neglect of it, in some form that avoided those difficulties about logical form. Here are five conditions that capture that conception while abstracting from those problematic specifics.

First, beliefs are interlinguistically ascribable. While Ramsey appeared to have doubts about this condition with regard to complex beliefs, his framework suggests (as we can see in the final reconstruction) a way of making the condition fully general. Secondly, beliefs are not relations to propositions, Fregean senses, Meinongian objectives, and so on. Thirdly, a belief ascription does not give the content of a belief by referring to a sentence or utterance of the ascriber's *as having a certain meaning*. Fourthly, an adequate theory of belief yields as a corollary a theory of truth, one moreover that is, in a strict sense to be defined, a redundancy theory. Fifthly, beliefs are naturalistically defined states; more specifically, having a belief is a matter of being in a state with certain causal properties – *e.g.* having certain direct or indirect relations to perception, and having certain relations to behaviour. The third condition, which establishes a major difference between Ramsey's theory and the two best known non-propositional theories (Carnap 1947; Davidson 1969), would permit belief to have a foundational status in the theory of meaning. For the concept of belief could then quite straightforwardly be used in the explication of such semantical concepts as that of a sentence's having a certain meaning in a certain population or in the mouth of a certain speaker. It is safe to say that, for Ramsey, as for Russell, the theory of belief or judgement is the foundation of the theory of meaning; indeed one might even say that for them it *is* the theory of meaning. The theory of belief that I shall outline later in this paper satisfies those five conditions and, except in certain rather superficial respects, is quite in the spirit of Ramsey's theory.

As for Ramsey's account of truth, when properly understood it stands in marked contrast to another famous redundancy theory – namely, Quine's disquotational theory. Indeed the two are exactly poles apart, despite Ramsey's theory's usual image; to this contrast I shall turn at the end of this paper.

The logical form of belief ascriptions. Probably the best known feature of Ramsey's theory of belief is his account of the logical form of a belief-ascription. Following Russell, he takes it to assert a "multiple relation" between the believer and (what I shall henceforth simply call) the referents of the belief, including not only the particulars the belief is about but also whatever properties and relations are expressed by predicates in the that-clause. Thus Ramsey would take 'Othello believes that Desdemona loves Cassio' to have the form B (Othello, Desdemona, love, Cassio). Naturally the information contained in the belief ascription is not exhausted by listing the referents; among other factors to be mentioned, their order is important, since the beliefs that aRb and that bRa may be distinct. But somehow the belief-relation does the ordering, so that 'B(x, a, R, b)' and 'B (x, b, R, a)' differ appropriately.

Ramsey did not discuss the possibility that belief is a relation to a sentence or utterance of the ascriber's. But he gave reasons for rejecting propositions as the objects of beliefs, and they were two. First he perceived, with Russell, "the incredibility of the existence of such objects as 'that Caesar died in his bed' which could be described as objective falsehoods" (p. 138). Outdoing Russell, he rejects even facts as entities, maintaining that 'the fact that. . .' does not denote. Secondly, and perhaps more importantly in this context, taking propositions to be the objects of belief would make truth and falsity into "unanalysable attributes". (His subsequent remark, 'truth and falsity are primarily ascribed to propositions' is best read as a manner of speaking; on this, more below.)

The multiple relation theory of belief has commonly been thought to lead to insurmountable problems, because it requires having to introduce a multitude of belief-relations. But that consequence is eliminable. There are two rather different sources for this multiplicity of belief relations, and eliminating them can be achieved by the use of two complementary devices, both technical tricks, one of which is more a real reformulation of Ramsey's theory than the other.

The first source of multiplicity is simply that beliefs can have different numbers of referents. So 'Henry believes that Suzanne admires Archibald' expresses a four-place relation: B $(h,s,$ admiration, $a)$; while 'Henry believes that Suzanne prefers Archibald to William' expresses a five-place relation: B$(h, s,$ preference, $a, w)$. But eliminating this multiplicity is very easily achieved, simply by gathering the referents of those beliefs into ordered n-tuples, so that we have: B$(h, \langle s,$ admiration, $a \rangle)$, and B$(h, \langle s,$ preference, $a, w \rangle)$. If it appears that this is too much of a trick, perhaps it will help to reflect that, on certain views, propositions themselves are complex entities, and that in any case, what will do as the objects of B requires a lot more to be said about B.

The second source of multiplicity lies in what Ramsey regards the contribution of logical operators to the that-clause to be. In 'Henry believes that Suzanne does not love Archibald', the 'not' does not name anything as 'love' does. So, that asserts the relation of disbelief among Henry, Suzanne, love and Archibald, which is a different relation from that asserted by the corresponding love-ascribing-belief-sentence. On Ramsey's theory there is no way of making the difference a matter of a difference in the relata, so it must be a difference in the relation. But that leads to a gigantic awkwardness. For it is clear that to every distinct logical form in the that-clause (where the distinctness is not due to the number of referents) there must then correspond a distinct belief-relation. So 'x believes that either y is φ to z or w is not ψ to u' expresses the two-placed relation B' $(x, \langle y, \varphi, z, w, \psi, u \rangle)$, while '$x$ believes that y is φ to z and w is ψ to u' expresses the distinct two-placed relation B‡ $(x, \langle y, \varphi, z, w, \psi, u \rangle)$. Nothing in Ramsey's theory suggests how at the level of logical form we might treat B' and B as being logically complex; and, if matters are left thus, we have on our hands a rather large, some would say infinite, number of semantically simple belief-relational expressions.

There is a quite simple device for introducing logical structure into the relational expressions that result from deleting the names of the believer and the referents of the belief. While clearly departing from the letter of what Ramsey says, it is compatible with the spirit both of his remarks about what belief-ascriptions do *not* refer to and, as I shall later discuss in detail, how they are to be explicated in terms of the causal properties of beliefs. At this point I shall introduce it merely at the superficial level of logical form without indicating how it connects up with the analysis of the relation.

The trick is of course to take the relevant structure to be metalinguistic. (Why this does not stand in the way of the theory's satisfying the third condition on being a Ramsey-type theory that I gave at the outset will, again, have to wait for the analysis.) The idea is that, for example, 'x believes that y is not φ to z' has the form: B(x, [——— is not . . . to – – –], $\langle y, \varphi, z \rangle$), or, if we now introduce metalinguistic letters into the blanks:

$$B(x, \ulcorner \alpha \text{ is not } \beta \text{ to } \gamma \urcorner, \langle y, \varphi, z \rangle).$$

The middle term of this relation is a structural description, a logically complex way of picking out classes of sentences in a way that exhibits their syntactical relations to other classes of sentences. The relational expression corresponding to B′ is then logically complex: $B(x, \ulcorner \alpha$ is β to γ or δ is not ε to $\xi \urcorner \langle \gamma, \varphi, z, w, \psi, u \rangle)$, where the '$x$' and the letters in '$\langle . . . \rangle$' are variables, and the expression in the middle place denotes an open sentence. And so we have just one three-place belief-relation. This could seem a rather substantial departure from Ramsey's account, but in the light of its final incorporation in the analysis of belief it will not, I think, appear so.

Ramsey's redundancy theory. Ramsey presents his account of truth simply as an obvious point to be noted before pursuing the main task of the analysis of belief. Now his account has not seemed to everyone to be impeccable in its use of variables; but there are ways of interpreting what he says so that instead of our finding use–mention confusions, all that needs to be attributed is a certain controversial attitude towards quantification. In this spirit it seems there are two ways of interpreting Ramsey's theory of truth, one in terms of substitutional quantification and the other in terms of higher-order quantification.

First, he writes: 'truth and falsity are ascribed primarily to propositions' (p. 44. This and subsequent page references are to Ramsey 1978). That happens in two contexts. In one, truth is ascribed to the "explicitly given" proposition, as in: 'It is true that Caesar was murdered', which, Ramsey says, "means no more than that Caesar was murdered". In the other sort of context, truth is predicated of "described" propositions, as in 'He is always right', which is initially to be read as 'for all p, if he asserts p, p is true.' But the point then is that 'is true' is not really required in a well understood logical notation after 'p', for "the propositional function p is true is simply the same as p, as, *e.g.*, its value 'Caesar was murdered is true' is the same as 'Caesar was murdered' " (p. 45). Thus we may simply drop 'is true'. Given Ramsey's quite determined earlier rejection of propositions as entities, the remark 'truth and falsity are ascribed primarily to propositions' can be only understood as a grammatical claim; then the use of the variable 'p' must be substitutional, which makes good sense of dropping 'is true'.

In another passage we find something that is intended as a clarification of the foregoing but which, when the quantification is rectified, is a slightly different theory. Suppose the only form of proposition were aRb; "then, 'He is always right' could be expressed by 'For all a, R, b, if he asserts aRb then aRb', to which 'true' would be an obviously superfluous addition" (p. 45). Now it is pretty clear that the variables here are quite objectual; the actual items a, R, b are being quantified over, and not just some sentence that mentions them. On that understanding we should regard 'R' as a higher order variable in 'then aRb'.

What general theory of truth is to be had from generalising this last device? Consider this suggestion: somehow you use higher-order variables over all possible properties, relations, *etc.*, that might occur in the n-tuples of the referents of beliefs. We needn't worry too much about the difficulties in that, for, even if something could be done with it, it still would be far too restricted to give us a general account of truth for beliefs. The reason we have in effect already seen: the referents of a belief and their order do not in general determine the truth-conditions of a belief. Whether a belief is negative is not thereby captured, and so for all complex logical forms. So the use of higher-order quantification over properties and relations to define truth would require defining it separately for every logical form: for all a, R, b, the belief that not aRb is true iff not aRb, and so on *ad infinitum*. An awkward theory.

That gives the substitutional interpretation the edge in respect of manageability, but it is not that intuitive an interpretation of Ramsey's view, given his strong emphasis on the referents of a belief as determinants of truth conditions. The conflict gets resolved on the reconstruction I later present of the redundancy theory, on which the referents certainly come into the picture.

But Ramsey's theory on either sort of quantification will appear to many, as it does to me, not to yield a solid basis for eliminating 'true'. For while there is nothing wrong with substitutional or higher order quantification, they require (according to my intuitions) a gloss in terms of ordinary first-order metalinguistic or objectual quantification when they are used in philosophical explication. So, 'iff aRb', for variable a, R, b, means: 'iff R is true of $\langle a, b \rangle$'; and the substitutional '$(\forall p)$ the belief that p is true iff p' makes good sense if the right-hand 'p' is elliptical for 'p is true'. Thus we have no elimination of 'true' by those devices, according at least to my intuitions about quantification. Naturally if it were thought that, say, substitutional quantification is as primitively comprehensible as the objectual sort, the Ramsey theory could be accepted as an eliminative theory. But I shall be proposing another redundancy theory of truth for beliefs which requires nothing controversial in the way of theories of quantification.

Ramsey's analysis of belief. Ramsey distinguishes two factors in a belief, the mental and the objective. The mental factor comprises the words or the sentence one assents to or accepts, or better the whole state of affairs of one's accepting such and such a sentence. The objective factor consists of everything about the belief that on a propositional theory is contained in the proposition; as we have seen, that is not exhausted by the belief's references. Ramsey's mental factor is what now we would call a sentential attitude – a relation between a person and a sentence of that person's own language. On the metalinguistic interpretation of belief-sentences, the objective factors are captured, somehow, by the n-tuple of references together with the open sentence that is, under a certain structural description, the middle term of the relation. (On Ramsey's unreconstructed account the objective factors are partly a matter of the belief's referents, partly a matter of how the belief-relation orders the referents, and partly a matter of what belief-relation is involved, *e.g.*, 'disbelieves'.) Let me emphasise that the (open) sentence that occurs on the metalinguistic account is not thereby being referred to as a component of the mental factor, for it is in our language, while the mental factor is in the believer's language.

An analysis of belief for Ramsey would be an account of what it is about z's having a certain attitude towards a sentence of z's that constitutes z thereby as believing that p. Ramsey's proposal is this: it is a matter of z's state, his attitude toward that sentence, having certain *causal properties*. The causal properties of the mental factors of a belief determine its objective factors – *i.e.* what proposition captures the content of the belief. It seems fair to say that for Ramsey the theory of *belief* and the theory of *meaning* are one and the same: what makes a certain sentence of z's mean p is whatever constitutes a mental relation to that sentence as being the belief that p. (This explains Ramsey's ending a paper devoted entirely to the subject of belief thus: 'The essence of pragmatism I take to be this, that the meaning of a sentence is to be defined by reference to . . . its possible causes and effects' (p. 57).)

The passages in which Ramsey discusses the causal properties theory of belief-content and meaning all concern logical operations: negation, truth-functions in general, and universal quantification. In these discussions something like the following thesis is strongly suggested, although not explicitly enunciated: each aspect of the logical form of a belief corresponds to a distinct systematic aspect of its causal properties. So, as regards negation, there is some systematic relation between the causal properties, for all p, of the belief that p and the belief that not p. If this is Ramsey's idea, any general systematic account of the causal properties of beliefs would have to be able to generalise over belief-pairs so as to take into account only that one is the negation of the other. Now negation, as we saw, is not, on Ramsey's theory, an entity that is to be counted among the referents of a belief, but must be built into the belief-relation, as in 'x believes that not y is φ to z'. Moreover there is not just one such disbelief relation, since other elements of logical form have to be built into the relation within the scope of negation, and they vary. The metalinguistic reconstruction of these multiform belief relations provides the basis for getting the right systematic generalizations for the full range of belief ascriptions, so that any belief that not p can be registered as being structurally thus related to the belief that p. Naturally this is essential to the causal analysis only if it is envisaged that there is some regular relation between the causal properties, for all p, of the belief that p and the belief that not-p.

What, for Ramsey, makes a certain particular or property or relation count among the referents or objects of a belief? It is a matter of its *name's* occurring among the mental factors. At certain points one might get the impression that Ramsey treats the concept of the name-relation as prior to the causal properties idea. But it seems unlikely that he would not have made the connection there as well; and there is the following very condensed passage, which is directed to the question what else is it about the belief that not aRb, apart from what makes it negative, that establishes its content: 'We can say that the causal properties are connected with a, R, and b in such a way that the only things which can have them must be composed of names of a, R, and b' (p. 155). This might be interpreted as saying that some causal relation between 'a' and a is sufficient, given the rest of the causal properties of the belief, for 'a' to be the name of a.

The fact that Ramsey's treatment of atomic beliefs is not

explicitly in terms of their causal properties leads to an awkwardness that the causal analysis would make quite unnecessary. About
the belief that aRb, Ramsey writes: 'the names must be united in a
way appropriate to aRb rather than to bRa; this can be explained by
saying that the name of R is not the word 'R', but the relation we
make between 'a' and 'b' then determines whether it is a belief that
aRb or that bRa' (p. 47). But the problem is not solved by making
something that is syntactically more comprehensive than 'R' the
name of R. For the problem is precisely how a mere collection of
names, of whatever form, can determine that the belief is true iff
aRb rather than iff bRa. Secondly, it seems natural, given the causal
property theory, to interpret 'the sense in which this [syntactical]
relation unites 'a' and 'b'' as referring to a causal property of the
mental state involving those names thus united. The difference then
between the belief that aRb and the belief that bRa lies in their causal
properties, for example in the former's being, among other things, a
state that tends to be brought about by a certain perceptual contact
with the fact that aRb rather than the fact that bRa.

As Ramsey emphasises, all this is more a sketch of an analysis
than an analysis. The general idea, couched in terms of the metalinguistic adjustment of Ramsey's belief-relations, is that some-
thing of the form $B(x, \ulcorner F\alpha_1 \ldots \alpha_n \urcorner, \langle y_1 \ldots y_n \rangle)$ is true of a believer
x just when x is in a state involving words of x's own language that
has such and such causal properties. For such an analysis to yield
sufficient conditions for having a specific belief, somehow distinct
complexes of the form $\langle \ulcorner Fa_1 \ldots a_n \urcorner, \langle y_1 \ldots y_n \rangle \rangle$ must systemati-
cally be associated with distinct causal properties.

Redundancy and correspondence. Ramsey's famous dictum that there is
"no separate problem of truth" (that is, separate from the problem
of belief) could lead one to expect him to proceed first by presenting
the theory of belief and then on that basis the theory of truth. But it
seems that he does precisely the opposite, presenting the redundancy theory first in such a way that it depends not at all on even the
general nature of the analysis of belief. Not only, it may seem, is
there no separate problem of truth, there is no problem at all. This is
not the most interesting way to read Ramsey, but to show that takes
some preliminary explanations.

An important difference among theories of truth has been as
follows. (1) On the one hand, truth conditions have been seen as

quite substantive, contingent properties of their bearers (sentences, utterances, sentential attitudes) which they have by virtue of social and/or psychological facts that in part consist in certain non-trivial (*e.g.* causal) relations between aspects of the bearers of truth and extralinguistic items that figure in the truth conditions. The contingent truth of *s* then is a matter of the correspondence, in part determined by those non-trivial relations, of two quite different contingencies, *viz.*, the one that consists in *s*'s truth conditions, and the extralinguistic fact. (Austin's theory (Austin 1950) is a paradigm of this genre.) (2) On the other hand, truth-conditions have been seen as trivial facts about their bearers, which have them non-contingently or essentially. Paradigms of this category are the otherwise quite different theories of Strawson, that truth is predicated of statements (= propositions) (Strawson 1950), and of Quine, that 'true' is a device of disquotation (Quine 1970). Not too surprisingly, it has usually been supposed that redundancy theories are always of type (2). Ramsey's theory of truth has, I think, usually been seen thus.

When I think of what it might mean to say that truth consists in some sort of correspondence between language and the world I think of theories of type (1). Some have seen matters differently. Perhaps out of scepticism that a substantive account of truth-conditions can be worked out, or fear of adverse epistemological consequences, what there is intuitively in the idea of correspondence has at times been thought to consist simply in redundancy. Thus Prior describes Ramsey's theory as a correspondence theory merely on the grounds that it holds that " '*x* says (believes) truly that *p*' means '*x* says (believes) that *p*, and *p*' " (Prior 1967).

While of course Ramsey does hold the latter theory, 'Facts and propositions' bears an interpretation under which it is also a correspondence theory in a stronger sense, a correspondence theory in a sense which merely being a redundancy theory is not sufficient for, in other words, a theory of type (1). If that is so, not all redundancy theories are of type (2); a theory of truth can be both a redundancy theory and a correspondence theory in the strong sense.

Here is the key passage:

if we have analyzed judgment we have solved the problem of truth; for taking the mental factor in a judgment (which is often itself called a judgment) the truth or falsity of *this* [my italics] depends also on what proposition it is that is judged, and what we have to explain is the meaning of saying that the judgment is a judgment that *a* has *R* to *b*, i.e. is true if *aRb*, false if not (p. 45).

It would seem that '*this*' refers to the mental factor, the sentential attitude, which is then being described as itself having truth or falsity. Now, a reasonable interpretation to place on all of this is as follows. The real problem of truth is what makes the mental factor, the sentential attitude (as opposed to the proposition) true or false. Think of a belief as a certain event or state that has different descriptions. One description applies to it in terms of the intrinsic details of the mental factors involved: 'Pierre's acceptance of the French sentence *s*.' Another mentions no intrinsic details of the mental factors, but describes the state entirely relationally – *i.e.* as a belief that such and such, this involving mention (on the meta-linguistic reconstruction) both of some open sentence of ours, and of the references of the belief, thus: 'Pierre's belief that not *aRb*.'

Under the latter description the predication of truth-conditions is trivial: 'Pierre's belief that not *aRb* is true iff not *aRb*.' Under the former description it is not trivial: 'Pierre's acceptance of the French sentence *s* is (of something) true iff not *aRb*.' Thus the bearer of truth-conditions, the mental factor, has those truth conditions contingently. So we have: (1) It is not contingent that if *x* = *z*'s belief that not *aRb* then *x* is true iff not *aRb*; (2) It is a contingent fact about *x* that *x* is a belief that not *aRb*, for that depends upon its causal properties, which are contingent. (3) Hence, it is a *contingent* fact about the belief *x* that *x* is true iff not *aRb*. The non-contingency in (1) and the contingency in (3) are quite compatible, the former being *de dicto* and the latter *de re*.

So although the predication of 'true' of the belief that . . . is, under that description and given the existence of the belief, equivalent simply to . . ., the truth-conditions of the belief are no trivial property of it. In a perfectly straightforward sense, the theory of truth would have as a major component the theory of what it is for something to be the belief that . . ., which is hardly a trivial matter.

What is a redundancy theory of truth? Let 'Φ . . .' stand for descriptions of the bearers of truth that contain either the sentence '. . .' or a structural description thereof. A redundancy theory will at least imply, for some such Φ and for every relevant '. . .' something of the form '$\square$ if *x* = Φ . . ., then *x* is true iff . . .' It would be incorrect to put the requirement thus: '$\square \Phi$ . . . is true iff . . .' For suppose 'Φ . . .' has the form of a definite description: to read it as having wider scope than '$\square$' would not cover the redundancy theory that has just emerged, on which such and such truth-conditions are only contingent properties of their bearers. But to give 'Φ . . .' narrower scope than '$\square$' might then yield equivalences such as: '$\square$ z's belief that snow is white is true iff snow is white' which has the consequence that necessarily if snow is white z believes it. The idea should rather be that necessarily *if* z believes that snow is white then z's belief is true iff snow is white.

Now the form given does not exclude theories on which truth-conditions are *essential* properties of their bearers: that is the case when 'Φ . . .' non-contingently denotes whatever it denotes. So, for example, on Strawson's theory the bearer of truth is the statement that p, which is to say, what is said rather than the saying of it, the proposition p. Since the statement that p has that property essentially, it has its truth-conditions essentially.

So we may distinguish two kinds of redundancy theory. The first kind, to which Ramsey's theory as I have interpreted it belongs, we might call *de dicto* redundancy theories, because the term 'Φ . . .' occurs merely *de dicto* in the modal statement that gives specific truth-conditions; the necessity in which the redundancy consists is not a matter of the essential properties of the bearer of truth but stems rather from how it is described. The second kind may be called *de re* redundancy theories, of which Strawson's theory is a paradigm. The necessity is *de re*; and truth-conditions are essential properties of their bearers. It is important to notice about *de dicto* theories that they would in general also be (what I have called) strong correspondence theories: truth-conditions depend upon contingent properties of the bearers of truth, properties that then must be accounted for in a fully explicative theory.[1]

---

[1] It is interesting to note that a *de dicto* redundancy theory using Ramseyan quantification is easily constructed in terms of Austin's theory of truth (Austin 1950), a paradigm strong correspondence theory. His theory was: a statement (= utterance) is true just when the state of affairs correlated with the statement by the demonstrative conventions is of the type correlated with the sentence by the descriptive conventions. Suppose we identify a state of affairs with a space–time region t. Then let us say that if t is correlated with U by the demonstrative conventions and P is correlated with the relevant sentence by the descriptive conventions, then U is a statement that Pt. Then 'true' may be defined thus: U is true iff, for some P and t, U is a statement that Pt, and Pt. The difference between Austin's and Strawson's theories then would lie in a disagreement not about redundancy but simply about what the bearer of truth is; that disagreement of course implies a further disagreement about whether the explication of the notion 'statement that Pt' or something like it must be part of the definition of 'true'.

We do not yet have a sufficient condition for a redundancy theory; the case by case redundancies in '$\square$ if $x = \Phi$ . . . then x is true iff . . .' are not enough. For if 'true' is redundant it must be eliminable from all contexts, including those in which 'Φ . . .' is not "explicitly given", *e.g.* in generalizations such as 'Whatever he believes about the corruption of officials is true'. Moreover, on any eliminative explication of a term the concern is not just to eliminate that term alone, but to do so without using similarly problematic terms. That means that the context 'Φ . . .' itself requires scrutiny. Even if, for example, one could accept substitutional quantification as not in need of further objectual (*i.e.* metalinguistic) clarification, Ramsey's general account still would pass muster as an adequate theory only if it contained an explicative account of belief that relied on no concept like truth. That is, of course, the point of the causal properties theory. In general it seems reasonable not to accept as a fully adequate theory of truth a theory that relies on unexplicated uses of 'believes', 'says' and so on. It may be precisely there that the real work for a theory of truth lies. So, finally, an adequate redundancy theory would satisfy these two conditions. First, it should be a genuinely eliminative explication of 'true' in all contexts, relying on no unexplicated semantical or mentalistic notions. This is a very strong condition indeed. Secondly it should entail all case by case redundancies – that is, for every relevant '. . .', something of the form '$\square$ if $x = \Phi$ . . ., then x is true iff . . .'. (I say every *relevant* '. . .' to cover problems about the semantical paradoxes, about which more below.)

My characterisation of *de dicto* redundancy theories raises this question. If it is *via* the necessary equivalence of 'Φ . . . is true' and '. . .' that the concept 'true' is to be understood, what role does '. . .' play in descriptions of the states denoted by 'Φ . . .' that makes it interesting or *use*ful to have a predicate, such as 'true', whose predication on '. . .' is equivalent to '. . .'? Without an answer to that question the redundancy of 'true' would be far from the illuminating fact it has been taken to be; on the contrary it would be very puzzling indeed.

The situation then, on Ramsey's theory, given the adjustment of the account of the logical form of belief descriptions, is this. Somehow sentences of the form $\ulcorner B\ (x, \ulcorner F\alpha_1 . . . \alpha_n \urcorner, \langle y_1 . . . y_n \rangle) \urcorner$ capture the causal properties of certain mental, linguistic states of x. And somehow the predicate 'true' is to be defined on these states so that its application to one of them is equivalent to the corresponding non-semantical condition. Ramsey appears to have assumed that to give these relevant causal properties of the state is *thereby* to give the truth-conditions; but as we shall see it is not quite as simple as that.

Defining 'true'. Suppose there is a sense of 'true' on which it applies only to beliefs. As surprising as it may be, there is a quite simple procedure, which uses only quite familiar materials, including nothing but ordinary first order quantification, which is based on the metalinguistic account of the logical form of belief ascriptions, and which yields a genuine redundancy theory of 'true' – an eliminative explication that implies the relevant necessary equivalences. The explicative conditions that emerge are quite easily shown to be strongly equivalent to the pre-analytic predicate 'true' of beliefs on one quite simple assumption about it. Let it be clear that I am speaking of a definition of truth not for sentential attitudes (thus described) but for propositional attitudes which, I am assuming, we ascribe to others by, in part, explicitly referring to sentences of our own.

The basic datum or assumption of the theory is this: we have, for every s: $\ulcorner \Box$ the belief that s is true iff $s \urcorner$. Or, if it is the datable beliefs of individuals and not types that are to be counted as true, the relevant intuitive schema is: $\ulcorner \Box$ if $x = z$'s belief (at t) that s, then x is true iff $s \urcorner$. If there are referential positions in $\ulcorner$ that $s \urcorner$, *e.g.* demonstratives, token reflexives, and so on, then those schemata hold, for each s, for every consistent assignment of references to both occurrences of s. The point I shall make is simplest with respect to the former schema, where it is belief types that are the subjects of predication, but that doesn't really matter. Let us, for simplicity's sake, also restrict attention first to the non-Ramseyan case, if it exists, in which the belief is purely *de dicto*, *i.e.* the only thing referred to in the that-clause is our sentence s. Then we may generalise.

Let T be the homophonic truth-predicate defined, à la Tarski,[2] over all sentences in the range of the belief relation. Naturally the question of the semantical paradoxes arises. But so that I might launch the basic idea without immediately facing squalls, let me assume the range of 's' to have somehow been appropriately restricted; any further full treatment of truth for beliefs will then

---

[2] (Tarski 1956). For useful accounts of what a Tarski-type truth predicate is, see Quine (1970, pp. 12–13 and ch. 3), and Field (1972).

depend upon some independently motivated treatment of 'true' that deals with the paradoxes. Now the definition of the homophonic predicate T deductively implies every instance of $\ulcorner$T $\bar{s}$ iff $s\urcorner$, where $\bar{s}$ stands for a structural descriptive name of s; we then have $\ulcorner\square$ T $\bar{s}$ iff $s\urcorner$ for every s. But that together with the earlier strong equivalence of $\ulcorner$the belief that s is true$\urcorner$ and s, for every relevant s, permits defining truth for beliefs very straightforwardly: 'x is true' $=$ $_{\text{def.}}$ '($\exists s$) x is the belief that s and Ts'. If the bearers of truth are the "mental" factors of states of individuals, we need something relativised to persons at times, thus 'x is true' $=$ $_{\text{def.}}$ '($\exists s$) x is z's belief at t that s, and Ts.' (The believer's sentence is the mental factor x or some component of it; s is *our* sentence.)

We may now generalise in the obvious way to those more Ramseyan beliefs the specification of which requires mentioning their references. Let s range over not only closed sentences but also pairs consisting of an open sentence s' and a sequence of referents $\langle x_1 \ldots x_n \rangle$, and let T$s$ be defined for those cases as 'Sat $(s', \langle x_1 \ldots x_n \rangle)$' where 'Sat' is the homophonic Tarski-type satisfaction relation. The definition of 'true' as stated thus covers all cases.[3]

(This suggests yet a further revision of Ramsey's theory. Ramsey counted among the referents of a belief the properties and relations expressed by predicates in the that-clause. Without higher-order quantification the truth-conditions of the belief that aRb are then that *a has R to b* – i.e. that $\langle a,b \rangle$ instantiates R, or that R is *true of* $\langle a,b \rangle$. The satisfaction relation can be used to well known good effect here. Parse 'z believes that aRb' not as 'B $(z, \ulcorner\alpha$ has φ to $\beta\urcorner$, $\langle a, R, b \rangle)$' but as 'B $(z, \ulcorner R\alpha\beta\urcorner, \langle a, b \rangle)$'. That belief is true just when Sat $(\ulcorner R\alpha\beta\urcorner, \langle a, b \rangle)$, which eliminates 'true of' from the truth conditions.)

Is the above definition of 'true' a redundancy theory? Certainly it succeeds in eliminating 'true' at least superficially from all contexts, for the Tarskian definition of T relies on nothing semantical. And it does imply case by case redundancies, at least superficially – that is, the definition of 'true' implies, for each s, $\ulcorner\square$ the belief that s is true

---

[3] To those familiar with Hartry Field's 'Tarski's theory of truth' (1972), a question may have arisen at this juncture which the following may help to answer. The Tarskian constructions whose adequacy I have argued for here are the pure Tarski-type truth and satisfaction predicates. They do not require for their definition any independent semantical notions, such as Field's primitive denotation, and a glance at the argument shows that they are all we need here. As regards non-trivial, naturalistic reference, the items in $\langle x_1 \ldots x_n \rangle$ after B are the references of the belief, according to the subsequent theory, by virtue of some sort of functional and/or causal relations to the belief.

iff $s^\lceil$. But I say 'at least superficially' since we do not yet know whether something semantical lurks beneath the surface of 'believes', and, as I earlier maintained, we should not be impressed by an explication of 'true' that relies on unanalysed occurrences of 'believes' or 'says'.

To the question of 'believes' I shall shortly turn. But if that is all right, we are in the following situation with regard to truth. It will for many come as no surprise that the Tarski-construction turns out to be essential to a redundancy theory (*i.e.* given the unacceptability of taking substitutional or higher-order quantification as basic.) But it may seem odd that, first, our own homophonic T can be used in a theory of *interlinguistically* ascribable truth-conditions, and, secondly, that a theory of interlinguistically ascribable truth can be a redundancy theory. We are used to thinking of Tarskian truth-predicates in two connections. First there is the Quinean use, in explicating 'true' as a disquotation device. Given the assumption that there is a predicate 'true' in English that applies only to English, so that every instance of '$\Box$ $\bar{s}$ is true iff s' holds, the Tarskian construction T fully captures it, and we have redundancy. Secondly, there is the interlinguistic 'true in population P or language L' for variable P and L. This is not *defined* by any Tarskian technique; rather we have for each P or L a finite set of Tarskian conditions that specify the extension of 'true in P or L'. In that case we don't have *redundancy*; for, even if P is identical with *us*, $\lceil\bar{s}$ is true in P iff $s^\lceil$ holds only contingently. So redundancy and an interlinguistic truth predicate have not normally gone hand in hand in a Tarskian framework. But if in saying 'x believes that s' we refer to our s, then even though x speaks no English we are ascribing s interlinguistically (somehow). And if the relation 'believes' can be accounted for without presupposing anything semantical, then the Tarskian constructions may be used, as we have seen, to capture strongly whatever it is that we normally are ascribing to a state when we say it is true, *over and above* what we have already ascribed in calling that state the belief that s.

So we have a theory that is very much like Ramsey's. On it truth is predicated of beliefs, which are interlinguistically ascribable, and the definition of 'true' is a redundancy theory *given* a satisfactory account of 'believes'. Whatever is true or false has that property by virtue of contingently satisfying whatever conditions make it a belief that such and such. And while the elaborateness of Tarski's construction contrasts strikingly with the simplicity of Ramsey's direct attempt, the idea of defining 'true' by somehow just summing up the case by case redundancies, with no further ingredients, is fundamental to both constructions. The rapprochement comes with noticing how the Tarskian device may apply to beliefs.

Functional role and the content of beliefs. So we have: (1) a certain suggestion about the logical form of belief-ascriptions: they assert a relation B to pairs of the form $\langle s, \langle x_1 \ldots x_n \rangle \rangle$, where s is a sentence or open sentence of ours and $x_1 \ldots x_n$ are the referents of the belief (it may happen that $n = 0$); (2) a thesis about the analysis of 'believes': somehow what it is to believe such and such is to be defined in terms of being in a state with certain causal properties; and (3) a thesis about the analysis of 'true' in terms of a Tarskian construction defined over the relata of B.

That brings us to the following two questions. First, how might references to sentences of ours be involved in ascribing to others (who may not speak our language) states with certain causal properties? Secondly, what have truth-conditions to do with such ascriptions?

Suppose we think of the relevant causal properties of the mental factors in a belief as being its *functional role* in a certain functional theory of individuals. That functional theory might involve, say, certain input conditions relating types of perceptual circumstances and certain belief types, certain output conditions relating belief and desire to decision, and decision to action, and certain internal constraints – *e.g.* rationality constraints on the cooccurrence of beliefs, in terms of their logical form. ('Causal' might be too narrow, for functional role may involve, in addition to causal relations, also relation simply of cooccurrence, succession, *etc.*) Now if the content of a belief is determined by its functional role, the functional theory must generate as many distinct functional roles as there are distinct beliefs. That will happen only if fairly specific constraints are part of that theory, *e.g.* in the input-conditions, and in certain "meaning postulates" that are among the internal constraints. But suppose the functional theory, the belief–desire theory, somehow manages to associate a unique functional role with each distinct belief.

Where does the reference to sentences of ours come in? Suppose we take those pairs of sentences and n-tuples of referents (sentential complexes) that are the relata of belief-ascriptions to be *indices* of functional roles, rather in the way numbers are supposed to be indices of temperatures. What number gets assigned to which temperature is determined by the structure of the theory that determines the interpretation of temperature ascriptions. So what sentential complex gets assigned to which functional role is determined by the structure of the belief–desire theory, in which the relations 'x believes that s', 'x desires that s', occur. Why such a system of indices? The idea is that the *structural* relations among the indices, which are primarily their *syntactical* relations, mirror the causal, transitional and cooccurrence relations that determine the functional roles of beliefs. Reference to the sentential complex is then a handy way of picking out a particular causal role.[4]

Now, functional roles are properties of the underlying state-types that have those roles. In the case of beliefs, presumably the internal states that have the relevant functional roles are, at least often, in some important sense (to be clarified in a psychological theory) linguistic states. Those underlying states are Ramsey's *mental factors*; in a belief ascription we give, not the linguistic specifics of the mental factors, but their functional roles. In specifying the functional roles which make those underlying states specific beliefs, we refer to certain sentential complexes, which are the indices of those functional roles and which constitute Ramsey's *objective factors*.

The relation captured by 'believes' to those objective factors is interlinguistically ascribable; while the objective factors involve sentences of our language, those sentences are not the sentences in which the subject's underlying state is couched, are not the mental factors. Those sentences of ours are interlinguistically ascribable as indices of functional roles.

This brings us to what is perhaps the most important aspect of this 'sentential index' theory of belief ascription for the eliminative explication of 'believes' (and therefore of 'true'). It is by virtue of the *syntactical* structure of the sentences referred to in that–clauses that they can serve as indices of functional roles. But that means that it is not by virtue of what those sentences mean in English, or among us, that they play that role. How can that be? The point is that only structural interrelations of indices are needed in assigning them to

---

[4] This sentential index theory of belief ascriptions, together with an account of the structure of the relevant functional theory, is presented in some detail in Chapter III and Chapter V, sections 1 and 2 of my (1981) *Mind and Meaning*.

functional roles, and their syntactical structure is enough. The upshot is that nothing that is problematically *semantical* is presupposed in the explication of B. The referential semantical properties of the belief are captured by two factors: first, what items occur in the n-tuple $\langle x_1 \ldots x_n \rangle$ that belongs to its index; and, secondly, what truth-condition T assigns to the whole sentential complex that is the index. As we have observed, nothing semantical is presupposed in giving a Tarskian definition of T. The earlier theory of truth in this context then qualifies, not merely superficially, as a genuinely eliminative redundancy theory.

There is a final puzzle about truth which, put baldly is: what is the concept for? It is fair I think to say that Ramsey thought it was intimately connected with capturing the causal roles of beliefs. Quite naturally, he took the belief's truth-conditions to be determined by its objective factors, and they are of course determined, on his theory, by the causal properties of the belief. So it would be natural to conclude that in specifying the relevant causal properties of a belief one somehow specifies in its truth-conditions.

The problem is that if those causal properties are identified with functional roles in the sort of functional system I sketched, at least for some beliefs it appears that truth-conditions are irrelevant to their functional roles. The idea is simply that some beliefs' (*e.g.* universal generalisations') relevant functional relations are only to other beliefs and not directly to say, extra-mental perceptual circumstances. But if what I earlier claimed about the adequacy of the syntactical structural properties of sentential indices in mirroring functional roles was correct, capturing the functional role of such a belief does not require specifying anything that seems to yield its truth-conditions. The lateral connections with other beliefs and desires are what matter to its relevant functional role, and not vertical relations to the world.

What this shows, I suggest, is this. The Tarski-predicate T on beliefs captures a certain correlation, between *independently defined* functional roles on the one hand and possible states of affairs (in a manner of speaking) on the other, that is of such importance, for some *further* reason, that we have promoted it to a quite special status, dubbing it 'true'. It is by virtue of this dubbing of T that the redundancy theory holds; and so in a perfectly logical sense, even though in a sense truth-conditions don't need to be mentioned in specifying the functional roles of those beliefs, those functional roles *determine* the beliefs' truth-conditions. That is how defining belief in terms of functional roles can be itself part of the definition of 'true'. What is true is a state that has a certain sort of functional role; the index both encapsulates the functional role and serves as the intermediary in the assignment of truth-conditions to that state.

What then motivates our interest in T? This is a large question. One possible answer is that the beliefs of our fellows, those functional states, tend to be quite reliable under T, that is, are reliable indicators of the obtaining of those states of affairs with which T associates them.[5] Whatever the account is to be of what makes T so special, let me emphasise that no such account is needed for the definition or explication of 'true'. As I have argued, all that is needed for that is the functional theory of beliefs, together with the Tarski predicate T on the standard indices of the functional roles that define specific beliefs. It is a quite separate question what makes T of such great interest that we have apotheosised it under the uniquely special term 'true'.

A genuinely deep dispute about truth. Finally I would like to point out that the distinction between *de re* and *de dicto* redundancy theories of truth is not a very important one, and that a far more fundamental divergence between theories of truth cuts across that distinction. Suppose we had interpreted Ramsey's theory so that it was not the mental factor that is true, *i.e.* the state that contingently is a belief that *s*, (the "first order" state that has that functional role) – but, instead, it is the functional state of *x*'s believing that *s* (the second order state) that is true. That state has an essential property that it is *x*'s state of believing that *s*, and since functional role determines truth-conditions (in the relevant sense) the truth-conditions of that second order state are among its essential properties. We would then have a *de re* redundancy theory. Now I do not think that it is an objective question which of these two theories is correct; it seems rather a matter of taste to prefer one to the other. What they have in common is substantial: on both, truth is interlinguistically ascribable, and, on both, a necessary condition of there existing something with such and such truth conditions is that someone be in a certain psychological state.

But consider Quine's disquotation theory of truth. On it, no

[5] For further motivations for having a truth predicate see Loar (1981) sections V.4 and V.5.

sense is made as such of interlinguistically ascribable truth-conditions; and nothing psychological, social, or involving the use of language comes into the account of 'true'. In effect that was demonstrated earlier when it was shown that, given that there is a predicate 'true' that applies to English sentences in such a way that, for every s, $\ulcorner \Box (\bar{s}$ is true iff $s) \urcorner$ is true (and it is hard to see how one could show there is not such a predicate), then T is strongly equivalent to it. Nothing psychological *etc.* has to be true of s for T to apply to it. Is Quine's theory *de dicto* or *de re*? This hardly matters; but if sentences are types, the theory is *de re*, for their syntactical properties are their essential properties; if sentences are tokens, the theory is *de dicto*.

Quine's theory of truth is radically different in its philosophical consequences from Ramsey's, despite their both being redundancy theories. On Quine's theory virtually nothing of the metaphor of truth's consisting in a correspondence between language or thought and the world is motivated. But, on Ramsey's theory, a reasonably substantial notion of correspondence is implied, with the contingent causal properties of a certain linguistic state corresponding, via the correspondence encapsulated in T, to aspects of the extramental world, aspects to which some of those causal properties may involve causal relations.

University of Southern California

REFERENCES

Austin, J. L. 1950. Truth. *Aristotelian Society Supplementary Volume* **24**, 111–28.
Carnap, Rudolf. 1947. *Meaning and Necessity*. Chicago.
Davidson, Donald. 1969. On saying that. In *Words and Objections*, ed. D. Davidson and J. Hintikka, pp. 158–74. Dordrecht.
Field, Hartry. 1972. Tarski's theory of truth. *Journal of Philosophy* **69**, 347–75.
Loar, Brian. 1981. *Mind and Meaning*. Cambridge.
Prior, A. N. 1967. Correspondence theory of truth. *The Encyclopedia of Philosophy*, ed. Paul Edwards, vol. 2, pp. 223–32. New York.
Quine, W. V. O. 1970. *Philosophy of Logic*. Englewood Cliffs, N.J.
Ramsey, F. P. 1927. Facts and propositions. In his *Foundations*, ed. D. H. Mellor, pp. 40–57. London.

4   Ramsey on belief

JOHN SKORUPSKI

In the semantics of intentional attitudes it is common to find a distinction drawn between two questions. There is the question of logical form, the proper concern of semantics as such – what objects must instantiate what properties or relations if S *hopes* or *believes* or *desires* that *p*. And then there is a question of broader philosophical import: what is it to hope, believe, desire? The distinction, or at least this way of stating the questions distinguished, leaves the character and point of the latter question obscure. We shall have more to say about it below. It also assumes a certain view of semantics. The task of semantics according to this view is to provide – in an illuminatingly systematic way – extensional truth conditions for all the sentences of whatever language may be in question. I shall call this the extensionalist programme. Note that it is the statement of the truth conditions which must, according to this programme, be extensional; so a wide variety of semantical approaches, which diverge in other respects, for example as to the kind of systematising truth conditional theory required, would fall within the programme.

An extremely intuitive philosophical conception informs the extensionalist programme. It is that whenever a sentence has a meaning, the question, what properties must be instantiated by what objects for the sentence to be true, can be properly posed and answered, and that in answering it, perhaps in some suitable theoretical framework, one determines the meaning of the sentence. This is a kind of "realism"; there can be a good deal more to realism of course.

Frank Ramsey's 1927 paper, 'Facts and propositions', is mainly concerned with the "logical analysis" of belief. His theory divides, not altogether cleanly, but neatly enough, into two parts, which one can see as respectively providing answers to the two questions I distinguished. On the one hand, influenced by the *Tractatus*, notably by 5.542, Ramsey proposes a picture theory of thought. (By the *thought that p* I mean any intentional attitude – or where context requires, the content of any intentional attitude – that *p*. In fact Ramsey discusses belief or judgement, but what he says can easily be extended to other intentional attitudes.) On the other hand, influenced by pragmatism, Ramsey puts forward a dispositional view of what it is to believe that *p*.

This summary both simplifies and idealises, as we shall see. But it does put Ramsey's account in an attractive light. Initially at least, three very natural requirements suggest themselves for a theory of belief – or, in general, of intentional attitudes. We want such a theory to bring out in some way the representational character of thought – its character as being in some way *about* the world, and we want it to do justice to the explanatory function of intentional attitudes, as items playing a certain sort of causal role *in* the world. And finally, if we endorse "realism", we want it to do these two things within the constraints set by the extensionalist programme. The logical atomism of Ramsey, Russell and Wittgenstein encompassed the extensionalist programme – it went beyond it in envisaging a reduction of all sentences to truth-functional compounds of atomic sentences, that is, of sentences formed from names and semantically simple *n*-place predicates. So Ramsey's theory promises to meet all three requirements. We shall consider whether it does. But of course requirements on philosophical theories can be hard to reconcile, and further philosophical reflection can overturn initial requirements.

In the first paragraph of 'Facts and propositions' Ramsey writes:

the problem with which I propose to deal is the logical analysis of what may be called by any of the terms judgement, belief, or assertion. Suppose I am at this moment judging that Caesar was murdered: then it is natural to distinguish in this fact on the one side either my mind, or my present mental state, or words or images in my mind, which we will call the mental factor or factors, and on the other side either Caesar, or Caesar's murder, or Caesar and murder, or the proposition Caesar was murdered, or the fact that Caesar was murdered, which we will call the objective factor, or factors; and to suppose that the fact that I am judging that Caesar was murdered consists in the holding of some relation or relations between these mental and objective factors. The questions that arise are in regard to the nature of the two sets of factors and of the relations between them, the fundamental distinction between these elements being hardly open to question (Ramsey 1978: 40. Subsequent reference to this edition of Ramsey's papers will be by page numbers only.).

Ramsey dismisses in fairly brisk style the suggestion that the objective factor is a proposition, on grounds of incredibility and obscurity; he also dismisses the suggestion that the objective factor is a fact (to which a judgement is related by one of two relations, depending on whether it is true or false) on the grounds that such a phrase as 'Caesar was murdered', in the context 'He believes that', cannot be either a name or a description of a fact. He concludes that "we are driven . . . to Mr Russell's conclusion that a judgement has not one object by many, to which the mental factor is multiply related" (44). And he asks what relation this is, and "how it varies when the form of proposition believed is varied" (44).

Ramsey thinks it necessary to distinguish two kinds of belief:

it is, for instance, possible to say that a chicken believes a certain sort of caterpillar to be poisonous, and mean by that merely that it abstains from eating such caterpillars on account of unpleasant experiences connected with them. The mental factors in such a belief would be parts of the chicken's behaviour, which are somehow related to the objective factors, viz. the kind of caterpillar and poisonousness. An exact analysis of this relation would be very difficult, but it might well be held that in relation to this kind of belief the pragmatist view was correct, i.e. that the relation between the chicken's behaviour and the objective factors was that the actions were such as to be useful if, and only if, the caterpillars were actually poisonous. Thus any set of actions for whose utility p is a necessary and sufficient condition might be called a belief that p, and so would be true if p, i.e. if they are useful.

But without wishing to depreciate the importance of this kind of belief, it is not what I wish to discuss here. I prefer to deal with those beliefs which are expressed in words, or possibly images or other symbols, consciously asserted or denied; for these beliefs, in my view, are the most proper subject for logical criticism.

The mental factors of such a belief I take to be words, spoken aloud or merely imagined, connected together and accompanied by a feeling or feelings of belief or disbelief, related to them in a way I do not propose to discuss. (46)

Ramsey proposes to deal with this latter type of belief by considering first atomic, and then truth-functionally compound thoughts.

By means of names alone the thinker can form what we may call atomic sentences, which from our formal standpoint offer no very serious problem. If a, R, and b are things which are simple in relation to his language, i.e. of the types of instances of which he has names, he will believe that aRb by having names for a, R, and b connected in his mind and accompanied by a feeling of belief. This statement is, however, too simple, since the names must be united in a way appropriate to aRb rather than to bRa; this can be explained by saying that the name of R is not the word 'R', but the relation we make between 'a' and 'b' by writing 'aRb'. The sense in which this relation unites 'a' and 'b' then determines whether it is a belief that aRb or that bRa. (47)

An element of confusion is engendered by Ramsey's shift from talk of names for a, R, and b in the *thinker's mind* to talk of the relation which *we* make between 'a' and 'b' by *writing* 'aRb'. According to what I shall call Wittgenstein's picture theory of *sentences*, any sentence-token which expresses the thought that aRb must consist of tokens which signify a and b by dint of direct correlation with them, and which stand in a certain relation to each other. The fact that these tokens stand in this relation, *e.g.* the relation of being written left and right of some given expression, pictures that aRb.

This theory has nothing directly to say about the *thought* that aRb. But it is clear that Wittgenstein, and, in this passage, Ramsey, also held what I shall call a picture theory of *thought*. (Not that Wittgenstein would have thought there were *two* theories here.) According to the picture theory of thought, when S thinks that aRb primitive signs for a and b must in some way be tokened in his mind (strictly, it needn't be "his", and it needn't be his "mind") and related in a certain manner: the fact of their being so related then pictures that aRb.

In the context of Wittgenstein's atomism, the picture theory of sentences gives a satisfying answer to a clearcut problem (*cf.* Geach 1976; Stenius 1976). What on the other hand is the picture theory of thought designed to do? To give the question edge, let us compare the picture theory with Russell's "multiple-relation" theory (Russell 1910). It will be interesting, however, to consider what is in effect a current version of Russell's theory: Wallace's suggestion (1972) as to the logical form of *de re* belief reports.

Wallace proposes to treat belief – initially *de re* or "relational" belief – as "a four-place relation between a person, a finite sequence of individuals, a time, and an attribute" (Wallace 1972: 86). For present purposes I shall ignore the temporal argument place; Wallace also proposes a treatment of *de dicto* belief, which I shall also for the moment ignore.

The statement that S has the (atomic) belief that aRb can be represented on Wallace's proposal as follows:

$$B(S, \langle a, b \rangle, xy \, [xRy]).$$

('$\langle a, b \rangle$' names the sequence a, b, '$xy \, [xRy]$', the relation R – the square brackets are Quinean notation for intensional abstraction, the variable letters preceding the left-hand square bracket indicate the order in which the members of the sequence are to be taken as satisfying the relation.)

Wallace's treatment, like Russell's "multiple-relation" theory, treats a thought as a relation between the thinker and certain other items. Ramsey's theory falls between Russell's and Wittgenstein's in that like Russell (and Wallace) he treats a thought as a relation between a thinker and other items, as against Wittgenstein who eliminates the thinking subject; and like Wittgenstein, as against Russell (and Wallace), he introduces mental tokens as featuring among these other items.

Wallace's treatment has the advantage of eliminating a problem, or at least an implausibility, which is created by Russell's and Ramsey's approach: the "variable polyadicity of belief". The multiple relation Russell and Ramsey envisage will have to be a different relation, with a different number of places, for thoughts which differ in themselves containing relations with different numbers of places: the thought that Fa, that $F'ab$, that $F''abc$, and so on. (Thus the relation "varies when the form of proposition believed is varied" (44).) By introducing sequences, Wallace's treatment has the same three-place relation involved each time (ignoring again the temporal argument place).

Note that the Russell/Wallace style treatment of belief sentences is compatible with picture theory of sentences: that 'S', '$\langle a, b \rangle$' and '$xy[xRy]$' are united in a given sense says that S believes that aRb.[1] This last point is of some significance. It is sometimes held that Russell's multiple-judgement theory is defective because it cannot distinguish the respective logical forms of 'S believes that aRb' and

---

[1] Not strictly compatible: a feature of Wittgenstein's theory is that items of a given category *must* be named by items of the same category: but here a relation is named by a linguistic object. However, it is compatible with a solution of the same problem as the picture theory deals with along the same lines as the picture theory. The feature of Wittgenstein's theory is supposed to be a consequence of this solution; I do not think it is, but cannot argue that here.

'*S* believes that *bRa*'. It even seems that when Russell gave up his theory it was partly on some such grounds: and Ramsey seems to refer to the point in the passage I quoted on p. 5. (See Russell 1956: p. 226.) There is no such problem, as is already suggested by the metaphorical way in which the problem is usually expressed. There is, that is to say, no *philosophical* problem – only the need for a convention. *Any* form of representation requires a convention determining the manner in which possible relations between the primitive signs are to be co-ordinated with possible relations between objects. Given a different convention, 'John loves Mary' could have said that Mary loves John, just as 'Peter believes that John loves Mary' could have said that Peter believes Mary loves John, or 'Believes (Peter, John, loving, Mary)' could have said that Peter believes Mary loves John, or 'B (Peter, ⟨John, Mary⟩, *xy* [*x loves y*])' could have said that Peter believes that Mary loves John. The fact remains that by actual conventions they do not.

Then does the picture theory of thought solve any problem which is not solved by the Russell/Wallace account? We shall begin by taking each as a proposal about logical form, made in the context of logical atomism. So we assume that all thoughts are either atomic or truth-functional compounds of atomic thoughts. Consequently all can be treated as *de re:* a *sine qua non* for the general applicability of either proposal.

The difficulty for the picture theory can then be put in this way. Only if thought is at bottom *de re* can the picture theory of thought be correct. For if the picture theory applies, then every thought reduces to a combination of primitively signifying mental tokens, to each of which there must be correlated an object. But if thought is at bottom *de re*, the Russell/Wallace account can also apply. Nor, as we shall see, does any advantage for the picture theory emerge when we consider compound as well as atomic thoughts. On the other hand, the picture theory goes beyond the Russell/Wallace account in being committed to the existence of mental tokens. Some justification for this is needed.

Would it help to switch attention from the question of the logical form of sentences reporting intentional attitudes to a broader question in the philosophy of mind? We would then take the picture theory of thought as entering, at a level of analysis deeper than that required for purposes of logical syntax, to explain what it must be to have the thought that *p*. (This approach would therefore be compatible with the Russell/Wallace treatment of the logical syntax of intentional attitude sentences.) But why should one suppose that there *is* a deeper level of analysis which informs one more fully about what *must* be involved when a subject has the thought that *p*? And why should one think, if there is a deeper level, that it is the picture theory which enters at this deeper level? The sense that thought has a "representational" character, which we noted at the outset, gives the picture theory some initial credit here, but that could only be redeemed by more specific argument.

Ramsey's account gives one no assistance. As we have seen, he distinguishes between chicken beliefs and human beliefs. He seems to dismiss chicken beliefs with a purely dispositional theory, and to reserve the picture theory for human beliefs. This makes it look, contrary to my initial summary, as if picture theory and dispositional theory were substitutes rather than complements (though reading the rest of Ramsey's paper makes it clear that this can't be right either). But if the human belief that *aRb* requires a picture theory of thought, why doesn't the chicken belief that *aRb* (*e.g.* that the coop is to the left of the gate)?

These obscurities stem from a confusion on the part of Ramsey which cannot be laid at the picture theory's door. Ramsey thinks that human beliefs are couched in introspectively accessible mental symbols (words, images) whereas chicken beliefs are not. In the passage we are considering he gives the appearance of thinking that the picture theory is required only for the kind of judgement which is couched in introspectively accessible symbols. But this locates the picture theory at too contingent a level. On this account, some particular intentional states as against others (e.g. human as against chicken beliefs) do, as a matter of fact, involve the generation of an internal token which "says" something, and to which the picture theory of sentences must therefore be extended. Now either this difference is simply irrelevant to semantic analysis – and Ramsey plainly does not think that – or one will have to conclude that 'belief', 'desire' and so forth are all ambiguous as between their human and their chicken sense. But it will remain open for anyone to deny, as against Ramsey, that the belief that *p* involves in *his* case any generation of internal tokens which say that *p*, and to hold that *his* belief is a "chicken" belief. And since the distinguishing test rests on the introspective accessibility of internal symbols, no-one can gainsay him. We seem to have postulated a semantic distinction which does no work at all.

Compare what Ramsey has to say in his review of the *Tractatus*. He thinks Wittgenstein holds that

a thought is a type whose tokens have in common a certain sense, and include the tokens of the corresponding proposition, but include also other non-verbal tokens; these, however, are not relevantly different from the verbal ones, so that it is sufficient to consider the latter. He says "It is clear that 'A believes that *p*' 'A thinks *p*', 'A says *p*', are of the form '"*p*" says *p*'" (5.542), and so explicitly reduces the question as to the analysis of judgement, to which Mr Russell has at various times given different answers, to the question "What is it for a proposition token to have a certain sense?" This reduction seems to me an important advance (Ramsey 1931: 275).

This accurate statement of Wittgenstein's thesis makes it clear that on Wittgenstein's conception the picture theory applied in a unified way to sentences *and* thoughts, and that it applied to *anything* that could be called a thought. But as to the reduction of intentional concepts to semantic concepts: it will not seem an important advance to anyone who is inclined to think that semantic concepts are on the contrary reducible to, or at least supervenient on, psychological concepts. In any case it presupposes that reasons can be given for applying the picture theory to thoughts; it does not give the reasons.

Perhaps Wittgenstein's main reason for extending the picture theory to thought was his insistence on the impossibility of *thinking* a nonsense. That is a fundamental thesis of the *Tractatus*: 'What makes logic *a priori* is the *impossibility* of illogical thought' (5.4731). Of course this impossibility, like any other, has to show itself in the logical form of propositions: in this case, of "propositions in psychology" (5.541). Wittgenstein criticised Russell's 1910 theory of judgement on just this score – as making it possible to judge a nonsense (5.5422; letter to Russell, June 1913, in von Wright & Anscombe 1961: 121).

The point is strictly a negative one: Russell's analysis of "propositions in psychology" gives them a logical syntax which does not *show* the *im*possibility of thinking nonsense. One would have to stipulate separately that certain otherwise well-formed propositions are ruled out: just the kind of artificial device which Wittgenstein objected to in *Principia Mathematica*.

These grounds for introducing a picture theory of thought are not at all without weight. But they do depend on two general philosophical theses: that illogical thought is impossible, and that impossibility must show itself in logical form. (The second of these makes the picture theory a proposal about logical form.) Neither thesis is obviously acceptable: particularly if one thinks the *apriority* of logic can be secured by another route, or if one thinks logic is not *a priori* in any case.[2]

So far we have explicitly considered only the logical form of atomic thoughts. Clearly the atomist argument requires to be completed by an account of truth-functionally compound thoughts: neither Russell's theory not the picture theory can be accepted if it cannot be extended to these. Ramsey begins by considering negation. To believe ~*p*, he thinks, is equivalent to disbelieving *p*,

the difference between assertion and denial thus consisting in a difference of feeling and not in the absence or presence of a word like 'not'. Such a word will, however, be almost indispensable for purposes of communication, belief in the atomic sentence being communicated by uttering it aloud, disbelief by uttering it with the word 'not'. By a sort of association this word will become part of the internal language of our thinker, and instead of feeling disbelief towards '*p*', he will sometimes feel belief towards 'not-*p*'.

If this happens we can say that disbelieving '*p*' and believing 'not-*p*' are equivalent occurrences, but to determine what we mean by this 'equivalent' is, to my mind, the central difficulty of the subject (49).

Ramsey thinks the equivalence "is to be defined in terms of causation, the two occurrences having in common many of their causes and many of their effects" (50). The suggestion is interesting for what it shows about Ramsey's conception of the relation between the two ideas: that beliefs are pictures, and that beliefs are dispositions. But it is nevertheless a solution to a non-problem: the appearance of a difficulty arises only because of the weakness we

---

[2] In 5.542 Wittgenstein treats the rejection of the empirical self as in some way a consequence of the picture theory of thought. But for independent reasons the self could not be a Tractarian object – the empirical self does not exist necessarily, the transcendental self is not in the world. So Wittgenstein could not in any case accept Russell's 1910 theory, or Ramsey's hybrid. Perhaps *this* provides an underlying route to the picture theory of thought, despite the fact that Wittgenstein seems to argue in the opposite sense.

It would be interesting to consider, in relation to this, what Dennett calls the "subpersonal" level of "intentional theory", and whether at this level there are systematic reasons that lead one to conceive of intentional states – or some of them – as physically realised by representational states of the brain, *i.e.* by patterns of significant physical elements which depict states of affairs. See Dennett 1978.

have noticed in Ramsey's presentation of the picture theory – the notion that the theory is to be introduced to deal with a type of situation in which mental symbols are consciously present in the thinker's mind. This naturally invites not just the idea that belief in such a case involves a relation between the thinker and mental symbols; but that the relation involved *is* that of belief. Now on Ramsey's version of the picture theory, a human belief involves a relation between the thinker, certain primitively signifying mental items, and the object signified. But it does not follow – *i.e.* it would not follow in a properly thought-through statement of the theory – that that relation, which holds between the thinker and these mental items, is the relation of *believing*, any more than it follows on Wallace's treatment that the relation which holds between S, $\langle a, b \rangle$, and xy [xRy], when S believes that aRb, is the relation of *believing*. S does not believe anything about sequences on the Wallace theory – and he should not be held to believe anything about mental tokens on the Ramsey theory – when he believes that aRb (unless a or b are themselves sequences or mental tokens). Nor should it follow, on Ramsey's version of the picture theory, that the mental tokens involved differ when S believes that $\sim p$, and when S disbelieves that p. Consequently there is no difficulty about the nature of the equivalence between the two: the suggestion that Ramsey needs is simply that they constitute the same intentional state, so that 'S disbelieves p' and 'S believes $\sim p$' have the same truth condition.

But why is the suggestion needed? To meet a central requirement of logical atomism: that atomic sentences be logically independent of each other. Any atomist theory of the logical form of intentional attitude sentences must be consistent with this. But if one treated the thought that $\sim aRb$ (where 'aRb' is an atomic sentence) as involving a mental token correlated with an item denoted by '$\sim$', then '$\sim$' would have to be accepted as a primitive name. Similarly, on Russell's theory, if one treated '$\sim$' as denoting one among the items to which the thinker was multiply related. In each case 'aRb' and '$\sim aRb$' would both be atomic sentences, which would conflict with the requirement. The same point holds for the suggestion that one should treat '$\sim R$' as a name of a negative relation. It then becomes a brute fact about the world that it is not the case that aRb & $\sim aRb$. There can be no logical constants or complex properties or relations, and so there can be no names of them either.

Ramsey's way of meeting this requirement works well enough

for negation. (It gives rise to some artificiality when generalised to other intentional attitudes – desiring that ~p, hoping that ~p, wondering whether ~p, etc. – but not to a degree which seems intolerable.) The general idea is to replace the *single* attitude of belief towards *compound* thoughts by a *multiplicity* of attitudes towards *atomic* thoughts.

Note that the difference between the picture theory and Russell's theory can drop out of consideration here, since Ramsey's approach can equally well be adopted, and for the same reason, on either theory. Here again the picture theory does no work that Russell's theory cannot do: we shall discuss Ramsey's treatment of compound thoughts in the framework of the Russell/Wallace approach. Thus in the case of negation, the proposal is to represent the logical form of '*S* believes ~aRb' as follows:

$$D(S, \langle a, b \rangle, xy \, [xRy])$$

which holds just when *S* disbelieves that *aRb*.

Meeting the requirement gets a good deal more difficult when we consider disjunctive thoughts. Ramsey suggests that

to believe *p* or *q* is to express agreement with the possibilities *p* true and *q* true, *p* false and *q* true, *p* true and *q* false, and disagreement with the remaining possibility *p* false and *q* false (51–2).

This may not seem to advance the problem. For example, doesn't disagreeing with the possibility that *p* is false and *q* is false amount (by Ramsey's redundancy theory) to disbelieving that ~p & ~q? But here the negations occur within the scope of the conjunction operator – and disbelief that (~p & ~q) cannot be identified with disbelief that ~p and disbelief that ~q, so one is left with an uneliminated compound thought.

However this objection misinterprets Ramsey's proposal, which is to define an attitude towards a set of atomic propositions,

in terms of the truth-possibilities of atomic propositions with which it agrees and disagreees. Thus, if we have *n* atomic propositions, with regard to their truth and falsity there are 2^n mutually exclusive possibilities, and a possible attitude is given by taking any set of these and saying that it is one of this set which is, in fact, realized, not one of the remainder (51; cf. Dummett 1973: 325).

From this it would follow that there are 16 possible attitudes towards a pair of atomic propositions, and in general 2^{2^n} towards a set of *n* atomic propositions: but Ramsey goes on to rule out any attitude that constitutes belief in a tautology or contradiction.

This proposal has to be reconciled with the thesis of the *de re* character of atomic thoughts, and the rejection of propositions, which are central to both the picture theory and Russell's multiple judgement theory. Thus, on Russell's theory, belief in the compound proposition *aRb* & *cR'd*, for instance, will have to consist, not in a relation between a thinker and a pair of propositions, but in a relation between the thinker, *a*, *b*, *c*, *d*, *R*, and *R'*. In terms of Wallace's treatment, one would have to accept a relation between the thinker, a plurality of sequences, and a plurality of attributes: in this case, $\langle a, b \rangle$, $\langle c, d \rangle$, $xy[xRy]$, and $xy[xR'y]$. (The relation involved will then vary in its number of places, depending on the number of atoms in the compound thought, but this is no longer directly objectionable, since a distinct set of relations, differing in cardinality, will in any case have to exist for every variation in the number of atomic propositions involved in a thought.)

Given the treatment of universal and existential propositions as logical products and sums of atomic propositions, the extension of this treatment to them would seem to involve in the case of Russell's theory a perhaps uncountably infinite set of relations between the subject and *all* objects, and in the case of the picture theory, between the subject, all objects and all names for all objects. Not surprisingly, Ramsey steers clear of this conclusion:

Feeling belief towards 'For all *x*, *fx*' has certain causal properties which we call its expressing agreement only with the possibility that all the values of *fx* are true. For a symbol to have these causal properties it is not necessary, as it was before, for it to contain names for all the objects involved combined into the appropriate atomic sentences, but by a peculiar law of psychology it is sufficient for it to be constructed in the above way by means of a propositional function (55).

But a "peculiar law of psychology" will not help if what is in question is the logical syntax of '*S* believes $(x)(fx)$'; and it is impossible to see a reason for holding the picture theory with respect to the logical form of *any* thoughts which does not also apply to *general* thoughts. (Though one could perhaps try denying that there literally *are* general thoughts.)

The object of Ramsey's proposals for dealing with compound and general thoughts is to avoid the introduction of logical constants, complex properties, or propositions. Wallace's theory, in 'Belief and satisfaction' is of course not presented in the context of logical atomism; he handles complex *de re* and *de dicto* thoughts quite differently.

(i) In the case of truth-functionally complex *de re* thoughts, *e.g.* 'S thinks, of John and Mary, that either he loves her or she loves him', Wallace introduces a complex attribute –

$$B(S, \langle John, Mary \rangle, xy \ [x \ loves \ y \ or \ y \ loves \ x]).$$

(ii) In the case of *de dicto* beliefs, Wallace proposes treating them as a special case of *de re* belief, by analogy with the Tarskian view of truth as a special case of satisfaction. *De dicto* belief becomes a relation between a thinker, the empty sequence, and a proposition –

$$B(S, \langle - \rangle, [p]).$$

These proposals avoid the extraordinary proliferation of cognitive relations to unlimited numbers of objects implied by Ramsey's approach, while remaining within the extensionalist programme. But they do so only at the cost of infringing the atomist ban on propositions and complex attributes. The ban is not arbitrary: the introduction of propositions, complex attributes, or logical constants, gives rise to special problems in the epistemology of logic, over and above any which are raised by introducing simple attributes.

On the other hand, the fact is that Ramsey's treatment of compound and general thoughts is unsuccessful. In particular the account of general thoughts is doubly unacceptable: general propositions are in any case not reducible to logical products or sums of atomic propositions, but, even if they were, there seems to be no clear and workable interpretation of Ramsey's analysis of the logical form of general *thoughts*.

To sum up so far then. Ramsey attempts to sketch out a general logical syntax for belief sentences which will be consistent with the requirements of logical atomism. The basis for Ramsey's general account is a picture theory of thought; but we have found nothing in his discussion which shows that a picture theory of thought is required at the semantic or at any other level. Given atomist assumptions, Russell's multiple-judgement theory would constitute an equally good, and in fact more intelligible, basis for Ramsey's discussion of compound and general thoughts, which could then quite smoothly be taken as an attempt to extend Russell's theory to the general case.

What of the dispositional conception of belief, which Ramsey touches on in 'Facts and propositions' and develops more fully in 'Truth and probability'? It is most naturally seen as providing further characterisation of the relation which his semantic theory posits as holding between the thinker and the objects of his thought. Actually, the dispositional view of belief and degrees of belief developed in 'Truth and probability' marries more neatly with the multiple-judgement theory than with the picture theory – whose redundancy it serves only to underline. It does not in fact presuppose an atomist semantics at all; and in what follows I shall take it as supplementing an account of the semantics of intentional attitudes along Wallace's lines.

In 'Facts and propositions' chicken belief and human belief are contrasted. But let us ignore this, and take what Ramsey says about chicken belief as the core of a dispositional account of belief in general.

The chicken belief that p is "any set of actions for whose utility p is a necessary and sufficient condition". To make this more generally plausible, we make the belief a disposition to action rather than a set of actions, drop the necessary condition, and make the sufficient condition explicitly modal. The belief that p is then a disposition towards any action which would be useful if it were the case that p. But for further elucidation, in particular of what is meant by 'useful', we must turn to the more elaborate and sophisticated treatment Ramsey gives in his 1926 paper 'Truth and probability'. Here Ramsey sets out "to find a method of measuring beliefs as bases of possible actions" (74), and proposes

to take as a basis of general psychological theory, which is now universally discarded, but nevertheless comes fairly close to the truth in the sort of cases with which we are most concerned. I mean the theory that we act in the way we think most likely to realize the objects of our desires, so that a person's actions are completely determined by his desires and opinions. This theory cannot be made adequate to all the facts, but it seems to me a useful approximation to the truth . . . I only claim for what follows approximate truth, or truth in relation to this artificial system of psychology, which like Newtonian mechanics can, I think, still be profitably used even though it is known to be false (75).

Ramsey calls the things a person ultimately desires 'goods', and suggests

that we introduce as a law of psychology that [the subject's] behaviour is governed by what is called the mathematical expectation; that is to say that, if p is a proposition about which he is doubtful, any goods or bads for whose realization p is in his view a necessary and sufficient condition enter into his calculations multiplied by the same fraction, which is called the 'degree of his belief in p' (76).

The agent acts in such a way as to maximise expected utility: what 'useful' in this context means is what satisfies his desires – *i.e.* what stands in a certain relation to certain of his intentional attitudes.

Both Ramsey's approach and his emphasis on its approximative or idealising character seem to me just right. Let us call an ascription of intentional attitudes to an agent whose behaviour one wishes to understand an 'interpretation'. Our interest in interpretation involves elements beyond the need to explain and predict behaviour; or, at least, elements only loosely or derivatively related to that need. Yet the primitive justification of an interpretative scheme must be its capacity to provide such explanations.

For the sake of initial simplicity, then, let us take an interpretation of an agent as nothing other than a theoretical scheme of a certain kind – involving ascription of intentional attitudes – suitable for giving explanations of the agent's behaviour. Then it reduces to two essential elements, a set of beliefs and a set of preferences. One can take these two elements as involving intentional attitudes of two kinds, *belief* and *desire*, without taking sides about, *e.g.*, Humean versus rationalist conceptions of practical reasoning. The "desire that p" may for present purposes be taken as a Humean desire that p, or a belief that there is reason to bring it about that p, or something more primitive than either, according to preference.

At the primitive level which we are considering, belief and desire get introduced as interlocking explanatory notions, in something like the following way:

I. For S to desire that p to such and such a degree is for S to be in a state which proportionately increases the likelihood of his doing whatever he believes would make it most likely that p.

II. For S to believe that p to such and such a degree is for S to be in a state which proportionately increases the likelihood of his doing whatever would maximally satisfy his desires if his beliefs were true and if it were the case that p.[3]

The distinction between *de re* and *de dicto* intentional attitudes can be accommodated in I and II as follows: if the intentional attitude is, e.g., of a that it Fs, then the term 'a' appears with large scope in the intentional contexts in both I and II. Then if 'a' has no reference, I and II fail to be true.

It is clear that I and II cannot be seen as providing analyses of 'belief' and 'desire' in the sense of providing *definitions* which eliminate them: they do provide accounts of belief and desire, but intentional concepts appear ineliminably in these accounts. Nor are they analytically true. They are to be taken, as Ramsey says, as "a general psychological theory" (which he shows how to use as a basis for measuring degree of belief). No doubt they are both more definite and more simple than anything one could seriously advance as implicit in ordinary interpretation. But any alternatives would have the same features: they would contain intentional concepts ineliminably, and they would not be true by virtue of the *meaning* of 'belief' and 'desire'. There *is* no analysis of these expressions, in the sense of an account which yields analytic truths about belief and desire, supplementary to an account of the logical form of belief or desire sentences.

However, I and II can still be seen as contributions to philosophical analysis in a broader sense, of elucidation or perspicuous display of philosophically interesting concepts. I suggest that they have, or that something like them has, a "contextually *a priori*" status in interpretation. (This is to go beyond what Ramsey says.) If a principle is contextually *a priori* in a theory, the principle is true if the terms of the theory have reference at all. It should be understood that the application of this notion is in real cases extremely rough – it need not be clear what principles if any have such a status, and a principle may lose or acquire the status. Further elaboration would

---

[3] These statements assume that S's beliefs and desires are consistent. The problems of inconsistent beliefs and desires do not belong to the primitive level of interpretation.

'Maximal satisfaction of desires' takes into account S's desires as a whole each weighted by its degree. The analogous remark applies to 'what S believes would make it most likely that p'.

Note that 'A increases the likelihood/makes it more likely that B' may be understood in *prima facie* "epistemic" and "ontic" senses. In the former sense, A need not be in any degree or sense *productive* of B. I am using these expressions in the latter sense.

Finally, I and II assume, as does Ramsey, that S maximises expected utility, rather than, e.g., following a maximin strategy. This is no accident: on the latter assumption, his behaviour would not suffice for measuring his degrees of belief.

invite examples from the history and philosophy of science: the need for such a notion emerges *e.g.* when one tries to explain why we sometimes say 'There are Ts, but they do not have the properties we thought they had', and sometimes 'It turns out there are no Ts'. (The history of ideas in general could hardly do without a notion of this sort – it is often introduced as a matter of the essential 'meaning' a term may have in a given historical period or social group; but one need not take 'meaning' here as a strictly semantic concept.)

So the suggestion is that I and II introduce the notions of belief and desire at the primitive level of interpretation: but, in Kripke's terms, by fixing their reference, not by giving their meaning.

If these are the only principles determining the character of interpretation (as we are assuming for the moment) then an interpretative explanation of an action of X-ing explains it in terms of a desire that p and a belief that X-ing will most likely bring it about that p. That is, in terms of a desire which, given the belief, is likely to cause the agent to X, and a belief which, given the desire, is likely to cause the agent to X. (There is point in distinguishing these two complementary states because each can match with other intentional attitudes in its complementary class to explain other actions.)

However, on the present suggestion, I and II are not necessary truths; nor is it necessary that the given desire and belief cause the given action. There could, as a matter of metaphysical possibility, be a situation correctly described as one in which *the belief that X-ing will bring it about that p* combines with *the desire that p* to cause some action quite different from X-ing. In such a case, there would be a true causal statement linking the belief and desire with this quite different action – but it does not follow that it would constitute an acceptable interpretative explanation of the action. To borrow terms from the sociologist Max Weber, it would be "adequate at the level of causality", but not "adequate at the level of meaning".

In reality, our interpretative resources are much richer than I have allowed. We ascribe an indefinitely large range of intentional attitudes, not just desire and belief. Or rather, 'desire' and 'belief' have to be reconsidered in the light of the fact that we ascribe more than two types of intentional attitude. This in turn expands the possible ways of securing 'adequacy at the level of meaning'; so the interpretative scheme itself has resources for explaining why S does not do what as a maximiser of expected utility he should do.

However, it still remains possible that S does not do what he should do, for no *reason: i.e.* without his ommission being explicable in terms of the interpretative scheme at all ("adequately at the level of meaning"). Only this will not be the rule if intentional concepts have application.

Interpretation is not anchored only to behaviour, nor only *via* interpretative explanations. Apart from principles relating to the "output" of intentional states, there are also principles relating to the "input": *e.g.* about the relation of perception and belief. (It seems at least contextually *a priori* that the object about which a subject thinks is among the causal antecedents – mediated by perception – of the thought. However, one needs an explanation of why this principle should seem so *central* to the notion of *de re* thought.) And finally, interpretative theory is required to tie in with other, non-interpretative theories about the creatures being interpreted: that may affect the content of interpretative theory itself. In all these ways the simplicity of a scheme based only on I and II is lost; but it remains, as Ramsey says, "a useful approximation of the truth . . . which like Newtonian mechanics can . . . still be profitably used even though it is known to be false".

At the beginning of this paper, I said that one might initially expect a theory of intentional attitudes to meet these three requirements: it should elucidate the representational character of intentional attitudes, do justice to their role in explaining behaviour, and do so in the context of the extensionalist programme.

The suggestion that thought has a representational character is not, as it turns out, easy to pin down. Does it mean no more than that intentional attitudes *are* intentional? Or is it an attempt to get at what *explains* their intentionality, by introducing the idea of an inner, or mental, item which represents, or pictures – in some sense is *about* the outer?

I feel uncertain about the whole question. On the one hand, I am inclined to say that we have reached a point from which the attempt to "explain" intentionality in terms of any definite notion of representation can be seen to be chasing a will o' the wisp. When one has characterised the logical syntax of intentional attitudes (which calls for no picture theory), and established their explanatory function (which calls for no picture theory either), has one not said what there is to be said of their representational character? Yet on the other hand an uneasy sense remains, of some underlying issue which has somehow not been touched.

It is unquestionably illuminating to see interpretation as an objective theoretical enterprise, and the philosophical questions which can be raised about it as special cases of general issues about explanation and theory. But rightly or wrongly this mode of approach has little to say about the reflexivity of interpretation. *I* have intentional attitudes (to ascribe them to others is to treat objects in my world as like me, subjects with a point of view on the world). I can abstract, in thinking about my thoughts, from any role they may have in explaining my behaviour in the world, and indeed from any relation to the world they seem to represent; but even after this bracketing they retain their intentional character, from which I cannot abstract. The point that intentionality is in this sense of the real essence of thought follows neither from what can be said about the explanatory function of intentional attitudes, nor from the semantic analysis of sentences reporting them. It is what gives rise, I suspect, to the feeling of an underlying question which has not been touched; but I am not sure whether there really is a question here which one should try to pin down and answer, or whether one should try to dispel the feeling that there is a question.

University of Glasgow

REFERENCES

Dennett, D. C. 1978. *Brainstorms*. Hassocks, Sussex.
Dummett, Michael 1973. *Frege: Philosophy of Language*. London.
Geach, Peter 1976. Saying and showing in Frege and Wittgenstein. In *Essays on Wittgenstein in Honour of G. H. von Wright*, ed. J. Hintikka, pp. 54–70. Amsterdam.
Ramsey, F. P. 1931. *The Foundations of Mathematics*, ed. R. B. Braithwaite. London.
Ramsey, F. P. 1978. *Foundations*, ed. D. H. Mellor, London.
Russell, B. 1910. On the nature of truth and falsehood. In *Philosophical Essays* (Revised edition 1966) pp. 147–59.
Russell, B. 1956. *Logic and Knowledge*, ed. R. C. Marsh. London.
Stenius, Erik 1976. The sentence as a function of its constituents in Frege and in the *Tractatus*. In *Essays on Wittgenstein in Honour of G. H. von Wright*, ed. J. Hintikka, pp. 71–84. Amsterdam.
von Wright, G. H. & Anscombe, G. E. M. (eds.) 1961. *Notebooks 1914–16* by Ludwig Wittgenstein, Oxford.
Wallace, John 1972. Belief and satisfaction. *Noûs*, IX, 85–95.

5   Inference, partial belief and psychological laws

CHRISTOPHER HOOKWAY

1 *Ramsey's "pragmatism"*. Ramsey described himself as a pragmatist, while granting that his pragmatism was "vague and undeveloped". Although he attributed it to the influence of Russell, it is clear that this aspect of his views derived substantially from his reading of Peirce: for example, his pragmatist justification of induction in the closing paragraphs of 'Truth and Probability' is taken from Peirce's discussion in 'Illustrations of the Logic of the Sciences'.[1] He follows the pragmatists, rather than his Cambridge contemporaries, in his conception of Logic. Logic is held to be a normative science, the business of which is "to tell us how we ought to think" (Ramsey 1978: 86). Moreover, "the most generally accepted parts of Logic, namely Formal Logic, mathematics and the calculus of probabilities, are all concerned simply to ensure that our beliefs are not self contradictory" (*ibid.*: 93). His pragmatism emerges most strongly in some highly allusive and unformed views about the nature of mental activity and the theory of meaning:

The essence of pragmatism I take to be this, that the meaning of a sentence is to be defined by reference to the actions to which asserting it will lead, or, more vaguely still, by its possible causes and effects (*ibid.*: 57).

What Ramsey offers as examples of "pragmatist" analysis is, perhaps, a better guide to his understanding of the doctrine than this opaque and confused remark. In this section I shall offer an account of some of the different lines of thought that are involved here: this will enable us to formulate some problems that confront broadly

[1] For a useful, albeit sketchy, discussion of how the influence of Peirce reached Ramsey and his Cambridge contemporaries, see the first edition of Thayer's *Meaning and Action* (Thayer 1968)

"pragmatist" accounts of belief, and the remainder of the paper will investigate these problems.

It will help us to do this if we distinguish a number of themes involved in Peirce's thought about belief and meaning. He held, as is well known, that a belief is a "habit of action": this suggests a broadly behaviourist picture, beliefs being construed as dispositions to behave in certain ways. It is in accord with this line of thought that Braithwaite held that to believe a proposition is to "act as if that proposition were true" (Braithwaite 1932). Beliefs, are manifested in broad patterns in the believer's behaviour: it is a view that is attractive to naturalistically inclined philosophers. Peirce, but not Braithwaite, supplemented this view in two ways that are relevant here. First, he derived from it an account of meaning (indeed the plausibility of the account of belief is established in part by the fact that it yields this independently plausible theory of meaning). The meaning of a sentence is determined by the content of the belief that it can be used to express: our psychological theory is supposed to yield a criterion of identity for habits of action which in turn supplies a criterion of identity for beliefs. Thus, in order to clarify the meaning of a particular sentence, we describe the habit of action associated with it. This will involve listing conditional expectations concerning the experiential consequences of actions that the agent could perform: if I think that an object is *hard* I expect that it will not be scratched if I scrape it with something, for example[2] (Peirce 1935–56: 5.388–410).

Peirce also provided a theory of mental activity which was not behaviouristic, a theory of thoughts and inferences. He took conscious episodes to be *signs* of what they were "of", and it was an essential feature of signs that they determined some other episode (their "interpretant") to be a sign, perhaps in some other respect, of the same thing. One sees here the makings of a functionalist theory of the intentionality of psychological episodes: the identity of a judgement (for example) being determined by its tendency to initiate other mental states and processes in inference and communication. Now, and this is the second point I wish to make about Peirce's supplementation of his behaviouristic theory of belief, it is clear that he thought that the account of belief, and the pragmatist

---

[2] This rough sketch ignores much that is important in Peirce's philosophy of mind which is, in most respects, more subtle than Ramsey's.

theory of meaning could be derived from this semiotic theory of inference. The three themes in Peirce's thought that concern us are:

(i) A broadly behaviouristic or dispositional account of belief.
(ii) A functionalist account of inference and judgement.
(iii) A theory of meaning that derives from these psychological theories.

It is, I think, true that Peirce regarded (ii) as fundamental.

The same themes are present in Ramsey's work. He states his "pragmatist" articles of faith at the close of a discussion of the theory of *judgement*, in a paper concerned with themes familiar from Wittgenstein's *Tractatus*. To judge that *aRb* one must publicly or privately assert a sentence which contains names of *a* and *b* which are related by being "written" either side of the predicate '*R*'. He hopes that his pragmatism will provide a means of avoiding some of the difficulties facing this account, by explaining what it is for a sentence to "agree with certain truth possibilities", and how logical constants do not represent. He also expects his psychological theory to provide a causal account of the projections that hold between names and objects in the world. The psychological theory will be a body of laws with the aid of which we can define notions such as 'being a name of *a*'. Consequently, we can explain the meaning of an expression by reference to the psychological laws which explain the occurrence of judgements containing public or private articulations of that expression: we explain the meaning of a sentence by reference to psychological laws that indicate the causal conditions and consequences of assertions of that sentence. An example of this form of analysis is provided by Ramsey's treatment of generality, which we shall discuss further below (section **2**). The laws which explain the meaning of the quantifier 'all' require that an agent believes that all *A* are *B* if, and only if, he is disposed to assert, publicly or privately, that all *A* are *B*, and to judge, concerning anything that he takes to be *A*, that it is also *B*. The meaning of 'all' is explained by reference to such laws governing inferential behaviour. Ramsey appears to see inference as a process involving causally related public or private "pictures" succeeding one another according to the laws of psychology. When we ascribe a belief to an agent by saying *A believes that p*, we provide a sample sentence of our language *p* and assert that *A* is in a state which is causally similar to the state which, in us, is manifested in assertions of *p* (Ramsey

1978: 51; cf. Davidson 1968). The approach to the analysis of mental states that views them as characterisable in terms of causal roles owes much to Ramsey's work; the causal roles in question frequently being described using the technique of *Ramsey sentences* (Lewis 1966; Grice 1977).

Ramsey's discussion of partial belief accords better with a behaviouristic approach to belief. Seeing that how one acts results not only from what one believes and desires, but also from how confident one is of the beliefs, and how attached to the desires, Ramsey attempted to develop an account of the quantity or degree of belief and desire. He provided means for measuring degrees of belief, which built upon

a general psychological theory, which is now generally discarded, but nevertheless comes, I think, fairly close to the truth in the sorts of cases with which we are most concerned. I mean the theory that we act in the way most likely to realise the objects of our desires, so that a person's actions are completely determined by his desires and opinions (Ramsey 1978: 75).

Degrees of belief are discerned in broad patterns in preference and choice, rather than in specific causal processes in inference and judgement; and this is done by ascribing them to the agent in a way that rationalises his behaviour. Degrees of belief and utilities are ascribed to the agent so that his behaviour is viewed as maximising expected utility.

I do not intend to discuss fully the adequacy of causal accounts of intentionality, or to consider the details of Ramsey's accounts of general belief and partial belief. Rather, there are two points of *prima facie* tension in his position which raise problems that are of more general interest. The first of these is between his "pragmatism" and the normative theory of Logic described in the first paragraph. If there is to be any point in the activity of criticising thought and inference, then, clearly, our inferential practices must sometimes fail to conform to the standards of rational performance prescribed by the formal sciences; psychology will deal with how we actually do think and reason, whereas logic will concern itself with how we should think or reason. One question concerns whether laws of any generality dealing with how we actually do think will be available; some remarks upon that will be made in section **4**. It is striking that when philosophers attempt to provide a general characterisation of a notion such as belief, they find it difficult to do so other than for idealised "rational agents" who always do think what they should (Hintikka 1962; but *cf.* Hintikka 1978). Furthermore, Ramsey's "general psychological theory" mentioned in the last paragraph is fairly glossed as the claim that people usually act as they *should*: if it were really true, decision theory would have no *critical* function in evaluating human decision making. A second difficulty derives from the fact that in clarifying the meaning of a notion it is plausible that we should spell out how it ought to be used, rather than how it is used by fallible cognitive agents.

A related problem faces the more behaviouristic formulations of the theory: if we determine an agent's degrees of belief, for example, by attempting to rationalise his choices, then on what basis can we regard a manifestation of apparent irrationality as evidence of genuine irrationality rather than as a refutation of our ascription of degrees of belief? Ramsey's discussion of irrationality is limited, but we shall discuss some remarks that he does make in the following section, which deals with his account of general beliefs. (It is not clear that these problems are as serious for Peirce as they may be for Ramsey: his account of inference is part of "normative science", and he does not share Ramsey's conception of psychology as a body of laws.)

The second point of tension concerns the relations between those discussions that focus upon broad behaviouristic features of the functioning of beliefs, and those that concern inferential behaviour. It is plausible to think that Ramsey regards inference as part of a mechanism linking retained beliefs and desires to action. If degrees of belief are effective in the determination of behaviour, then their functioning should be evident in the process of inference, but this is not so. The degree of a belief is not a feature of the content of the belief: we say

A believes-to-degree-n-that p

rather than

A believes that it-is-true-to-degree-n-that-p.

Thus the degree is not represented in the premiss or conclusion of the inference. Nor are we conscious of its influence upon the inference: degree of belief is a theoretical innovation that Ramsey proposes for its explanatory advantages. Therefore we must provide a more sophisticated account of how these features of the position hang together.

The two tensions are related. In the following section, we shall examine Ramsey's view of general beliefs and the criticism of cognitive activities. We shall then be able to turn to the relation between partial belief and inference in section **3**.

2 *General beliefs and logical criticism.* In 'Law and causality' Ramsey writes:

> To believe that all men are mortal – what is it? Partly to say so, partly to believe in regard to any x that if he is a man he is mortal. The general belief consists in
>   (a) A general enunciation
>   (b) A habit of singular belief.
> These are, of course, connected, the habit resulting from the enunciation according to the psychological law which makes the meaning of 'all' (Ramsey 1978: 136–7).

We generally do articulate our general beliefs, but the question could be raised why the habit of singular belief would not suffice: if an agent never volunteered that all swans were white, but automatically expected any swan he encountered to be white, would we hesitate to ascribe to him the belief that all swans are white? Surely not, and Armstrong has claimed Ramsey's authority in urging that general beliefs are simply habits of singular belief (Armstrong 1973: 89). However, notice first of all that Ramsey believes that the "general enunciation" is not just an avowal of the belief, but is involved in the realisation of the habit of singular belief; the habit results from the use of the general proposition in inference, and so the enunciation need not even be in public language. Secondly, while Ramsey holds that the beliefs of animals, for example, may just be behavioural states,

> I prefer to deal with those beliefs which are expressed in words, or possibly images or other symbols, consciously asserted or denied; for these beliefs, in my view, are the most proper subject for logical criticism (Ramsey 1978: 46).

In this section, we shall consider the question what difference the enunciation of a general belief, for example, makes to the possibility of the belief being subjected to logical criticism.

Logical criticism involves both the detection and the correction of logical error: when we discern a logical confusion it is often possible to bring this to the notice of the agent concerned, and that is usually sufficient for the correction of the error. It is a reflection of the extent to which our thoughts and beliefs are under our control, and of our responsibility for them, that inconsistencies do not often survive their discovery. Ramsey, as we saw in section **1**, granted that the logical critic must try to weed out contradictions – he detects logical falsehoods that are believed, and logically inconsistent sets of beliefs. In addition he can determine when beliefs that result from inference derive from a mistake in reasoning; when beliefs are thought to be based upon what will not support them.

The enunciation may be required in order to make sense of differences between belief states which appear to involve the same habit of belief or inference, as, for example, the difference between believing all swans to be white, and being agnostic about that, while not expecting to encounter any non-white ones. Alternatively, and more relevantly, it may facilitate the detection of inconsistency: if an agent asserts that there are black swans, but infers of any swan that it is white, we may charitably assume that he merely does not expect to encounter a black one; if he also asserts that all swans are white, this avenue is not open. We shall return to this point in section **4**, pointing out here that a refusal to reason in accord with the law that determines the meaning of the sentence asserted would, for Ramsey, show merely that we had misidentified the content of the believer's assertion.

Stich has suggested that full blooded beliefs are distinguished from belief-like states that feature in the aetiology of beliefs, what he calls 'subdoxastic states', because the believer has conscious access to them and they are 'inferentially integrated' with the rest of his beliefs (Stich 1978: 503). Examples of subdoxastic states might be the competent speaker's "grasp" of the syntactic rules of his language which is invoked to explain his linguistic behaviour, or the "knowledge" that is made use of in processing the deliverances of the senses. If general beliefs were merely habits of singular belief, they would resemble subdoxastic states. If the speaker does not, or cannot, articulate these beliefs to himself, then he can only come to know that he has them by observing the patterns in inference or behaviour that outside observers must rely upon. As the beliefs are not articulated, they cannot occur as premises or conclusions in inferences: if we accept Fodor's hypothesis of the Language of Thought, they may be used in "inferences" of which the believer is not conscious; but, in that case, they must receive an enunciation, albeit an unconscious one, and their inferential functioning is limited by the fact that they cannot occur in conscious inference (Fodor 1975; see also Stich, 1978: §7).

General beliefs could function in inference in a way analogous to rules of inference: the agent infers, 'Buttercup is a cow, so she is a mammal', thus manifesting his belief that all cows are mammals. They might then be inferentially integrated with other beliefs in that they would be invoked on any occasion to which they would be relevant: thus, it would, apparently, not matter that they could not function as premisses of inferences. However, they could not function as conclusions either; the agent could not consciously derive his general beliefs from other beliefs, and could not evaluate their reasonableness. If a habit of inference is to be derived as the conclusion of something that can be regarded as deliberation, it too must be articulated. Although we speak of deriving rules of inference from the other rules and axioms of a Logical system, this derivation must be carried out by constructing a metatheoretical proof in which the rules of inference are represented. But, perhaps our psychological theory could be developed so that we could predict that agents with certain habits of inference, and particular singular beliefs, would naturally acquire further habits of inference. Given a background of habits and beliefs, the acquisition of a further habit or belief would thus occasion the acquisition of a particular habit of inference. Would this serve as a model for the derivation of a general belief from other beliefs in a process of deliberation? Much would depend upon the details of any proposal that was made along these lines. However, this would be a kind of inference markedly different from the paradigm examples of conscious inference that we have discussed. Given that the whole inference could not be disclosed, we should have no means of establishing exactly what were the premisses upon which the deliberation rested, and the deliberator himself would be in no better position than us to determine this. In that case, it is hard to see how we could discern specific *mistakes* in inference. This is for two reasons. First, such inferential errors would only be discoverable indirectly from an attempt to rationalise an agent's other inferential behaviour which does not wholly succeed. Insofar as the error is attributed to a logical slip, it is likely that various slightly flawed inferences would equally account for the phenomena, and little sense can be made of an inquiry into the question which of these slips was actually committed.

The second reason provides support for the first, but is concerned with the notion of a *mistake*, and with the correction of logical error, rather than with its detection. As was mentioned above, agents normally readily acknowledge their logical slips and rectify their errors. Moreover, we hold them responsible for their mistakes. This suggests that inferential behaviour is somehow "under the control" of the reasoner: deliberating is something we *do* (*cf.* Bennett, 1976: §55). It is consciously monitored, and controlled, so the reasoner must have some access to his reasonings. Unless the premisses and conclusions are articulated, we cannot account for this. We can account for mistakes in reasoning because the monitoring reasoner is prepared to acknowledge that the slip occurred, and because, as controller of the inferential process, he accepts responsibility for it. Because the monitoring is causally involved in the process of inference, the reasoner's conception of what the terms of the inference are contributes to determining what in fact they are. Thus we can see that there is a dimension of rational criticism of beliefs to which only beliefs that are articulated can be subjected, and there is a form of participation in the process of inference which would not be available to general beliefs if they were merely habits of singular belief. I do not know whether this was the argument that Ramsey had in mind in urging that a general belief involved a general enunciation: it does make use of materials that are to be found in his work.

3 *Inference and partial belief.* We turn now to the second problem mentioned in section **1**. If we agree that beliefs can be formed on the basis of deliberation, and that deliberation and practical reasoning can issue in action and decision, then, if partial beliefs are operative in the formation of belief and decision, we should be able to say something about how they feature in inference. However, it is hard to see how that can be done, granted that the degree of a belief is not represented in the premisses and conclusions of inferences, and that we do not have access to it. The degree of a belief is not closely related to the frequency with which it is deployed in inference; a belief which is held without confidence may be used more frequently than one upon an abstruse subject of which the believer is convinced. Nor is it helpful to say that a belief is used on a particular occasion if, in the context, its degree is *sufficient*: what degree would suffice may depend upon the agent's other degrees of belief and preferences, whereas we frequently introduce a belief into an inference before it is clear what other beliefs will occur in the process of deliberation of which it is a part. Furthermore, we frequently conduct inferences on the basis of propositions that we do not believe, in order to determine their consequences. This last consideration reminds us that the relation of inference to decision may be more complex than we have so far assumed: when this complexity is recognised, the present suggestion, that the degree of belief is reflected in the importance that we attach to it in inference, may yet prove to be along the right lines.

First, however, we should notice that degree of belief can receive a partial expression in judgements of the forms:

It is likely that p.

It is more likely that p than that q.

It is certain that q.

We have access to how sure we are of propositions in such terms, we make use of such claims in monitored inference, and it is easy to derive, from the calculus of probabilities, principles that we employ in inference when using these vague probabilistic qualifiers. We should not, for example, judge p & q likely when we do not judge p to be likely; if we judge p to be likely, we should judge $\sim p$ to be unlikely; and so on. The problem arises because by attending to the patterns displayed in the decision making of agents, we can apparently discern additional information about their degree of belief which is not manifested in their avowals using these non-specific probabilistic qualifiers. Using methods analogous to those proposed for the purpose by Ramsey in 'Truth and probability', we can establish that an agent's degree of belief falls within a certain numerical range, associate numerical intervals with the utilities he attaches to particular projects, and thus make qualified predictions about his behaviour. I am not here concerned with the details of these proposals for measuring beliefs and desires.

Following Ramsey, we have tended to view conscious deliberation as a procession of mental "pictures", leading from beliefs plugged in to the sequence as premises to conclusions or decisions, each step giving way to the next according to psychological law, each transition justified by a principle of inference. Granted that picture, it is hard to account for partial belief, but if we adopt a

different, and more complex, idealisation of the nature of deliberation, then progress can be made. Suppose that I have to travel to *A*
by train or by bus. I may reason about the likely consequences of
travelling in each of these ways; I establish the relative advantages of
each. I can explain why I concluded that each would have the
features I took it to have, and I can reconstruct the reasoning that led
me to conclude that each form of travel had its characteristic advantages. Finally I must decide which form of travel to adopt.
Although I am guided by the considerations that have been
rehearsed and regard myself as judging reasonably in the light of
them, I do not have access to *why* they lead me to choose as I do. I
cannot say what tips the balance one way or the other. This distinction within deliberation between monitored reasoning and blind,
yet reasonable, decision making can also be drawn when the deliberation issues in belief rather than action. Wanting to work out
which form of transport will be faster, I reflect upon what has to be
taken into account, and then decide that, in all probability, the train
is faster: I believe that my decision was reasonable, but I cannot say
why I decided as I did. (Dennett 1979: 302–3, makes some similar
remarks in a discussion of how *de dicto* desire is transformed into *de
re* desire.)

We can detect among an agent's cognitive capacities both an
ability to construct and recognise valid or good arguments, and a
judgemental capacity which is reflected in his practice in determining his opinions and courses of action in the light of the arguments
and other considerations that are relevant. (By calling this a 'judgemental capacity', I mean to stress that it is non–discursive: the agent
cannot volunteer his reason for judging as he does, beyond indicating the arguments and other considerations that have been taken
into account.) Partial belief may be manifested in the functioning of
this judgemental capacity: it is revealed in the importance we attach
to different beliefs and arguments in forming opinions and decisions on the basis of them. The broad behavioural patterns we
exploit in discovering degrees of belief reflect, as well as our capacity to construct good arguments, our inchoate and tacit habits of
forming opinions and intentions on the basis of relevant considerations. Thus we use decision theory and the probability calculus to
evaluate patterns that reflect features in the aetiology of an agent's
decisions to which he has no access.

The judgemental capacity can be subjected to logical criticism. If we cannot accuse the agent of misapplying the principles implicit in some features of his practice, and thus cannot discover mistakes in his judgements, we can discuss which judgemental capacities it would be good to have. We may discover that an agent would allow a Dutch book to be made against him, or find evidence of an incoherent preference function. His degrees of belief may not reasonably reflect the evidence that he has available, or he may fail to take into account all of the relevant information that he has in making his decision. We will criticise an agent if he ignores relevant information, if his degrees of belief are not appropriate to his evidence, or if his decisions reveal patterns that clearly conflict with his interests. We may hold him responsible for these faults because the incoherent pattern in his decision making should have been evident to him. It may be possible to construct a theory which predicts and explains poor judgement. However, the fact that degrees of belief are not articulated in inference makes a clear difference. On the basis of information about an agent's beliefs and preferences, we can construct an argument which shows what it would be reasonable for him to do or believe in his circumstances. If he fails to do as we predict, we may decide that he is irrational. However, the inference we use to determine what he should do is not one that he would normally be able to rely upon himself in deciding how to act. In framing the decision theoretic argument, we have relied upon our knowledge of a pattern in his decision making to which he does not have immediate access; it is a pattern in his thinking which is not consciously monitored. The arguments we use to determine what an agent should believe using the predicate calculus or the logic of non-specific probabilistic qualifiers are of just the kind which the agent himself will often use: the premisses represent beliefs to which he has access and can articulate. Thus whereas the latter can be used to criticise an agent's reasoning, we can use decision theory only to discern inconsistent patterns among his beliefs and decisions; it does not indicate to us particular slips or mistakes in deliberation.

4 Psychological laws.

(1) $(x)(y)$ (If x believes that all A are B, and x believes that y is A, then x believes that y is B).

We may grant (1) should be true of all rational agents; we may even grant that it is approximately true of cognitive agents in certain normal or favoured situations and must be if consistent belief ascription is to be possible. It is also plausible that our grasp of this last claim is central to our grasp of the notion of generality. But, is (1) a psychological law? Human fallibility suggests that it probably has counter-instances. Now consider (2):

(2) (x)(if x's degrees of belief are given by F, and x's utilities are given by G, then x will do H)

where (2) is derived from decision theory. It seems that analogous remarks could be made. (2) looks normative, but must be approximately true in normal circumstances or we would not be able to make consistent attributions of degrees of belief. We can be confident that it too has counter-examples. If the phenomenon of irrationality means that neither (1) nor (2) holds as a deterministic law, we can feel sure too that they cannot be reformulated as precise statistical laws. Differences between the inferential capacities of different individuals and species suggest that no such laws will be available. It *may* be possible to formulate such a law restricted to a species, or to an individual, or to a stage in the history of an individual, but in that case the law would not be sufficiently general to be used to *define* psychological notions such as that of a general belief. The familiar point that psychological states can be variously realised physiologically in different organisms, together with the plausible suggestion that the realisation is likely to be imperfect in certain respects, ensures that no general laws obtain which can be used for definitional purposes. (For a discussion of the philosophical significance of the variable realisability of psychological states, see McGinn 1978.)

My concern here is with some differences between (1) and (2). If the universal quantifier in (1) were replaced by the vague pluralistic quantifier 'most', then the result would be a true generalisation that would sustain probabilistic counterfactuals of the form:

(3) If c, who believes that all A are B, were to believe that d were A, then he would probably believe that d were B.

The case with (2) is more complex. Experimental evidence suggests that decision making approximates to the requirements of decision theory only in a restricted range of cases. Even in simple artificial experimental conditions, it is found that degrees of belief do not conform to the probability calculus where the probabilities involved are particularly large or small. (For a discussion of this, see Edwards 1960 and Davidson & Suppes 1957; Kyburg 1978 provides a useful discussion of some of the difficulties involved in interpreting the related notion of subjective probability.) Thus, (2) would have to be substantially restricted in application to obtain a generalisation that would sustain counterfactuals. (I am ignoring here difficulties for the theory of partial belief that suggest that decision making is so unstable that reliable measures of degree of belief cannot even be obtained.) A limited parallel does remain: the probability that a believer holds that d is B conditional upon his holding that d is A and that all A are B, is high. That explains the assertibility of the probabilistic counterfactual. The probability that he believes that d is B conditional upon his holding that d is A, that all A are E, that all E are F, and that all F are B, is less high and the counterfactual may not obtain. We know that some inferences are so complex that we cannot grasp them and see their validity. But the parallel is limited: the complex quantificational inference is composed of a string of simple quantificational inferences, or, at least, it can be represented as having that form. The kinds of decisions that decision theory poorly predicts cannot be construed as composed of a sequence of inferences or decisions which are, for example, probabilistically sound: the contrast between simple and complex inferences sits less happily with these cases.

The discussion of sections **2** and **3** suggests two relevant differences between the uses made of statements (1) and (2). First, notice that (1) is one of our common sense psychological beliefs. We would all acknowledge that (1) was roughly true, and we all know that we all know this. (2) relates to a body of theory which, we saw, was a theoretical innovation which purported to go behind our conscious inferential practice to explain certain features of that practice. The normative principle underlying (1) is a principle that we all use in monitoring our own reasoning, and in criticising the reasoning of others. If an agent did not accept it, he could not be brought to admit and correct logical slips in his reasoning. Whereas (2) derives from a body of theory which can be used for the rational assessment of human decision making, the principles involved are not ones that we generally *use* in our deliberations. We could be said to "know" (2) only in that attenuated sense in which we can be said to know the syntactic rules of our native language: there might be subdoxastic states involved in the causation of our behaviour which "represent" decision theoretic principles. (See Fodor 1975: ch. 1.)

Secondly, whereas (2) articulates a body of laws which can be used to explain to us the theoretical notion of degree of belief, the laws from which (1) is derived not only explain what it is to have a general belief, but also yield a semantic account of the meaning of 'all'. The two points are connected: for insofar as we attempt to make our use of language conform to the use of others in the community, our usage must be guided by tacit or reflective knowledge both of how it actually is used in the community and of the general consensus about how it ought to be used. In part, it is because the approximate truth of (1) is generally recognised that (1) is approximately true. (1) is something that must be known to be approximately true by anyone who understands the quantifier 'all'. In that case, we could expect that the related statement (1') would be true without exception:

(1') (x) (y) (If x believes that all A are B, and x believes that y is A, then x would acknowledge that he could retain those beliefs consistently only if he believed that y was B).

The consequent of the conditional requires a spelling out that I shall not provide here: the point is that if somebody has the beliefs mentioned in the antecedent then he can come to recognise the fact, and the principles he grasps by virtue of understanding the notion of generality enable him to deduce immediately that he should have the belief that the object in question was B. The principle applies only to full blooded conscious beliefs. (1') does not entail (1) because the believer need not reflect upon his beliefs as he must if he is to acknowledge that he ought to adopt the further belief. This suggests that it is possible that the normative theory of logic may be reconciled with the causal theory of belief and meaning, once it is granted that the laws used to explain meaning would be complex, as (1') is; but it provides no reason for us to anticipate that psychological laws will be found which do not derive from bodies of common knowledge concerning how expressions will be used. Ramsey would hold that such laws can be found which are related to the meanings of all words, but 'all' is special because it is a logical constant. We can perhaps find laws concerning certain adverbs – if x believes that y is *very* A, and he believes that z is *fairly* A, then he would acknowledge that y was A-er than z – and for a number of semantic features of many other expressions. However, doubts about the analytic–synthetic distinction suggest that the approach may not be generalised. If Putnam's suggestion that our understanding of many expressions involves the grasp of a stereotype to which not all members of the extension of the term will conform is correct, it is unlikely that laws of the kind we are considering will be derivable from these stereotypes (Putnam 1975: 247–52).

The approximate truth of (2) is to be accounted for differently. We may grant that natural selection should favour species whose beliefs were probabilistically consistent, and whose actions derived from their beliefs and needs roughly as decision theory enjoins. There is room for dispute about what criterion of choice should be adopted, but that does not weaken the general point: it is relevant that ethologists have found it fruitful to employ decision theory and cost–benefit analysis in studying animal behaviour (MacFarland 1976). The point is simply that we expect species to evolve in an optimal way, and decision theory provides criteria of optimality. A creature of which (2) was not approximately true would pursue its ends in a grossly inefficient manner. Our judgemental capacities result from a compromise between the need to approximate to (2) and other evolutionary pressures: thus it has not proved a disadvantage that our decision making is inefficient where probabilities are particularly high or low. It is a task for psychology to provide a description of these capacities which will account for the extent to which they fall short of the requirements of decision theory: I shall not speculate about the kinds of psychological mechanisms that might be involved beyond mentioning that it may prove unnecessary to introduce degrees of belief as a theoretical magnitude in order to explain the rough and ready appropriateness of talk of degrees of belief. If this psychological theory consists in a system of laws, they need not embody normative principles as Ramsey's theory of degrees of belief appeared to.

5 *Conclusions*. I have not been concerned with the general question of whether there are any psychological laws, but rather with the acceptability of some specific proposals for such laws produced by Ramsey. The laws he sketched concerned rational belief formation and decision making, and each law was intimately related to certain normative principles of consistency and reasoning. We considered the nature of this relation, and tried to establish whether it was compatible with the putative law having a nomological status. The relation between the "law" and the normative principle was relevantly different in the two cases we examined. Where the law dealt with inferential behaviour that could be monitored by the reasoner,

then part of the explanation of the approximate truth of the law Ramsey produced was that it was known to be approximately true by the reasoners whose behaviour it governed. We saw that in such cases it may prove possible to construct a genuine deterministic law, although a more complex one then Ramsey envisaged. However, as it seems that this law would derive from the semantic knowledge of believers, it seems unlikely that the law governing inference produced could be used, as Ramsey wished, to explain semantic phenomena in psychological terms. With laws that concerned the exercise of what I have called 'judgement' rather than monitored inference, there is no reason to expect to find a more complex genuine deterministic or statistical law corresponding to the putative law that Ramsey proposed. Our predictive grasp of the behaviour of the judger rests initially upon our justified presumption that his organisation of his activities will not depart too far from the standards of efficient and optimal organisation codified in decision theory. Experience of an agent's actual decision making enables us to modify these expectations, but there is no reason to expect to be able to construct general laws of behaviour by these means.

University of Birmingham

REFERENCES

Armstrong, D. M. 1973. *Belief, Truth and Knowledge*. Cambridge.
Bennett, J. F. 1976. *Linguistic Behaviour*. Cambridge.
Braithwaite, R. B. 1932. Belief and action. In *Knowledge and Belief*, ed. A. P. Griffiths, pp. 28–40. Oxford.
Davidson, D. 1968. On saying that. In *Words and Objections*, ed. J. Hintikka and D. Davidson, pp. 158–74. Dordrecht.
Davidson, D. & Suppes, P. 1957. *Decision Making*. Stanford.
Dennett, D. C. 1979. *Brainstorms*. Hassocks.
Edwards, W. 1960. Measurement of utility and subjective probability. In *Psychological Scaling*, ed. Gulliksen & Messick, pp. 109–28. New York.
Fodor, J. 1975. *The Language of Thought*. Hassocks.
Grice, H. P. 1977. Method in philosophical psychology. In *Proc. & Addresses of the Am. Phil. Soc.*
Hintikka, K. J. J. 1962. *Knowledge and Belief*. Ithaca.
Hintikka, K. J. J. 1978. Impossible possible worlds vindicated. In *Game Theoretic Semantics*, ed. E. Saarinen, pp. 367–79. Dordrecht.

6   *Higher order degrees of belief*

BRIAN SKYRMS

It is hardly in dispute that people have beliefs about their beliefs. Thus, if we distinguish degrees of belief, we would not shrink from saying that people have degrees of belief about their degrees of belief. It would then be entirely natural for a degree-of-belief theory of probability to treat probabilities of probabilities. Nevertheless, the founding fathers of the theory of personal probability are strangely reticent about extending that theory to probabilities of higher order. Ramsey does not consider the possibility. De Finetti rejects it. Savage toys with it, but decides against it. I. J. Good (1965) and E. T. Jaynes (1958) put the mathematics of higher order probability to work, but remain rather non-committal about its interpretation. This reticence is, I believe, ill-founded.

I will argue here that higher order personal probabilities are legitimate, non-trivial, and theoretically fruitful. In part **I** I will defend the conception of higher order personal probabilities against charges of inconsistency, illegitimacy and triviality. In part **II** I will illustrate one aspect of their theoretical fruitfulness in connection with the question of the laws of motion for rational belief, and the relations between probability kinematics, the information theoretic approach to statistics, and conditionalisation.

I *The legitimacy of higher order personal probabilities.* The worst suspicion that has been voiced about higher order probabilities is that they lead to an actual *inconsistency*. Thus, in the development of his

I would like to thank Zoltan Domotor, Glenn Shafer, and Bas van Fraassen for letting me see copies of papers not yet published. Each of these illuminates some of the issues discussed here, and each represents a different philosophical viewpoint. I would also like to thank Richard Jeffrey for discussion of some of these ideas.

theory in terms of conditional probabilities of propositions in *Probability and the Weighing of Evidence*, ch. III, I. J. Good takes pains to exclude higher-order probabilities: 'it will be taken that the propositions *E, H, etc.* never involve probabilities or beliefs' (Good 1950: 19). With regard to this restriction he makes the following comment:

The development of the abstract theory must follow the rules of ordinary logic and pure mathematics. Hence we could, at this stage, hardly allow the propositions E, F, H, etc. to involve probabilities . . . To what extent this restriction may be relaxed is an interesting question. If it were entirely relaxed . . . the resulting theory would have some convenience, but it would also be confusing and might even be self-contradictory (Good 1950: 20).

Good does not spell out the inconsistency that he has in mind, so we can only speculate as to the nature of the perceived danger. It is, of course possible to blunder into an inconsistency when treating propositions and propositional attitudes. Suppose one maintained that there is a set of all propositions *P*; that for any subset *S* of that set, there is a proposition to the effect that George believes just the members of *S*; that if *S* and *S'* are distinct sets, the propositions to the effect that George believes just the members of these sets respectively are distinct propositions. One would then be maintaining that there is a set *S*, whose power set can be mapped into it, which is impossible. There are various variations one can play on this. In particular, what can be done with belief can, *a fortiori*, be done with probability. The set of probability distributions over a given set of propositions is of greater cardinality than the initial set of propositions. There is some reason to believe that Good has this sort of difficulty in mind. He touches on the matter again in the next chapter. 'Perhaps the most obvious method would be to extend the meaning of the word 'proposition' so as to allow it to refer to probabilities, but this course may lead to logical difficulties', a remark which receives the following amplification in a footnote: 'it may require a 'theory of types' as in symbolic logic' (Good 1950: 41).

The moral of this story for those who wish to consider higher order probabilities is simply, 'Be careful'. We know how to avoid such contradictions. One can start with some ground level set of propositions (without any claims to exhaustiveness), and build a language–metalanguage hierarchy on top of it, adding at each level propositions about the probabilities of lower-level propositions. (I take it that this sort of idea is what is behind Good's reference to types.) This is not to say that the story is uninteresting for ontologists who wish to think in some sense about all propositions. And psychological theorists who are interested in propositional attitudes may well draw the conclusion that the hierarchy shouldn't be run up so high that the results won't fit in their subjects' heads. But the fear that considerations of probabilities of probabilities *must* involve presuppositions of the sort that led in our story to an inconsistency is groundless. (For an explicit construction of a system of higher order personal probabilities see Gärdenfors (1975).)

Another way in which probabilities of probabilities have been thought to cause logical difficulties is embodied in a paradox due to David Miller (1966). The paradox can be put as follows:

Premiss 1: $Pr(\text{not-}E) = Pr[E$ given that $Pr(E) = Pr(\text{not-}E)]$.
Premiss 2: $Pr[E$ given that $Pr(E) = Pr(\text{not-}E)] = 1/2$.
Conclusion: $Pr(\text{not-}E) = 1/2$.

Since the proof is for any proposition, E, we have not just an absurdity, but also an inconsistency with the rules of the probability calculus.

This paradox generated a surprising amount of discussion in the journals, but it really should be transparent to anyone who has paid attention to recent philosophy of language, for it rests on a simple *de dicto–de re* confusion. (Let us remember that the probability contexts at issue are intensional; the probability that the morning star = the evening star may not equal the probability that the morning star is the morning star.) Consider premiss 1. Its plausibility depends on the appropriate *de re* reading of the right hand expression: '$Pr[E$ given that $Pr(E) = Pr(\text{not-}E)]$'. That is, in Donellan's terminology, the embedded description '$Pr(\text{not-}E)$' is to be thought of *referentially*. If the actual probability of not-E has a certain value, say 3/4, then I think of the embedded description '$Pr(\text{not-}E)$' having as its sole function the designation of this value. There is nothing wrong with:

$$3/4 = PR[E \text{ given that } Pr(E) = 3/4]$$

or indeed with its generalisation:

$$a = PR[E \text{ given that } Pr(E) = a]$$

(assume that $PR[Pr\ (E) = 3/4] \neq 0$, so that the conditional probability is well-defined in the standard way) where 'a' is rigid designator: that is, a name which designates the same numerical value at every point in the space. I will call this principle *Miller's principle*. Those who have followed the development of modal logic will already know that we invite no additional difficulty by universally generalising Miller's principle to:

$$\text{for any } x,\ x = PR[E \text{ given that } Pr(E) = x]$$

provided that we restrict universal specification to rigid designators of the type indicated. We shall see that Miller's principle has a genuine significance independent of Miller's paradox.

The second premiss of Miller's paradox depends on a *de dicto* reading for its plausibility. It requires that the description, 'Pr(not-E)' be taken attributively rather than referentially. We are to think of it as designating at a point in the probability space the value of the random variable at that point in the probability space, not as a rigid designator of a numerical value. Likewise for the description '$Pr(E)$'.

It is evident, then, that Miller's paradox is simply a fallacy of equivocation. The plausibility of the first premiss depends on reading 'the probability of E' attributively and 'the probability of not-E' referentially. The plausibility of the second depends on reading them both attributively. If both are given a uniform attributive reading, and the probability of E is not, in fact, $1/2$, then the first premiss is false, and can be derived from Miller's principle only by a fallacious universal specification.

These are the two arguments I know that allege a formal inconsistency in the higher order probability approach. I would say nothing more about formal inconsistency were it not that some reputable philosophers continue to have suspicions (if not arguments) in these directions. Though it may be a case of bringing out a cannon to swat a fly, I therefore feel obliged to point out that there is implicit in de Finetti's work a proof of formal consistency for a theory of second order probabilities: simply interpret pr as relative frequency probability (*i.e.* probability conditional on relative frequency. Indeed any way of explaining pr as "objectified" probability relative to a partition will do. See Jeffrey (1965: ch. 12).). This is not the intended interpretation, but it suffices to settle the question of consistency.

One might, however, hold that, although formally consistent, a theory of higher-order *personal* probabilities is, in some way, *philosophically* incoherent. This appears to be de Finetti's position. De Finetti adopts an *emotive* theory of probability attribution (de Finetti 1972).

Any assertion concerning probabilities of events is merely the expression of somebody's opinion and not itself an event. There is no meaning, therefore, in asking whether such an assertion is true or false or more or less probable . . . speaking of unknown probabilities must be forbidden as meaningless.

If probability attributions are merely ways of evincing degrees of belief, they do not express genuine propositions and are not capable themselves of standing as objects of probability attribution.

De Finetti's positivism stands in sharp contrast to Ramsey's pragmatism:

There are, I think, two ways in which we can begin. We can, in the first place, suppose that the degree of belief is something perceptible by its owner; for instance that beliefs differ in the intensity of a feeling . . . of conviction, and that by the degree of belief we mean the intensity of this feeling. This view . . . seems to me observably false, for the beliefs we hold most strongly are often accompanied by practically no feeling at all . . .

We are driven therefore to the second supposition that the degree of belief is a causal property of it, which we can express vaguely as the extent to which we are prepared to act on it.

. . . the kind of measurement of belief with which probability is concerned is . . . a measurement of belief *qua* basis of action, (Ramsey 1926: 71).

For Ramsey then, a probability attribution is a theoretical claim. It is evident that on Ramsey's conception of personal probability, higher order personal probabilities are permitted (and indeed required). (It is perhaps also worth noting that anyone who takes Ramsey's view of degrees of belief, and is willing to accept personal probabilities of propensities, or propensities of propensities, must also accept second-order personal probabilities, for on Ramsey's view personal probabilities *are* a kind of propensity.)

Even from de Finetti's viewpoint, the situation is more favourable to a theory of higher order personal probabilities than might at first appear. For a given person and time there must *be*, after all, a proposition to the effect that that person then has the degree of belief that he might evince by uttering a certain probability attribution. De Finetti grants as much:

The situation is different of course, if we are concerned not with the assertion itself but with whether 'someone holds or expresses such an opinion or acts according to it,' for this is a real event or proposition (de Finetti 1972: 189).

With this, de Finetti grants the existence of propositions on which a theory of higher order personal probabilities can be built, but never follows up this possibility.

Perhaps this is because of another sort of philosophical objection to second-order personal probabilities which, I think, is akin to the former in philosophical presupposition, though not in substance. Higher order personal probabilities are well-defined all right – so this line goes – but they are trivial; they only take on the values zero and one. According to this story, personal probabilities – if they exist at all – are directly open to introspection; so one should be certain about their values. If my degree of belief in p is x, then my degree of belief that my degree of belief in p is x will be one, and my degree of belief that my degree of belief in p is unequal to x will be zero. Put so baldly, the objection may seem a bit silly, but I will discuss it because I think that something like it often hovers in the background of discussions of personal probability. But, first, I would like to point out that this objection has a much narrower scope than the previous one. According to the view now under consideration, it is perfectly all right to postulate non-trivial personal probabilities about personal probabilities, if they are my probabilities now about your probabilities now or my probabilities now about my probabilities yesterday or tomorrow. What become trivial, according to this view, are my probabilities now about my probabilities (that I am introspecting) now.

The foregoing objection is an expression of a form of positivism which most philosophers would consider a combination of bad psychology and bad epistemology. Ramsey's pragmatism is again good medicine. If we focus on degrees of belief *qua* basis of action rather than the intensity-of-feeling notion, there is much less reason to put so much weight on introspection. (It is perhaps worth a passing remark that those philosophers who argue that personal probabilities don't exist because they can't introspect them are relying on the same positivistic preconceptions.) For a dispositional sense of belief, the status of my beliefs about my beliefs now is not so different in principle from the status of my beliefs now about my beliefs yesterday, or indeed about the status of my beliefs now about your beliefs now (although there will typically be differences in degree). In a word, the dispositional sense of belief makes sense of the possibility that someone may not *know his own mind* with certainty, and thus makes sense of this last disputed case. (See Jeffrey (1974) for a discussion of second order preferences, desires and probabilities.)

I should mention at this point that some philosophers do adopt a pragmatic, dispositional sense of belief but do so in such a rigid operationist way that they are led to have verificationist doubts about the case in question. The following argument has been made to me in conversation:

Probability is a disposition to bet in certain ways. To test his second order degrees of belief, we must get him to bet on his first order degrees of belief. To determine the payoff on this bet we must test his first order degrees of belief. To do this we must get him to bet on ground level propositions. But the ratios at which he bets on these propositions may be distorted by his efforts to protect his previous higher order wagers.

To this objection there is both an internal and external reply. The internal reply is that we can ameliorate the bias by making the first order bets small with respect to the second order bets. The external reply is that one surely need not be so rigidly operationist as to assume that the *only* way that one can gain evidence for a degree of belief is by making a wager. The pragmatic notion of probability that Ramsey espouses in 'Truth and probability' is by no means so rigid. Ramsey thinks of personal probabilities as theoretical parts of an imperfect but useful psychological model, rather than as concepts given a strict operational definition. Ramsey's point of view is, I think, infinitely preferable to either the left-wing positivism implicit in the objection just discussed, or the right-wing positivism of the one preceding it.

There is some psychological evidence, however, which suggests that even Ramsey's modest claims of approximate truth for the theory of personal probability as a psychological theory may be overstated. Actual preferences often appear to be ill-defined, or, where defined, incoherent. Depending on how bad things really are (I will not try to evaluate that here), it may be better to stress the normative rather than the descriptive aspect of the theory of personal probability. According to this view, the theory of personal probability is a prescription for coherence, just as the theory of deductive logic contains prescriptions for consistency. It is this strand of thought that is really fundamental, I think, in 'Truth and probability' and it remains even if the average man proves more incoherent than Ramsey expected. Let us notice now that if the theory of personal probabilities is conceived of as medicine, then we need second order medicine for our second order degrees of belief just as we need first order medicine for our first order degrees of belief. Higher order personal probabilities remain a natural and indeed an inescapable part of the theory of personal probability.

I hope that in the preceding I have been able to sweep away some of the philosophical debris that has played a part in blocking the development of a theory of higher order personal probabilities. But even when one is convinced that the conception is consistent and philosophically legitimate, then the question remains as to whether they are of any special interest. Savage's brief discussion in *The Foundations of Statistics* is along these lines:

there seem to be some probability relations about which we feel relatively "sure" as compared with others. When our opinions, as reflected in real or envisaged action, are inconsistent, we sacrifice the unsure opinions to the sure ones . . . There is some temptation to introduce probabilities of a second order so that the person would find himself saying such things as 'the probability that B is more probable than C is greater than the probability that F is more probable than G.' But such a program seems to meet insurmountable difficulties . . .

If the primary probability of an event B were a random variable b with respect to secondary probability, then B would have a "composite" probability, by which I mean the (secondary) expectation of b. Composite probability would then play the allegedly villainous role that secondary probability was intended to obviate, and nothing would have been accomplished.

Again, once second order probabilities are introduced, the introduction of an endless hierarchy seems inescapable. Such a hierarchy seems very difficult to interpret, and it seems at best to make the theory less realistic, not more.

Finally, the objection concerning composite probability would seem to apply, even if an endless hierarchy of higher order probabilities were introduced. The composite probability of B would here be the limit of a sequence of numbers, $E_n (E_{n-1} (. . . E_2(P_1(B)) . . .))$, a limit that could scarcely be postulated not to exist in any interpretable theory of this sort . . .

The interplay between the "sure" and "unsure" is interestingly expressed by de Finetti thus: 'The fact that a direct estimate of a probability is not always possible is just the reason that the logical rules of probability are useful. The practical object of these rules is simply to reduce an evaluation, scarcely accessible directly, to others by means of which the determination is rendered easier and more precise' (Savage 1972: 57–8).

In this passage, Savage appears to have two rather different motivations in mind for higher order probabilities. The first is the consideration that he begins with: that there is a second-order aspect of our beliefs, *i.e.* "sureness" about our first order beliefs, which is not adequately reflected in the first order probability distribution alone. The second is the idea that second order distributions might be a *tool* for representing vague, fuzzy, or ill-defined first order degrees of belief with greater psychological realism than a first order distribution would provide. This second motivation is implicit in the discussion of the "insuperable difficulties", and becomes even clearer in a footnote to the second edition:

One tempting representation of the unsure is to replace a person's single probability measure P by a set of such measures, especially a convex set (Savage 1972: 58).

I think that it is very important to carefully distinguish these two lines of thought. Savage's "insuperable difficulties" are serious objections against the suggestion that second order distributions provide a good mathematical representation of vague, fuzzy, or ill defined first order beliefs. Indeed, an apparatus of second order distributions presumes more structure than conventional first order distributions rather than less, and the first order structure can be recovered as an expectation (providing we have Miller's principle: see Skyrms 1980: Appendices 0 and 1). But *however* we wish to model vague or fuzzy first order degrees of belief, we shall, given beliefs about beliefs, wish to model vague or fuzzy second order degrees of belief as well. Interval valued, fuzzy logical, and convex set representations of imprecise first order degrees of belief are not *competitors* with second order probabilities; they are aimed at a different problem. If we then return to Savage's first motivation, we find that *vis à vis* this problem, the "insuperable objections" are not objections at all. The extra structure of higher order probabilities is just what is wanted. That two second order distributions for $pr(p) = x$ can have the same mean but different variance gives us a representation of the intuitive phenomenon with which Savage broached the discussion: two people may have the same first order probabilities, but different degrees of sureness about them.

There is one further strand in the passage from Savage that invites comment. Savage speculates that the notion of sureness may give us some insight into probability *change*: 'When our opinions, as reflected in real or envisaged action are inconsistent, we sacrifice the unsure opinions to the sure ones.' One version of Savage's first objection might hold that everything that we can know about probability change is already encoded in the first order conditional probabilities, so that any second order information must be either redundant or irrelevant. Such a position rests on several questionable premises; but there is one in particular to which I would again like to call attention. That is, that second order probabilities should only be treated *instrumentally*, *i.e.* that the relevant inputs and outputs of probability change must always be first order. Once we take the philosophical position that higher order probabilities can refer to something as real as first order probabilities, it opens up the possibility of conditionalising at a higher level, *e.g.* conditionalising on some statement about the first order probability distribution. It therefore opens up possibilities that simply do not exist as we restrict ourselves to the first order setup. I believe that these possibilities do indeed illuminate questions of probability change. I will give a brief illustration of this in the second part of this paper.

II *Higher order personal probabilities and the question of the laws of motion for rational belief.* The 'rational' in 'rational belief' refers to *coherence*. The idea of justifying the probability calculus as embodying laws of *static* coherence for degrees of belief occurred independently to Ramsey and de Finetti. Each had the idea that qualitative constraints could lead to a representation theory for probability. And each had the idea of a Dutch book theorem; a theorem to the effect that if probabilities are taken as betting quotients, then someone who violates the laws of the probability calculus would be susceptible to a system of bets, each of which he considers fair or favourable, such that he would suffer a net loss no matter what happened. A great deal turns on the significance of these theorems, and indeed this has been the subject of some philosophical dispute. I think that the way in which Ramsey states the Dutch book theorem is enlightening:

If anyone's mental condition violated these laws, his choice would depend on the precise form in which the option were offered him, which would be absurd. He could then have a book made against him by a cunning bettor and would then stand to lose in any event (Ramsey 1926: 84).

It is clear that what is important for Ramsey about coherence, and what makes it for him a kind of consistency, is that someone who is incoherent is willing to bet on the same betting arrangement at two different rates, depending on how that arrangement is described to him. The remark about the cunning bettor is simply a striking corollary to this fundamental theorem. Thus, let the criterion of individuation of a *betting arrangement* be the schedule specifying the *net payoff* on each possible outcome. The additivity law for probability is then justified by the observation that the same betting arrangement may either be described as a bet on a disjunction of two mutually exclusive propositions, or as the upshot of separate bets on each of the two propositions. The condition that the betting arrangement be evaluated consistently, no matter which advertising brochure accompanies it, is just that the probability of the disjunction be equal to the sum of the probabilities of the disjuncts. Along the same lines, de Finetti provides a justification for the customary definition of conditional probability:

$$Pr(q \text{ given } p) = Pr(p \ \& \ q)/Pr(q)$$

via the notion of a conditional bet. A bet on q conditional on p is called off if p is false, otherwise won or lost depending on the truth value of q. Again such a conditional betting arrangement can be redescribed as the upshot of separate bets on $p \ \& \ q$ and against p, with the consequency that coherence *requires* the foregoing treatment of conditional probability.

I find these arguments very compelling. And I think that some philosophers who fail to find them compelling, fail to do so because they focus on the striking corollary about the cunning bettor rather than on the fundamental theorem. 'Must the rational man always behave,' they ask, 'as if the world were a cunning bettor, lying in wait to make a Dutch book?' Asking the question in this way appears to make the subjective theory of probability rest on a kind of methodological paranoia that is usually associated only with the theory of games. This is, I think, the wrong way to look at the question. Of course there are situations in which a little incoherence won't hurt you, just as there are situations in which a little deductive inconsistency won't hurt you. (Remember, it is Ramsey's remark that he believes each of his beliefs but believes that at least one of his beliefs is false.) Of course there are situations in which it would be too costly to remove an incoherence to be worth it, just as there are situations in which it would be too costly to remove a deductive inconsistency to be worth it. Ramsey's pragmatism is not William James' pragmatism! But this is all, I think, beside the point. At a deeper level, Ramsey and de Finetti have provided a way in which the fundamental laws of probability can be viewed as pragmatic consistency conditions: conditions for the consistent evaluation of betting arrangements no matter how described.

The question naturally arises as to whether there is any analogous coherence argument for ways of *changing* degrees of belief. Ramsey strongly suggests that he believes that there *is* such an argument for conditionalisation:

Since an observation changes (in degree at least) my opinion about the fact observed, some of my degrees of belief after the observation are necessarily inconsistent with those I had before. We have therefore to explain how exactly the observation should modify my degrees of belief; obviously if p is the fact observed, my degree of belief in q after the observation should be equal to my degree of belief in q given p before, or by the multiplication law to the quotient of my degree of belief in pq by my degree of belief in p. When my degrees of belief change in this way we can say that they have been changed *consistently* by my observation (Ramsey 1926: 94).

but does not explicitly set out any such argument. Hacking (1967) doubts if there can be such an argument, and regards it as a serious failing of Bayesian theory that this "dynamic assumption" lacks a justification. Nevertheless, David Lewis has produced a coherence argument for conditionalisation (reported in Teller (1973). See also Freedman and Purves (1969).) I would like to give the leading idea of Lewis' argument here, so that it may be compared with the static coherence arguments. Suppose that I am about to find out whether a certain proposition, p, is true or false (*e.g.* the result of a certain experiment is about to come in); that I have a rule or disposition to change my degrees of belief in a certain way upon learning that p is true; that PR represents my degrees of belief just before learning whether p is true or not and PR_p the degrees of belief that I would have according to the rule (or disposition) upon learning that p is true. The key point is this: prior to finding out about p, *the rule or disposition to change my beliefs in a certain way upon learning p is tantamount to having a set of betting ratios for bets conditional on p.* (Someone can achieve a betting arrangement for a bet on q conditional on p with me, at the betting ratio $PR_p(q)$, just by reserving a sum of money which he will bet on q with me *after* I change my degrees of belief if p turns out true, and which he will not bet at all if p turns out false.) But we also know from de Finetti's observation that PR alone commits us to betting ratios for conditional bets in a different way, with those betting ratios being reflected in the conditional probabilities of PR (assuming $PR(p) \neq 0$). For the conditional betting ratios arrived at in these two ways to coincide, PR_p must come from PR by conditionalisation on p (*i.e.* for all q, $PR_p(q) = PR(p \& q)/PR(p)$). (Obviously, the same argument can be repeated for $PR_{\sim p}$, and for the more general case where the experimental report may consist of any one of a set of mutually exclusive and exhaustive propositions.)

This observation yields a Dutch book theorem as a corollary. If someone does not change his degree of belief by conditionalisation, then someone who knows how he does change his belief can exploit the different betting ratios for bets conditional on p to make a Dutch book conditional on p, which can then be turned into an unconditional Dutch book by making an appropriate small side bet against p.

We can only speculate as to whether Ramsey had this sort of argument in mind. But it is clear that the Lewis argument is quite in the spirit of Ramsey, and rests on the same conception of pragmatic consistency as the static consistency arguments of Ramsey. It is, I think, undeniable that it establishes a special status for conditionalisation as a law of motion for rational belief in the cases which satisfy the conditions of the argument. But what of cases in which these conditions are not met? In particular, what about those cases to which Ramsey alludes, in which observation changes *in degree* my opinion about the fact observed, but where that change is not a change to probability 1 of some observation proposition? Richard Jeffrey (1965) introduces *probability kinematics* for just this purpose. Suppose that an observational interaction autonomously changes the probability of some proposition, p, but does not change it to 1. In such a situation we might plausibly decide to take as our final probability distribution a mixture (weighted average) of the probability distribution we would get by conditionalising on p, and the probability distribution that we would get by conditionalising on not-p. Then, for any q,

$$PR_{final}(q) = PR_{final}(p)\, PR_{initial}(q \text{ given } p)$$
$$+ PR_{final}(\sim p)\, PR_{initial}(q \text{ given } \sim p).$$

Under these circumstances, we say that the final probability distribution comes from the initial probability distribution by probability kinematics on p. More generally,

> *Probability Kinematics:* Let Pr_i and Pr_f be probability functions on the same field of propositions and let $\{p_j : j = 1, \ldots, n\}$ be a partitioning of that field such that $Pr_i(p_j) \neq 0$ and $Pr_f(p_j) = a_j$. Pr_f is said to come from Pr_i by *probability kinematics on* $\{p_j\}$ iff:
>
> For all propositions, q, in the field:
> $Pr_f(q) = \Sigma_j a_j Pr_i (q \text{ given } p_j)$.

This is equivalent (Jeffrey 1965: ch. 11) to:

> For all q and j : $Pr_f(q \text{ given } p_j) = Pr_i(q \text{ given } p_j)$.

Conditionalisation on p is a special case of probability kinematics where the partitioning consists of $[p, \sim p]$ and the final probability of p is 1. Probability kinematics takes a certain special kind of constraint on the final probability distribution as its input, the constraint as to the final probabilities of the p_js. E. T. Jaynes, the originator of the information theoretic approach to statistical mechanics, suggests a more generally applicable rule (Jaynes 1957): Maximise the relative entropy in the final distribution relative to the initial distribution subject to the stated constraints. Jaynes' maxim can be put roughly as: Be as modest as possible about the amount of information you have acquired. Several writers have recently pointed out that probability kinematics is a special case of Jaynes' rule (May & Harper 1976, Shafer 1979, and van Fraassen and Domotor, Zanotti and Graves in not yet published papers). But neither the maximum entropy rule in general nor the special case of probability kinematics has the kind of Ramsey–de Finetti justification that Lewis supplied for conditionalisation. True modesty is, no doubt, an epistemic virtue but false modesty is not, and the question is now to distinguish true modesty from false.

If only we had some proposition in our language which summed up the content of our imperfect observation, we could simply conditionalise on it. But the assumption that every observation can be interpreted as conferring certainty to some observational proposition leads to an unacceptable epistemology of the given. There is, however, another, entirely natural way in which the sorts of cases under consideration can be assimilated to conditionalisation.

Within the framework of second order personal probabilities, we can answer that in the case of probability kinematics there was, after all, something that we did learn for certain from the observation. We learned the values of the final probabilities of the members of the partition. The same remark generalises to other cases in which Jaynes' rule of maximising relative entropy relative to a set of constraints on the final distribution applies. In the higher order probability setup, we can conditionalise on statements specifying those constraints (by conditionalising on random variables on the second order probability space). I would like to proceed to discuss the relation between second order conditionalisation and the first order generalisations of conditionalisation suggested by Jeffrey and Jaynes. I will start with the case of probability kinematics, but much of what I have to say will carry over to maximum relative entropy inference as well.

I would first like to set out the formal connection between first order probability kinematics and second order conditionalisation, and then discuss the interpretation of this connection in the light of what I have said about higher order personal probabilities. First, the framework for second order probabilities:

Let L_1 consist of some field of propositions. We extend L_1 to L_2 by adding every proposition of the form: $pr(p) \in S$ where p is a proposition of L_1 and S is a subinterval of the unit interval, and closing under finite truth-functional combination. (We could iterate this process as far as you please.) I will here only discuss a probability distribution PR on L_2 with English being the language of discussion.

Suppose that $[p_i: i = 1, \ldots, n]$ is a partition such that $PR[p_i] \neq 0$ and let $[a_i: i = 1, \ldots, n]$ be numerical values such that $PR[\bigwedge_i pr(\bigwedge_i p_i) = a_i] \neq 0$. Under what conditions does conditioning on the second order proposition, $\bigwedge_i pr(p_i) = a_i$, which specifies probability values for every member of the partition, have the same effect at the first order level as probability kinematics on that partition $[p_i]$? By the characterisation (Jeffrey 1965: ch. 11) of probability kinematics on $[p_i]$ as a change which leaves the probabilities of propositions conditional on members of the partition unchanged, it follows that

Conditionalisation on $\bigwedge_i pr(p_i) = a_i$ is equivalent at the first order level to probability kinematics on the partition $[p_i]$ if and only if:

(SUFFICIENCY CONDITION): PR (q given p_j and $\bigwedge_i pr(p_i) = a_i$)

= $PR(q$ given $p_j)$ for all first order propositions, q, and all elements, p_j, of the partition.

For conditionalisation on $\bigwedge_i pr(p_i) = a_i$ to also be a change which leads to each member of the partition $[p_i]$ having as its final probability the corresponding a_i, we must also have:

(GENERALIZED MILLER) : $PR(p_j$ given $\bigwedge_i pr(p_i) = a_i) = a_j$ for all elements, p_j, of the partition.

(The special case of the foregoing observation, for probability kinematics on a partition consisting of $[p, \sim p]$ is discussed in Skyrms (1980: Appendix 1).)

This bit of mathematics is open to more than one interpretation. One could, for instance, use it to argue for probability kinematics in cases in which one, by reflection, comes to know his own mind a little better. But, here, I would like to focus on the sort of interpretation for which it was designed. Here, pr signifies the final probabilities that are the upshot of an observational interaction. Under this interpretation it is plausible that there should be a wide range of first order propositions for which the sufficiency condition holds. Notice that here the analogy with the de Finetti decomposition breaks down. In the de Finetti setup, relative frequency plays the role of our random variable, pr. De Finetti shows that an infinite sequence of exchangeable trials has a unique representation as a mixture of *independent* identically distributed trials. So our sufficiency condition fails: *e.g.* consider an infinite sequence of exchangeable tosses of a coin, which is an equal mixture of two Bernoulli sequences with $pr(\text{heads}) = 1/4$ and $pr(\text{heads}) = 3/4$ respectively. Then $PR[\text{Heads on trial 2 given } pr(\text{heads on 1}) = 3/4]$ = $3/4$; $PR[\text{Heads on trial 2 given heads on trial 1}] = 9/16$; but $PR[\text{Heads on trial 2 given both heads on trial 1 and } pr(\text{heads on 1}) = 3/4] = 3/4$. The plausibility of our sufficiency condition depends on the interpretation of pr as degree of belief. In the de Finetti setup, sufficiency runs the other way. There we have:

$$PR(q \text{ given } pr(q) = a_i \wedge p) = PR(q \text{ given } pr(q) = a_i) = a_i \text{ (for all } i)$$

where PR is concentrated on $a_1 \ldots, a_n$ as before. And thus

$$PR(q \text{ given } p) = \Sigma_i a_i PR(pr(q) = a_i \text{ given } p)$$

(First order conditionalisations) = (Second order probability kinematics)!

But for personal probabilities one is almost tempted to think of the sufficiency condition as a methodological postulate. My degrees of belief with regard to the p_is are irrelevant to the probability of q in the presence of the truth about the world regarding the p_is (*i.e.* p_j). This, however, would be going too far. Notice that the sufficiency condition would not be plausible if we allowed second order propositions to take the place of the q. But we can think of examples of first order propositions which are highly correlated with the second order final probability propositions in question, and for these the sufficiency condition may fail too. (*E.g.* my current probability that I will sweat at the moment of arriving at my final probability, conditional on the fact that Black Bart will not really try to gun me down *and* that my final probability that he will try to kill me will be 0.999, is *not* equal to my current probability that I will sweat, conditional on the fact that he will not really try to gun me down. The sweating is highly correlated with my final degree of belief rather than the fact of the matter.) So we must make do with the more modest claim that in typical situations there is a wide range of first order propositions for which the sufficiency condition holds. When our first order language consists of such propositions (relative to the probability measure and partition in question) we shall have probability kinematics on that partition as the first order consequence of second order conditionalisation. The generalised Miller condition is also highly plausible under this interpretation, though for different reasons. Here the plausibility depends on the interpretation of *pr* as my *final* probability, after the observational interaction. Under the assumption that my final probability is to be arrived at by conditionalisation on $\bigwedge_i pr(p_i) = a_i$, and under the assumption that *pr* is to be interpreted as final probability, the generalised Miller principle says that conditional on the final probability of p_j having a certain value (and a few other things), it has that value. Of course, we can invent cases, where these assumptions do not hold. I might have reason, for instance, to believe that my final probabilities would not be reached by conditionalisation, but rather would be distorted and biased in a foreseeable way by an evil force. Contemplating that sort of final probability distribution from my antecedent, clearheaded state, I would not have probabilities [PR] which exemplify Miller's principle, but rather probabilities which compensate for the projected bias in [*pr*]. The point I would like to make here is that the approach by way of higher order probabilities both shows us why probability kinematics is the right approach in a wide variety of cases, and enables us to isolate "pathological" cases in which it would give the wrong results. Furthermore, in the cases in which it is correct, it appears not merely as a successful *ad hoc* method, but rather as a special case of second order conditionalisation. As such, it inherits the force of Lewis' coherence argument.

I mentioned another way in which the generalised Miller principle might fail which leads to questions of independent interest. The Miller principle might fail if $[pr]$ were not interpreted as a final probability. Now the model that we have been studying, where the observational interaction forces *final* probabilities of the elements of a partition on you, and your final probabilities of all other sentences are then determined with reference to these, leaves something to be desired. It would be more informative if we could separate the observational input of a probability change from the final upshot. We might take as input the observational probabilities of the elements of a partition, *i.e.* the values that they would have on the basis of the observation alone – and then combine these with our prior information to get a final probability distribution. (I suggested in Skyrms (1975: 196–8) that such an analysis would be desirable, but could not see how to provide it. An observational parametrisation, at the first order level, has recently been provided by Field (1978).) Suppose, then, that we reinterpret *pr* as observational probability rather than final probability (which I will indicate with a subscript, o). How does this reinterpretation affect the sufficiency and generalised Miller conditions? The considerations that were adduced in favour of the sufficiency condition remain substantially unchanged; information as to the true member of the partition should typically swamp the effects of observational probabilities of members of the partition on the probability of a first order sentence, q. But under the reinterpretation, the generalised Miller principle is no longer plausible. I observe a piece of cloth by candlelight. My observational probability that it is black is 0.8; that it is purple 0.05; dark blue 0.05; other 0.1. I may, however, already have strong evidence that the cloth is blue, and perhaps also that the light is deceiving, *etc.* This prior evidence has been assimilated into my probability function PR. Under these conditions, my final probabilities for the members of the partition (black, purple, dark blue, other) will not equal the observational probabilities, but rather will be the end product of some way of weighing the observational probabilities against the other evidence. So here we can expect probability kinematics, by virtue of the sufficiency principle, but we should not expect:

$$PR(q \text{ given } \bigwedge_i pr_o(p_i) = a_i) = \Sigma_i a_i PR(q \text{ given } p_i)$$

because of the failure of the generalised Miller principle.

Suppose that p_1 and p_2 are mutually exclusive hypotheses and o is a piece of evidence. Then, by Bayes theorem, $PR(p \text{ given } o) = Pr(p)$ $PR(o \text{ given } p)/PR(o)$, so we have $PR(p_1 \text{ given } o)/PR(p_2 \text{ given } o)$ $= [PR(p_1)/PR(p_2)][PR(o \text{ given } p_1)/PR(o \text{ given } p_2)]$. That is, the ratio of the final probabilities of the hypotheses on the evidence can be obtained by multiplying the ratio of the initial probabilities by the *likelihood ratio*. Furthermore, if we have a series of pieces of evidence, such that the pieces of evidence are independent, conditional on the hypotheses, then the likelihood ratio for the conjunction of the pieces of evidence can be obtained by multiplying through, *i.e.*:

$$PR(p_1 \text{ given } \bigwedge_i o_i)/PR(p_2 \text{ given } \bigwedge_i o_i)$$
$$= [PR(p_1)/PR(p_2)]\pi_i[PR(o_i \text{ given } p_1)/PR(o_i \text{ given } p_2)].$$

If we want to "add up" evidence instead of multiplying through, we need only take logarithms of the terms (the choice of base being a matter of convention). Following I. J. Good (1950) (who was following a suggestion of Alan Turing) we focus on the logarithm of the likelihood ratio, $\ln[PR(o \text{ given } p_1)/PR(o \text{ given } p_2)]$ as the *weight of evidence* in o for p_1 as against p_2. For a series of observations which are independent, conditional on the hypotheses, the final relative probabilities $PR(p_1 \text{ given } \bigwedge_i o_i)/PR(p_2 \text{ given } \bigwedge_i o_i)$ can be recovered from the prior relative probabilities and accumulated weight of evidence as:

$$[PR(p_1)/PR(p_2)]\exp\Sigma_i\ln[PR(o_i \text{ given } p_i)/PR(o_i \text{ given given } p_2)].$$

Shafer (1979) shows how Field's model falls out of Good's Bayesian analysis, provided that there are propositions, o_i, in the domain of $[PR]$ which represent the results of the observational interaction. Thus, the Field's formula, $PR_f(p)/PR_f(\sim p) = [PR_i(p)/PR_i(\sim p)]e^{2\alpha}$, Field's parameter of observational input, α, is just $1/2$ Good's weight of evidence for p as against not-p. Shafer, however, is sceptical about the existence of such propositions.

If one adopts the point of view suggested in this paper, these propositions are not to be found among the first order propositions, but rather as statements of observational probability. That is, an observational statement, o_i, will consist of a conjunction of observational probability statements, $\bigwedge pr_o(p_j) = a_j$. We have already seen that the generalised Miller principle typically fails for observational probabilities. The question arises whether the partition independence of the generalised Miller principle survives, *i.e.* whether we have $PR(p_j$ given $\bigwedge pr_o (p_i) = a_i = PR(p_j$ given $pr_o(p_j) = a_j)$. I think that in general we do not. Suppose that the p_is are orange, red, pink, blue and black. Then the probability of red given an observation would plausibly depend not only on the observational probability of red but also on the distribution of observational probabilities among orange, pink, blue and black. What is more to the point is the likelihood $PR[\bigwedge pr_o(p_i) = a_i$ given $p_j]$ which evidently is typically not equal to $PR[pr_o(p_i) = a_j$ given $p_j]$. But the foregoing example also shows that typically we cannot even factor $PR[\bigwedge pr_o(p_i) = a_i$ given $p_j]$ as $PR[pr_o(p_j) = a_j$ given $p_j] [PR(pr_o(p_i) = a_j)/PR(\bigwedge_i(pr_o(p_i) = a_i)]$. Thus, the likelihood function will in general have to take into account interactions between the members of the partition, and these interactions will depend on the partition and observational situation at issue. These complications obligingly disappear when the partition in question has only two members, $[p, \sim p]$ since the observational probability of p determines the observational probability of its denial.

Another complication affecting the representation of observation is that some observations may count for more than others, even though the distribution of probabilities is the same. An observation in the light of three candles may count for more than an observation in the light of one; an observation made while sober may count for more than one made when drunk or while under the influence of hallucinogens, *etc.* This difference must show up in the likelihood, $PR(o$ given $p)$, and so a sufficient representation of observations should, in such cases, be capable of representing it. The minimal way to effect such a representation would be to add a weight parameter, I, to the statement of observational probabilities, *i.e.* $o = [\bigwedge_j pr_o(p_j) = a_j$ & weight $pr_o(p_j) = I_j]$ (I_j will often, but not invariably, be independent of j). This concept of weight is just Savage's intuitive concept of "sureness" which applies as much to observational probabilities as any other species of degree of belief. A deeper analysis would then represent an observation as a second order probability distribution over pr_o, with our old observational probabilities emerging as expectations, and (in cases where the second order distribution is nice enough) our weight being a function of its variance. Such a representation would then move our involvement with higher order personal probabilities to level three. I do not propose to develop this in detail here, but only to make the point that higher order personal probabilities provide a rich framework for analysis of what is going on inside Field's parameter α.

I offer one brief illustration of how the likelihoods might go in some cases, with no special claims as to the value of the illustration, other than as nostalgia. I will forgo higher order observational probabilities and keep weights, and confine myself to the partition $[p, \sim p]$. I will have both observational probabilities, pr_{o_i}, and final probability, pr_f, as random variables, and will deal with probability density functions PDF rather than probabilities on these random variables. By Bayes' theorem:

$$PDF\,[pr_f(p) = w \text{ given } o] \propto$$
$$PDF\,[pr_f(p) = w]\,PDF\,[o \text{ given } pr_f(p) = w]$$

(where the proportionality symbol indicates multiplication by a normalising term not dependent on w). Suppose that the likelihood function has a Bernoullian distribution:

$$PDF[o_1 \ldots o_n \text{ given } pr_f(p) = w] = w^\gamma\,(1 - w)^\delta$$

where $\gamma = \Sigma_1^n\,pr_{o_i}(p)\,I_i$ and $\delta = \Sigma_1^n\,pr_{o_i}(\sim p)\,I_i$ and that the prior distribution for $pr_f(p)$ is a beta distribution:

$$PDF[pr_f(p) = w] \propto w^{\alpha-1}(1-w)^{\beta-1}$$

(a case of some special interest being that in which $\alpha = \beta = 1$ which gives the "flat" or "uniform" prior, $PDF[pr_f(p) = w] = 1$). Then by Bayes' theorem, the posterior distribution, $PDF[pr_f(p) = w$ given $o_1 \ldots o_n]$, is also a beta distribution with parameters $\alpha' = \alpha + \sum_{i=1}^n pr_o(p)I_i$ and $\beta' = \beta + \sum_{i=1}^n [1 - pr_{o_i}(p)_i]I_i$. That is, in this situation, where the observations are Bernoullian in the sense indicated, repeated observations never move the probability distribution function out of the family of beta distributions, but only change the values of the parameters, alpha and beta. The family of beta distributions is called the family of *conjugate prior* distributions for samples from a Bernoulli distribution (Raiffa and Schlaifer 1961: ch. 3). We take the posterior probability of p to be the posterior expectation of pr_f (this being another form of Miller's principle).

$$PR[p \text{ given } o_1 \ldots o_n]$$
$$= \int w \, PDF[pr_f(p) = w \text{ given } o_1 \ldots o_n].$$

The expectation of a beta distribution is $\alpha/(\alpha+\beta)$. Therefore:

$$PR[p \text{ given } o_1 \ldots o_n]$$
$$= \alpha + \sum_{i=1}^{n} pr_{o_i}(p)I_i/[\alpha + \sum_{i=1}^{n} pr_{o_i}(p)I_i] + [\beta + \sum_{i=1}^{n} pr_o(p)I_i]$$

where α and β are the parameters of the prior PDF of $pr_f(p)$. In the case in which $\alpha = \beta$, we have:

$$PR[p \text{ given } o_1 \ldots o_n] = [\Sigma pr_{o_i}(p)I_i + \beta]/[\Sigma I_i + 2\beta].$$

If we consider the case where observational probabilities are always 0 or 1 and where I_i always equals 1, we have (letting N be the number of observations, $n = \Sigma pr_{o_i}(p)$, and $\lambda = \beta/2$):

$$\text{Carnap: } PR[p \text{ given } o_1 \ldots o_n] = [2n + \lambda]/[2N + 2\lambda]$$

(see Carnap (1952) and Jaynes (1958)), and taking the case of a flat prior:

$$\text{Laplace: } PR[p \text{ given } o_1 \ldots o_n] = (n+1)/(n+2).$$

We can recover the formula for $\alpha = \beta$ from Carnap if we take an observation, o_i, as equivalent to a virtual sample of size I_i and frequency pr_{o_i}. But in some situations, the likelihood may *not* be as if the observational probabilities were relative frequencies within Bernoullian samples, so I reemphasise that the foregoing is offered as an illustration rather than as methodology.

At the beginning of this section, I claimed that the points I made about the relation between probability kinematics and higher order conditionalisation would generalise to Jaynes' information theoretic approach to statistical inference (Jaynes (1957, 1979), Kullback (1959)). The extent to which the points made about probability kinematics generalise to inference maximising relative entropy is in fact quite remarkable. I will close this section with a brief sketch of their relation. I rely for this account on Halmos and Savage (1949), Kullback and Leibler (1951) and Kullback (1959). The question is there treated in a very general setting. We deal with abstract probability spaces, $\langle X, S, \mu_i \rangle$, where X is a set, S a sigma algebra of subsets of S, and μ_i a measure on S. The relative information of μ_1 with respect to μ_2 is defined as:

$$I(1:2) = \int f_1(x)\ln[f_1(x)/f_2(x)]d\lambda(x)$$

where f_1 and f_2 are generalised probability density functions whose existence is guaranteed under mild conditions of continuity. (We need only assume that μ_1 is absolutely continuous with μ_2. Then we can take $f_1(x)$ as the Radon–Nikodym derivative of μ_1 with respect to μ_2. $f_2(x)$ then equals 1, since it is $d\mu_2/d\mu_2$, so in this case $I(1:2)$ $=\int f_1(x)\ln[f_1(x)]d\mu_2(x)$; see Kullback (1959: 28–9). We can then take the information theoretic version of statistical inference as follows: starting from an initial probability distribution, μ_2, and a constraint of the form $\int T(x)f_1(x)d\lambda(x) = \theta$, and a set of eligible candidates for final probability distribution with respect to which μ_1 is absolutely continuous, infer that final probability distribution μ_2 such that among the candidates for final distribution which meet the constraint it minimises the relative information, $I(1:2)$. Here $T(x)$ is a measureable statistic, either real or vector valued and θ is a constant. For example: (1) suppose $T(x)$ is the characteristic function of measurable set, s; $\mu_2(s) > 0$; $\theta = 1$; and we take every μ_1 with which μ_2 is absolutely continuous as eligible. Then the final probability, μ_1^*, which minimises $I(1:2)$ comes from μ_2 by conditionalisation on s. (2) Just as (1), except that $\theta = a$ for some $0 \leq a \leq 1$. Then μ_1^* comes from μ_2 by probability kinematics on the partition $[s,\bar{s}]$ (see Kullback 1959: example 2.3, pp. 42–3). (3) As before except that $T(x) = \langle c_1(x) \ldots c_n(x) \rangle$, where each c_i is the characteristic function of an element, p_i, of a finite partition of X; $\mu_2(p_i) > 0$; $\theta = \langle a_1 \ldots a_n \rangle$ with $0 \leq a_i \leq 1$. Then μ_1^* comes fron μ_2 by probability kinematics on the partition $[p_i]$. (4) As (3) except that the partition may be countably infinite. Then μ_2^* still comes from μ_1 by probability kinematics, in a sense that I will explain. (5) However, the random variables are not limited to characteristic functions, or vectors whose components are characteristic functions, but may be any measurable functions, or vectors whose components are measurable functions.

To discuss the relation of probability kinematics to the maximum relative entropy (minimum relative information) rule, we need an equally general formulation of probability kinematics. Suppose that we have a countably infinite partition, $[p_i]$, such that $\mu_2(p_i) > 0$ for all p_i. Then we can say that μ_1 comes from μ_2 by generalised probability kinematics on the partition, $[p_i]$, if and only if for each element of the partition, p_i, the ratio of the posterior to the prior density at each point in $p_i, f_1(x)/f_2(x)$, is equal to the ratio of the posterior to the prior probabilities of that element, $\mu_1(p_i)/\mu_2(p_i)$. That is, the criterion of constancy of probability, conditional on members of the partition in the finite case, is simply generalised to constancy of conditional density. Given this generalised definition my remark under (4) above holds. Strictly speaking, I should add the qualification: *modulo* a set of points of measure zero in μ_2. In fact, the generalised probability distribution functions we have been using are only determined to within a set of measure zero in μ_2. This qualification should be understood to hold throughout. If $\langle X, S, \mu_1 \rangle$ comes from $\langle X, S, \mu_2 \rangle$ by probability kinematics on the countable partition, $[p_i]$, in the way indicated, we say that the partition is *sufficient* for $\langle \mu_1, \mu_2 \rangle$ because in this case measuring the relative information with respect to the partition $\Sigma_i \mu_1 \ln[\mu_1(p_i)/\mu_2(p_i)]$ gives the relative information, $I(1:2)$. If a partition is not sufficient, *i.e.* if μ_2 does not come from μ_1 by kinematics on that partition, then the information with respect to the partition is less than $I(1:2)$; measuring information relative to a insufficient partition causes loss of information (Kullback 1959: corollary 3.2, p. 16). It follows that if a constraint consists in specifying the final probabilities of each member of a countable partition each of whose members have positive prior probability, then the final probability measure comes from the initial one by minimising relative information *if and only if* it comes from the initial one by probability kinematics on that partition.

For a fully general formulation of probability kinematics, we need to remove the restrictions on the partition. Any statistic (measurable function) on a probability space *induces a partition* on that space, with the elements of the partition being the inverse images of the values of the statistic (*e.g.* if I have a probability space of baskets and the statistic 'number of eggs in', the statistic induces a partition of baskets such that two baskets are members of the same element of the partition if and only if they contain the same number of eggs. Notice that a vector valued statistic induces the partition that is the common refinement of the partitions induced by its components.) Conversely, any partition whose elements are measurable sets is induced by some statistic. (*n.b.* I have not made any limitation as to the types of values that statistics can take.) So we can have full generality if we formulate probability kinematics relative to a statistic. Let T be a statistic, with domain X and range Y, and let R be the class of measurable subsets of Y (*i.e.* $G \in R \longleftrightarrow T^{-1}(G) \in S$). Then starting with a probability space, $\langle X,S,\mu \rangle$. and a statistic, T, we can consider an associated probability space $\langle Y,R,\upsilon \rangle$ where the measure υ is derived from μ, by $\upsilon(G) = \mu(T^{-1}(G))$. Then $\upsilon(G) = \int_G g(Y)d\gamma(Y)$ where $\gamma(G) = \lambda(T^{-1}(G))$. The associated probability space can be thought of as representing the effect of consolidating the elements of the partition induced by the statistic into single elements. Let g_1 and g_2 be the generalised probability density functions for the spaces $\langle Y,R,\upsilon_1 \rangle$; $\langle Y,R,\upsilon_2 \rangle$ which corresponds to $\langle X,S,\mu_1 \rangle$; $\langle X,S,\mu_2 \rangle$ under the statistic T. (We may take them as the Radon–Nikodym derivatives of μ_1 and μ_2 with respect to μ_2.) Then we will say that $\langle X,S,\mu_1 \rangle$ comes from $\langle X,S,\mu_2 \rangle$ *by generalised probability kinematics on the statistic T* (or, if you please, on the partition induced by T) if and only if $f_1(x)/f_2(x) = g_1 T(x)/g_2 T(x)$. This is equivalent to saying that the conditional density conditional on $T(x) = y$, *i.e.* $f(x)/gT(x)$, remains the same before and after the change, and is thus clearly the correct statement of probability kinematics for this general case. If $\langle X,S,\mu_1 \rangle$ comes from $\langle X,S,\mu_2 \rangle$ by generalised probability kinematics on the statistic T, we shall say that *T is a sufficient statistic*, relative to them. Just as in the countable case, we have the result that the relative information measured on the partition, $I(1{:}2,Y)$, is less than or equal to the relative information, $I(1{:}2,X)$, with equality if and only if the statistic is sufficient (Kullback & Leibler 1951: theorem 4.1; Kullback 1959: theorem 4.1). A sufficient statistic is one which loses no information. It follows from this that, if the satisfaction of a certain constraint is a function of the posterior values of $g(\gamma)$ (*i.e.* the posterior values of the conditional expectation of $f(x)$ given that $T(x) = \gamma$), then the posterior distribution that comes from the prior by minimising relative information subject to that constraint comes from the prior by generalised probability kinematics on T. For consider the posterior distribution of values of $g(\gamma)$ in the minimum relative information posterior. By the hypothesis that the satisfaction of the constraint is a function of the posterior values of $g(\gamma)$, any posterior distribution with these values satisfies the constraint. Thus the posterior which comes from the prior by probability kinematics on T with this final distribution for $g(\gamma)$ satisfies the constraint. And, by the previous theorem, it must be the minimum relative information posterior.

But the constraints considered in the maximum entropy (minimum relative information) formalism are all of this character! Remember that the constraints all consisted in specifying the posterior expectation of a statistic:

$$\int T(x) f_1(x) d\lambda(x) = \theta.$$

This can now be rewritten as:

$$\int y g_1(y) d\gamma(y) = \theta.$$

So T is a sufficient statistic relative to a prior and a posterior which minimises relative information subject to the constraint that the posterior expectation of T has a certain value. (See Kullback 1959: 43–4; van Fraassen has also discussed a special case of this in a recent unpublished paper.) We have just established a theorem, which can be roughly put as:

JAYNES implies JEFFREY.

That is, if we start with a prior and move to that posterior (among those with respect to which the prior is absolutely continuous and which satisfy the constraint that a statistic T has a certain posterior expected value) which minimises relative information, then the posterior comes from the prior by generalised probability kinematics on the statistic, T. Conversely, we can say that if a posterior comes from a prior by generalised probability kinematics on T, then it minimises relative information subject to the constraint that $g(y)$ has those posterior values. In the finite or countable case, we could always put that constraint in Jaynes' form by considering a statistic T' which is a vector of characteristic functions of elements of the partition induced by T. But in the general cases it is not clear that we can always put the constraint in Jaynes' form (unless we use the same trick and countenance vectors of uncountable dimension). So it is only with some qualification that we can assert that JEFFREY implies JAYNES.

The point I made about the relation of higher order probabilities to probability kinematics carries over to this general setting. Let me explain why I called the sufficiency condition:

$$PR(q \text{ given } p_j \text{ and } \bigwedge_i pr(p_i) = a_i) = PR(q \text{ given } p_j)$$
$$\text{for all first order } q \text{ and all } j$$

by that name. Given that the change from the initial distribution to the final distribution is to be by conditionalisation on $\bigwedge_i pr\ (p_i) = a_i$, the condition can be rewritten as:

$$PR_{final}\ (q\ \text{given}\ p_j) = PR_{initial}\ (q\ \text{given}\ p_j)$$
$$\text{for all first order}\ q\ \text{and all}\ j$$

which means that if we look at the first order probability space, we have the condition for $[p_j]$ to be a sufficient partitioning for $(PR_{initial}, PR_{final})$.

It should be clear from the foregoing discussion that we can carry all this over to abstract probability spaces and generalised probability density functions. So we will be able to say in general that second order conditionalisation results in first order probability kinematics on a partition if and only if such a sufficiency condition is satisfied.

It would be of some interest to investigate the full structure of minimum relative information inference from the same point of view. That is, we look at a second order distribution where we can conditionalise on the constraint that the final expected value of a statistic has a certain value, and identify the characteristics that the second order distribution must have for such conditionalising to coincide at the first order level with minimum relative information inference. We have some of the answers already, but not all. It is a necessary condition for minimum relative information that we have generalised probability kinematics on T, the statistic of the constraint. We have this if and only if the second order probability distribution satisfies the proper sufficiency condition. To ensure that conditionalising at the second order level leads us to a distribution in which the constraint is in fact met requires a further generalisation of the generalised Miller condition. But there will be further requirements necessary to guarantee that the final density over the elements of the partition induced by T is of the proper exponential character required to satisfy the minimum relative information principle. (See Kullback (1959: ch. 3) for derivation and discussion of the exponential solutions.)

Conclusion

If I end with more questions open than closed, I hope this will only reinforce the point that second-order personal probabilities are not only legitimate, but also theoretically interesting. They provide a perspective from which the scope of applicability of first order generalisations of conditionalisation can be assessed. Counter

136   BRIAN SKYRMS

instances to the sufficiency condition are counter instances to both probability kinematics and the minimum relative information principle. The scarcity and peculiar nature of such counter instances explains the wide range within which probability kinematics can be plausibly applied. An analogous determination of the range of applicability of minimum relative information inference calls for further study.

University of Illinois at Chicago Circle

REFERENCES

Carnap, R. 1952. *The Continuum of Inductive Methods*. Chicago.
de Finetti, B. 1972. *Probability, Induction and Statistics*. London.
Domotor, Z., Zanotti, M. and Groves, G. (Forthcoming). Probability kinematics, *Synthese*.
Field, H. 1978. A note of Jeffrey conditionalization, *Philosophy of Science* **45**, 171–85.
Freedman, D. & Purves, R. 1969. Bayes method for bookies, *Annals of Mathematical Statistics* **40**, 1177–86.
Gärdenfors, P. 1975. Qualitative probability as intensional logic, *Journal of Philosophical Logic* **4**, 171–85.
Good, I. J. 1950. *Probability and the Weighing of Evidence*. London.
Good, I. J. 1965. *The Estimation of Probabilities*. Cambridge, Massachusetts.
Good, I. J. 1971. The probabilistic explication of information, evidence, surprise, causality, explanation and utility. In *Foundations of Statistical Inference*, ed. Godambe & Sprott. Toronto.
Hacking, I. 1967. Slightly more realistic personal probability, *Philosophy of Science* **34**, 311–25.
Halmos, P. R. and Savage, L. J. 1949. Application of the Radon–Nikodym theorem to the theory of sufficient statistics, *Annals of Mathematical Statistics* **20**, 225–41.
Hintikka, J. 1971. Unknown probabilities, Bayesianism and de Finetti's representation theorem. In *Boston Studies in the Philosophy of Science*, vol. 8. Dordrecht.
Jaynes, E. T. 1957. Information theory and statistical mechanics, *Physical Review* **106**, 620–30.
Jaynes, E. T. 1958. *Probability Theory in Science and Engineering*. Dallas.
Jaynes, E. T. 1979. Where do we stand on maximum entropy? In *The Maximum Entropy Formalism*, ed. R. D. Levine & M. Tribus, pp. 115–18. Cambridge, Massachusetts.
Jeffrey, R. 1965. *The Logic of Decision*. New York.
Jeffrey, R. 1974. Preference among preferences, *Journal of Philosophy* **63**, 377–91.
Kullback, S. 1959. *Information Theory and Statistics*. New York.

Kullback, S. & Leibler, R. A. 1951. On information and sufficiency, *Annals of Mathematical Statistics* **22**, 79–86.

May, S. & Harper, W. 1976. Toward an optimization procedure for applying minimum change principles in probability kinematics. In *Foundation of Probability Theory, Statistical Inference and Statistical Theories of Science*, vol. I, ed. W. L. Harper & C. A. Hooker. Dordrecht.

Miller, D. 1966. A paradox of information, *British Journal for the Philosophy of Science* **17**, 59–61.

Raiffa, H. & Schlaifer, R. 1961. *Applied Statistical Decision Theory*. Boston.

Ramsey, F. P. 1926. Truth and probability. In his *Foundations*, ed. D. H. Mellor, pp. 58–100. 1978. London.

Savage, L. J. 1972. *The Foundations of Statistics*, 2nd ed. New York.

Shafer, G. 1979. Jeffrey's rule of conditioning, *Technical Report 131*, Department of Statistics, Stanford University.

Skyrms, B. 1975. *Choice and Chance*, 2nd ed. Belmont, California.

Skyrms, B. 1980. *Causal Necessity*. New Haven, Connecticut.

Teller, P. 1973. Conditionalization and observation, *Synthese* **26**, 218–58.

7   *Consciousness and degrees of belief*

D. H. MELLOR

1 Many of our beliefs come by degrees. Do beliefs about beliefs, especially beliefs about our own present beliefs, do so? In other words, do we have "second order" degrees of belief? In chapter 6 of this volume, Skyrms defends the idea that we do "against charges of inconsistency, illegitimacy and triviality" and goes on to show its "theoretical usefulness in connection with the laws of motion for rational belief" (p. 109). I go further. The idea of second order beliefs is not only legitimate and useful, we positively need it in order to provide a theory of conscious belief. And with this theory we can ward off a recent attack on the theory that degrees of belief are subjective probabilities. Combining these two theories seems, however, to have some unattractive consequences; but none, I believe, that need force us to reject them.

In what follows I shall develop and defend these three claims in turn. In Part **I**, I develop a theory of conscious belief, and extend it to take in degrees of belief. In Part **II**, I shall use this theory as part of a general defence of subjective probability as a measure of degrees of belief. (I anticipate this result from time to time in Part **I** by taking degrees of belief to be subjective probabilities. But that is only to simplify the discussion; it is not essential, and does not beg the question.) In Part **III**, I show how the theories of Parts **I** and **II** together seem to entail that we consciously believe all the conse-

I am particularly indebted to Professor Kyburg for provoking me to try and answer his objections to subjective probability. In my hasty attempt to solve the problems posed in Part **III**, which surfaced at the last minute, I am indebted for helpful comments to Mr Anthony Appiah, Dr Jonathan Lear and, especially, Professor T. J. Smiley. They are not of course responsible for the errors it doubtless contains.

This work was done during my tenure of a Radcliffe Fellowship for which I owe thanks to the Radcliffe Trust.

quences of our conscious beliefs. This clearly false conclusion in fact follows, not from these theories, but from the easy but erroneous idea that we always believe definite propositions, *i.e.* that the contents of all our beliefs determine definite truth conditions for them. Not, however, wishing to pretend that I have worked out any better idea, I shall continue to use the term 'proposition' for the content of a belief.

I

2 Ramsey (1926) showed how to measure the degree of a belief by measuring how strongly its owner is disposed to act on it. Ramsey, apropos of its degree, and Braithwaite (1933) in general, identify belief with this disposition to act rather than with any conscious feeling of conviction. Feelings of conviction may accompany belief, but they need not: "the beliefs we hold most strongly are often accompanied by practically no feeling at all" (Ramsey 1926: 71). For example, "I believe quite thoroughly that the sun will shine tomorrow, but experience no particular feeling attached to the proposition believed" (Braithwaite 1933: 142). Feelings may no doubt be among the causes and effects of gaining or losing a belief, but it is the disposition which directly determines how the believer will behave. The disposition is what provides the proximate explanation of his actions.

This might be denied, on the grounds that, as Molière thought, it is vacuous to explain events by saying that things – or people – are disposed to make them happen. But this is not always so. The most reputable explanatory properties of people and things are just conjunctions of dispositions to bring about the events they explain (Mellor 1974). Even if a person's belief were just a disposition, using it to explain his behaviour would be no worse than using his weight to explain his effect on the bathroom scales. If anything, it should seem better to those who suspect dispositional explanation of vacuity, since a particular belief is not a disposition to any specific kind of activity: what its owner does will depend also on his desires and his other beliefs. So the beliefs and desires which are used to explain an action cannot be defined by it in the simple way in which Molière complains that 'dormitive virtue' can be defined. This is indeed an important fact about beliefs, and one I shall have need of later on. Meanwhile it will be convenient to mark the fact immediately by calling beliefs 'quasi-dispositions', and Ramsey's and Braithwaite's theory of them an 'action' theory rather than a dispositional theory.

It is in fact neither vacuous nor easy to characterise beliefs by the actions which, along with desires, they generate. In particular, it is not easy to say in general how changes in belief affect behaviour. Fortunately, we shall be concerned only with variations in the strength of belief, rather than in its content; and their effects are relatively easy to state. What they affect is betting behaviour, broadly conceived. As Ramsey put it, "all our lives we are in a sense betting. Whenever we go to the station we are betting that a train will really run, and if we had not a sufficient degree of belief in this we should decline the bet and stay at home" (1926: 85). And as the degree of our belief in the train's running gets less, we may add, so the journey has to matter more to us to get us to the station.

This is not meant to imply that we consciously calculate odds whenever our degrees of belief affect our activity. Degrees of belief can influence quite unselfconscious actions. That is indeed how degrees of belief are best revealed, since *ex hypothesi* such actions will not be being done deliberately in order to mislead.

It is precisely because an action theory does not invoke conscious feelings of conviction that it can readily allow beliefs to explain actions done while the agent's conscious thought is miles away. And so it should : that is how most actions are done. Crossing a two-way street in Britain, for example, I nearly always look right first, that being the direction I most strongly believe traffic on my side of the road will be coming from; but this thought crosses my conscious mind much less often than I cross British streets. Animals likewise, we suppose, can act on beliefs without having to be conscious of them. 'Often enough, my cat's behaviour makes it clear to me that he believes he is about to be fed', says Jeffrey (1965: 9), and I believe him. At least, I believe him more strongly than I believe his cat has any conscious thought about the matter. What is more, the animal could just as easily make it clear to me that he is none too sure of being fed, less sure for instance than he is of the prospects to be opened up by stalking a nearby thrush. In short, we readily grant some animals degrees of belief; and we grant them these degrees more readily than we should grant them conscious convictions. It is a virtue therefore in Ramsey's theory to let them have the one without the other.

3 Virtues, however, have their price. The price here is that an action theory does not as it stands make any sense of conscious belief. It is not, as Ramsey claims, "observably false . . . to suppose that the degree of a belief is something perceptible by its owner" (1926: 71). On the contrary, their being perceptible to us is what makes immediately obvious the truth of Ramsey's other claim that "the beliefs we hold most strongly are often accompanied by practically no feeling at all".

If belief were a feeling of conviction, the phenomenon of conscious belief would pose no problem, since kinds of consciousness are just what kinds of feelings are. But dispositions to act are not kinds of consciousness, and nor are the quasi-dispositional states of belief and desire that, according to the action theory, cause them. Such states of mind as these will not automatically intimate their presence to their owners as feelings do. Nor can we credibly claim a general ability to become conscious of our own properties, whether they be physical or mental. Fortunately for the medical industry, for example, I cannot detect by introspection either what my blood group is or whether I am colour blind. My beliefs, on the other hand, I can call into my consciousness almost whenever I like (doubtless with Freudian exceptions). The Humean idea of belief as a kind of self-intimating feeling still appeals precisely because it accounts immediately for this fact. And until the action theory can produce an alternative account of what conscious belief is and how it occurs, that Humean idea, for all its defects, will never be properly scotched.

Where should an alternative to the Humean idea of conscious belief be looked for? Armstrong, who espouses an action theory of belief, maintains that "an account of having a belief before the mind, as a current content of consciousness, does not demand development of the theory of belief but rather of the quite general notion of consciousness" (1973: 22). I disagree: the contents of consciousness are too diverse. The action theory is after all forced on us in the first place because even conscious belief is so obviously unlike a feeling. It seems evident to me that conscious belief should be explained by relating it to its "unconscious" action-producing counterpart, not by lumping it in a general theory of consciousness with items as unlike it as pains, visual sensations and emotions are. That at least is how I shall set about explaining it; it will be time to consider Armstrong's preferred alternative if and when it ever appears.

4 I need however to say a little more about conscious belief before offering a theory of it. I take it that a man's mind changes in some way when he acquires a conscious belief, even if he acquires it only by becoming conscious of a belief he already has. Suppose I walk towards the back of a room in order to get out of it. I walk that way because that is where I most strongly believe the exit to be. But this need not be a conscious degree of belief: consciously, I may be completely preoccupied with my reason for leaving the room. If I do start to think consciously about where the exit is, I shall come thereby into a new state of mind, different from the one which would in any case propel me towards the door.

For this new state, of conscious belief in the exit's whereabouts, I need a new name, in order to discourage the idea that it is just the quasi-dispositional belief state plus consciousness. This conscious state is actually what Hume called simply '*belief*, which is a term that every one sufficiently understands in common life' (1739: 629); and no doubt the conscious state is still what most people think of as belief. But since our account of belief is going to start from the basic concept of the action theory, 'belief' is best reserved for that "unconscious" quasi-disposition. As in my 1978 paper on conscious belief, therefore, I follow Price (1969: 189) and others in using Hume's other term, 'assent', to refer to conscious belief. The term is not ideal, as I remarked on first adopting it: in particular, its connotations of a public display of acquiescence need to be discarded. Still, as Hume said, "provided we agree about the thing, 'tis needless to dispute about the terms"; and the mental state I have in mind is as familiar in common life today as it was to Hume, despite having proved so elusive to analysis. Throughout what follows, therefore, it must be kept in mind that this familiar inner state is what I mean by 'assent', not any of its outward manifestations in behaviour; and by 'dissent' I shall likewise mean the inner state of conscious *dis*belief.

Assent, thus understood, evidently comes by degrees as much as plain belief does. Assenting to something is at least consciously believing it more strongly than its negation, and is quite often not much more than that. While between assent and dissent, as between belief and disbelief, there are the intermediate degrees of doubt, in this case conscious doubt. In order to talk about all these conscious states together I shall use 'assent' as 'belief' is also used: namely, not only for one extreme of this family of mental states, but also as a name for the family itself, ranging in degree from what we may call full assent, through increasingly sceptical shades of doubt, to outright dissent.

Not only can we assent in varying degrees to propositions of all sorts, we incessantly do. Almost whenever we are conscious, that consciousness includes assenting to something, or dissenting from it or consciously doubting it. This aspect of our consciousness moreover is what gives us an almost instant access to nearly all our own beliefs, which we have to no one else's. I may see some of your beliefs reflected in your behaviour (as Jeffrey sees his cat's), but I need not watch my own actions to get my own beliefs and doubts into my consciousness. Suppose for example I hear you put to me almost any question, 'h?', which I understand. I will at once be made conscious, as you will not, of whether I believe h, disbelieve it or doubt it: $i.e.$ I will at once assent to h in some greater or less degree. Now I may of course be wrong, not only about h itself but about the strength of my own belief in h. That is, not only may I assent to h when h is false, I may assent to h when I do not believe it. The degree of my assent, in other words, may differ markedly from the degree of plain belief which my unselfconscious actions would reveal to others. And it is an important fact that when this happens, we take it to be a case of self-deception: what we conclude is that I do not really believe what I consciously believe. This shows both how assent is thought to involve a fallible perception of belief, and how right the action theory is to take the unconscious state, and not assent, to be the paradigm of really believing something.

Self-deception about belief is, I suppose, almost always possible. But it is not common; and, right or wrong, my assent does at least tell me something about my belief, which it does not tell me about anyone else's. This is the familiar fact, referred to in 3, of our privileged access to our own beliefs. This is the fact that, on an action theory, needs accounting for – preferably, on an action theory, by construing assent also as some kind of disposition or quasi-disposition to action.

5 The cue for an action theory of assent is given by the fact that some behaviour needs assent, not just plain belief. In particular, linguistic behaviour needs assent. To talk or write to someone I have to be conscious of what I am talking or writing about. My plain belief, that traffic here keeps left in two-way streets, may steer me safely

through a town without it becoming a conscious belief, but it will not steer me through a conversation on the subject. For that I need assent. I do not mean that I need to assent fully to everything I say, since I can of course choose to lie. But what I lack when I lie is not consciousness of my state of belief. On the contrary, I have to be as conscious of what I believe in order to lie about it, as I do in order to tell what I believe to be the truth. What I lack when I lie is the degree of assent which is implicit in the remarks I choose to make. To lie, I must dissent from what I assert, or at least consciously doubt it more than my speech conveys. Plain disbelief is not enough.

Some degree of assent therefore is needed for every assertion. But assent is not a simple disposition to assert, as the case of lying shows. What I say depends not only on what I assent to, but on how I desire to affect my audience. I shall only assert what I assent to if I want to tell my audience the truth; otherwise I shall deny it, equivocate or say nothing at all. So no degree of assent, however high, can be defined as a disposition to make any specific assertion, any more than plain beliefs, however strong, can be defined as dispositions to do any other specific thing.

Assent, therefore, like belief, at least includes a quasi-disposition – only, to act in special ways, such as conversing, which call for it. Now if we actually identify assent with such a quasi-disposition, we can spare ourselves the unhopeful search for a special kind of consciousness to accompany, or partly constitute, assent. We already know that no feeling or sensation does so: the whole point of the quotations from Ramsey and Braithwaite in **2** was to invite us to make some strong belief conscious, *i.e.* to generate a high degree of assent, and then consciously to note the absence of any particular feeling.

Our problem then will be to relate these two quasi-dispositions, assent and plain belief. The problem is especially acute for those of us who wish to follow Ramsey in measuring the strength of a belief by the believer's choice of odds for a bet on its truth. For literally choosing odds, like talking, calls for consciousness of the proposition in question, *i.e.* it calls for assent, and not just for belief. We have to give some reason for assuming that a conscious choice between explicitly risky alternatives will reveal the strength of beliefs of which we need not, even in action, be conscious at all. Nor even perhaps, in the case of animals, be capable of bringing to consciousness. We have credited animals with beliefs, and with beliefs of variable strength, but not with what it takes to choose odds, not with degrees of assent. Why should the strength of an assent of which they are incapable be supposed to measure the strength of the essentially unconscious belief that they actually have?

6 I propose to solve these problems with the simplest possible action theory of assent: namely, that *assenting to a proposition is believing one believes it*. I put this theory forward first in 1978, when I deliberately confined it to the qualitative case of full belief and full assent. But since belief and assent do in fact come by degrees, the theory must be shown also to accommodate that fact; and this is my present task. First, however, I should summarise the qualitative theory, correcting some errors in the original version and dealing with some objections that have been made to it.

I write '*Btah*' for a person or animal a believing a proposition h at a time t. Where the identity of a, t or h is immaterial, I abbreviate this as convenient to '*Bth*', '*Bah*', '*Bh*', or just '*B*' Disbelief I take to be belief in the negation, which I write '*B~h*': '*~Bh*' means merely that h is not believed, which might mean disbelief, or doubt or merely a lack of any attitude at all to h. Originally I took a believing at t that he believes h to be *BtaBtah* (1978: 90–1), but this is wrong. Believing one believes something is an essentially indexical state: it is a believing at t that *he* believes h *now*. This is not the same as his believing that a believes h at t, as Perry (1979) has shown, even though he is a and t is the present time. For instance, a may have forgotten the time, or even who he is, and not believe *Btah* under any true non-indexical description of t and a. But he can still believe that he himself, whoever he is, believes h now, whatever the time now is; and this is the state that concerns me.

Since this state of believing one believes is indexed in this way to its owner and the present time, it will suffice for my purposes to write it simply as '*BtaB*h*', or '*BB**' for short, the '*' serving to indicate its indexicality in these two respects.

Then if A is the state of assent, as B is of plain belief, my thesis is that

$$(1) \qquad A = BB^*.$$

7 (1) involves two claims: (1a), that A entails BB^*; and (1b), that BB^* entails A. My argument for (1a) may be summarised by the following excerpts from my 1978 paper, duly modified to correct the error noticed above.

There is *prima facie* such a thing as believing one believes something. I have beliefs about all sorts of things: why not about my own beliefs? [Moreover] we recognise a difference [between BB^*h and Bh], as our concept of a state of self-deception shows. . . . A husband, we suppose, can (subconsciously) believe his wife to be unfaithful, while (consciously) believing that he believes nothing of the sort (1978: 91).

If we have such states [as BB^*h] at all, they surely occur when we assent to propositions . . . Assent is the conscious belief in h that is required for the sincere affirmation of h's truth. In coming to assent to h I have perceived (or in cases of self-deception, misperceived) my belief in h: if that does not involve believing one believes h, what does? (1978: 92)

In the original discussion, the following counter-example was proposed to this rhetorical question. Suppose I am reluctantly persuaded, *e.g.* by a psychoanalyst, that I subconsciously believe some nasty proposition about my parents. Since it makes no odds to the argument, I shall for ease of exposition represent this as subconsciously disbelieving its negation, the nice proposition h. Then, despite the analyst, I still *assent* to h; but, it was alleged, I no longer believe I believe it, which shows that (1a), and therefore (1), is false.

Not so: the case has been misstated. What we really have here is my assenting to a proposition h and also *assenting* to the indexical proposition $\sim B^*h$ ($=$ I don't now believe h). That is not Ah and $\sim BB^*h$ as was alleged; it is Ah and $A\sim B^*h$, which according to (1) is BB^*h and $BB^*\sim B^*h$, two perfectly compatible states of mind. Now I had indeed conjectured (1978: 92) "that we have in fact no more distinct states [BB^*B^*h, $BB^*B^*B^*h$] etc." beyond BB^*h; and this case perhaps shows that we must occasionally allow BB^*B^*h to be a state distinct from BB^*h. But my chief contention, (1a), survives unscathed: assenting entails believing one believes.

The converse contention, (1b), is less obvious. If Bh can exist without being my being conscious of it, as on an action theory it clearly can, one might ask why BB^*h cannot do so. And if it can, it can presumably exist without assent, in which case (1b) is false. But this suggestion misses the whole point of (1). The thesis is, after all, that for Bh to be conscious just *is* for the state BB^*h to occur. For *that* state in turn to be conscious would therefore be for BB^*B^*h to occur. But with the possible exception just noticed, I see little reason to suppose that there is any such state distinct from BB^*h itself. And of course this account does not invoke consciousness in saying what assent is. That is a virtue, not a defect, since its very object is to say in other terms what this elusive kind of consciousness is.

What a defender of (1) does need to do is, positively, to use it to explain why the kinds of behaviour that need assent do so, *i.e.* why they need BB^* and not just B; and, negatively, to explain away putative counter-examples. In my 1978 paper I undertook both of these tasks; here I shall briefly summarise the results.

Positively, I used a couple of Gricean truisms about language to show that sincerely communicating any h calls for BB^*h, not just Bh. (What I originally claimed in 1978 (§VII) was that communication needs BBh, but in fact the token–reflexive state BB^*h is what the argument really shows to be needed.) In being told that h, the hearer is intended by the speaker to be convinced that the speaker himself believes h as he speaks. To have this intention the speaker needs, if he is sincere, to believe that he himself now believes h, *i.e.* he needs to be in the state BB^*h. (If he is being insincere, the state he needs to be in is $BB^*{\sim}h$.) And if (1) is true, that fact explains why he needs to be in the state Ah $(A{\sim}h)$, because it is the very same state. The thesis does therefore explain why conversation needs assent, not just belief.

To dispose of most proposed counter-examples to (1b), it suffices to insist on the essentially indexical, present-tense nature of assent. Tenseless beliefs about beliefs, beliefs of tenses other than the present tense, beliefs about the beliefs of other people: none of these is assent, and any of them could exist without assent for all (1b) says. The suspicion that BB^* could do so stems largely from confounding it with other sorts of belief about beliefs.

But one apparent counter-example to (1b) is properly indexed: namely, self-deception itself. A man deceives himself if he believes he believes h when he does not believe h; *i.e.* $BB^*h\&{\sim}Bh$. But we should not normally say that he was self-deceived about his belief in h only when that belief was conscious. So it seems that he could be in the state BB^*h without being in any degree of the state Ah; so (1b) is false.

In fact this is not so. The state of self-deception that can exist even when the man is not assenting to h is not in fact $BB^*h\&{\sim}Bh$. Now in saying this I am not just trying to rescue (1b) by stipulation. Recall that our objective is to extend the action theory to cope with assent, and the basic concept of belief to be used must therefore be that of the action theory itself. We have already seen that it differs from everyman's concept in not implying consciousness; it differs also in not applying to this state of self-deception. This is because what the action theory calls belief is a quasi-disposition (see **2** above): *i.e.* how a belief displays itself in action depends on what else its owner believes and what he desires. But this is not true of self-deception and self-knowledge. They are straight dispositions. Like fragility and Molière's "dormitive virtue", these states always display themselves in the same way, by which therefore they can be defined. Regardless of what else he believes and desires, anyone who assents to (dissents from) *h* only when he believes it is, by definition, a man who knows (deceives) himself in this respect.

An action theory of belief that can cope with assent is thus automatically equipped to cope with self-knowledge and self-deceit. The man who believes *h* and knows himself in this respect, is a man *disposed* to assent to *h*, whether he is actually assenting to it or not. This indeed is a state distinct both from just believing *h* and from actually assenting to it, even though it is definable in terms of those two states. So there are three states to be accounted for altogether, but with the addition of our thesis (1), the action theory can account for all of them: the basic quasi-disposition, Bh; assent, BB^*h; and the disposition, to BB^*h (if $BB^*h \lor B{\sim}B^*h$) only if Bh. This disposition is not a belief as action theory construes belief. *A fortiori* it is not the belief $BB^*h\&Bh$; so the fact that it can exist without Ah is no objection to the thesis (1).

8 Although self-knowledge is definable in terms of belief and assent, it is nevertheless a distinct, and a real, property of those that have it. It is a property distinct from belief and assent in just the way the fragility of a glass is a property distinct from its being dropped and its breaking. And, like fragility, self-knowledge is a real property in the sense, for example, that changes in it are real events with causes and effects (Mellor 1974: 158). It has in fact a causal mechanism, whereby whenever one's belief about *h* comes to consciousness, the state Bh will cause the state BB^*h, and the state $B{\sim}h$ will cause the state $BB^*{\sim}h$. It is the means whereby, as Ramsey put it, "what determines how we should act determines us also directly or indirectly to have a correct opinion as to how we should act" (1926: 73); only not, as Ramsey thought, "without its ever coming into consciousness".

The mechanism of self-knowledge is like the mechanism whereby, when something we are looking at is red, it causes us to believe it is red, and when it isn't, to believe it isn't. In short, self-knowledge is a species of perceptual ability, which enables facts to cause us to believe in them. That is, its causal mechanism is a sense, just as eyesight is a sense. Only, since what it informs us of is one of our own inner states of mind, it is an inner sense. It will be embodied entirely within the brain, because that is where both its objects, B, and the perceptions it delivers, BB^*, are embodied. Its organs are therefore naturally unfamiliar to us, because they are less visible than those of our outer senses; its very existence, indeed, is for this reason quite easily overlooked. This inner sense is nevertheless crucial to my account of the relation between belief and assent, and in particular of the relation between first and second order degrees of belief. I must therefore beg leave to expatiate on it to some extent.

I mean the claim, that we have an inner sense, literally, not just metaphorically; and I defended it at some length in my 1978 paper (§IX), where I took the liberty of calling it 'insight'. Insight is the mechanism of the privileged access that we have to our own beliefs, and as such it completes in principle the account, with which I said in **3** the basic action theory must be supplemented, of the phenomenon of assent. Details of the working of our insight, like the working of our other senses, are for physiological psychology to supply; what matters here is that we recognise its existence, and thus that there is nothing either scientifically ineffable or infallible about introspecting our own beliefs. When we introspect beliefs, we are simply perceiving them with a special sense, just as with other senses we perceive visible and audible aspects of the outside world.

Now the outside world of course contains more visual detail than meets the naked eye. In the same way, our minds no doubt contain more cognitive detail than meets our unassisted insight. The extreme case, corresponding to literal blindness, would be that of animals who have beliefs but have no insight at all. Since they lack the means of perceiving their own beliefs, they cannot assent in any degree to what their actions show them to believe. This in turn explains why they have no language, being incapable of Gricean intentions to communicate their beliefs – and it explains that fact without depriving them at all of sensations, emotions and other important aspects of consciousness which languageless animals may well possess.

People, however, are not internally blind. We do have insight; but it is not perfect, any more than our eyesight is. At any time, most of our beliefs are not being perceived by us; and those that are will not be perceived in every detail. Thus, to anticipate an observation that is going to cause trouble in Part **III**, we are never aware of all the consequences of our conscious beliefs, not even of all those consequences which we do in fact believe. I believe, for example, that to drive quickly from Cambridge to London I should start off along the Barton Road; and given my other geographical beliefs, it follows that I should turn left from the end of Fen Causeway. But I can easily be conscious of the first of these beliefs without being conscious of the second.

Moreover, as we have seen, insight, like eyesight, is fallible. People can and do deceive themselves. And once we recognise that insight is just another sense, there is no more mystery about recognising self-deception than there is about recognising colour-blindness. Naturally neither state is directly perceptible to its owner. But both can be seen by others, and in essentially the same way, namely by comparing the patient's faulty perception with the thing perceived. And (*pace* Davidson and others) there is no special mystery about perceiving people's beliefs and assentings. Mostly we infer them from what we know they have seen and heard. For the rest, we infer people's beliefs from their unselfconscious actions, and what they assent to from their unstudied speech. That is why, when someone's seemingly sincere speech makes too little sense of the rest of his behaviour, we infer that he is self-deceived – as when we listen sceptically to the subconsciously suspicious husband's eager rationalisations of his incessant phone calls home.

Admitting the fallibility of insight is thus by no means admitting wholesale scepticism about its deliverances. Insight we know to be no less reliable than our outer senses: for one thing, they themselves rely on it in conscious observation, since that gives us assent as well as plain belief. And we know that our senses are reliable, that people mostly see things as they are and believe what they assent to, because we can see that they do. The reliability of our senses is a straightforwardly observable fact about the world of which we, and they, are perceptible parts. It is important to realise this, and moreover to realise that, as Grandy remarks in Chapter 9 of this volume, there is no epistemologically vicious circle or regress involved in it. It is because our senses are reliable that our seeing that they are amounts to our knowing it: *i.e.* it is a true belief got by a reliable process (Ramsey 1929: 126). We need not prove *a priori* that our senses are largely free of error before using them to confirm the fact.

It follows in particular that we need no special or *a priori* justification for assuming that insight generally reveals to us the degree of our plain beliefs. When Ramsey assumed that a conscious choice of betting odds generally reveals the degree of our unconscious belief, he assumed nothing that calls for *a priori* defence. He was simply, and rightly, taking for granted the observable reliability of one of our senses.

9 If (1) is true, and belief comes by degrees, assent should come by degrees in two distinct ways. Suppose my plain or "first order" belief in h is neither full belief nor full disbelief, but is of some intermediate degree of doubt. For that to be the conscious degree of my belief in h is, I take it, for me to believe fully that I have this degree of belief in h. That is the natural way to construe degrees of assent. Insight, like our other senses, usually delivers full belief about what we perceive by means of it. But, again like our other senses, it need not. Just as poor eyesight may leave me unsure of the colour of an object, so poor insight may leave me unsure of the strength of my first order beliefs. In that case, if my degrees of belief are subjective probabilities, I should have a subjective probability distribution over possible values of my first order degrees of belief in h. And this is a second way, according to the theory, in which assent should be capable of coming by degrees.

Is this really so? How, it will be asked, do we distinguish second order subjective probabilities from first order ones? What is the difference between being sure of doubting something and doubting that one is sure of it? It is natural to suspect second order probabilities of collapsing onto first order ones; and if they do collapse, so does my theory. So the suspicion needs to be dispelled. Let us therefore consider some *prima facie* cases of second order probabilities.

Suppose for example I know a coin to be fairly tossed but fear it may be double-headed. That is, I know the chance of heads is either 0.5 or 1, but am not sure which. Suppose I think each value equally likely. Here we have second order probabilities: degrees of belief in alternative values of the objective chance. (Actually, we have degrees of assent, in the first and straightforward sense; but therefore also degrees of belief if I am not self-deceived – and as the extra element of consciousness is immaterial, I shall discuss the case in the simpler terms of plain belief.) Now as far as my expectation of heads goes, these second order probabilities do indeed collapse onto first order ones. Their net effect on me is that I should bet on heads at 3:1 on, *i.e.* behave as if I thought the chance 0.75. So how do these supposed second order probabilities show up in my behaviour?

They show up, for one thing in how I should react to seeing the results of successive tosses: in particular, in how my degree of belief in heads resulting from the next toss should be affected by them. It affects, as Skyrms says, "the laws of motion for rational belief". Tails just once, for example, should instantly reduce the degree of my belief in heads to 0.5, by proving that the coin is not double-headed; whereas it should have no such immediate effect if I had merely thought the chance 0.75.

So the second order probabilities do not in this case collapse completely onto first order ones. But in this case the first order probabilities are objective. There is an objective difference between a coin's being double-headed and its merely being biased. Doubt about the one possibility is bound in the end to be distinguishable from certain belief in the other by how one reacts to evidence as to which is actually the case. When both first and second order probabilities are subjective, however, it is not so obvious how they are to be distinguished. If I doubt a proposition *h*, why should I react differently to fresh evidence for *h* or against it just because my doubt is second order rather than first? How, for example, will the alleged difference show up between (i) believing to degree 1 that I believe *h* to degree 0.75 and (ii) believing to degree 0.5 that I believe *h* to degree 1, and to degree 0.5 that I believe it to degree 0.5?

On the theory I am propounding, the difference will be a difference in consciousness and hence, in particular, in linguistic ability. In state (i), I am conscious of a precise degree of doubt in *h*, which I can if I wish sincerely report. I can predict exactly how I should react to options whose desirability depends on the truth of *h*. I would have no hesitation now in picking precise odds for a bet on *h*'s truth.

State (ii) is a very different, and a very odd state. What is odd about it is the discontinuous two-peaked second order probability distribution over the first order degrees of belief. Our senses, inner and outer, do not usually deliver such bizarre distributions. My eyes, for example, would rarely if ever make me see the colour of something to be possibly either pure white or pitch black but certainly nothing in between. They normally give me a roughly bell-shaped probability density distribution over a continuous range of colours similar in hue, brightness and saturation. That is, as the colour becomes more similar the degree of my assurance, that it isn't the colour I saw, diminishes more rapidly. And similarly with insight. My consciousness of my doubts usually consists in a roughly bell-shaped probability density distribution over my first order degrees of belief. That is, the closer two degrees of my first order belief become, the more rapidly does the degree of my assurance, as to which one I really have, diminish.

State (ii) seems bizarre simply because it is so rare. It is, nevertheless, a perfectly intelligible state, and there is no difficulty in saying how it differs from state (i). In state (ii) I should be less aware of what I believe about h. I could sincerely say that I do not totally disbelieve h. But all I could say positively is that, in unselfconscious actions to whose outcome h mattered, I should either act as if I were certain of h or dither in a way equivalent to betting on h at evens; and that, if asked now to bet on which of these two I would then do, evens are again the odds I should propose.

The oddity of (ii) does not therefore count against our theory of assent. On the contrary, that theory is what tells us what it would be like to be in state (ii), and what people in it would be apt to do and say; and this is how we know that state (ii) is so rare. We know we ourselves are almost never in states like that, and that other people are not apt to do and say such things. Our theory of assent, in short, makes plenty of behaviour and respectable introspection available to distinguish state (ii) from state (i) – and to distinguish both from the unconscious and inarticulate 0.75 degree of merely first order belief in h, which my unselfconscious action might reveal, with no degree (not even zero) of second order belief in h at all.

So second order subjective probabilities do not collapse onto first order ones. They are introspectably distinct states of mind and show up in quite different kinds of behaviour. But there are of course causal connections between them. They are connected one way by insight: with good insight, a degree of first order belief will produce a very high degree of second order belief in its true value. There are also connections the other way. Conscious thought is, amongst other things, a means of affecting our habits of action, *i.e.* our desires and the degree of our first order beliefs. After a shock from an electric kettle, considerable conscious reflection on the safety of the rewiring may be needed to make me pick it up again without hesitation, *i.e.* to drive the degree of my first order belief in its safety back towards 1. But it can be done: calculation can affect our beliefs just as observation can. I may not, by taking conscious thought, be able to add cubits to my stature, but I can add degrees to my first order beliefs. In other words, we are not only disposed to assent to what we believe: we are also disposed, on the whole, to believe what we assent to.

II

10 If the thesis (1) is true, we will have second order subjective probabilities if we have first order ones. Higher orders are more doubtful. I conjectured in **6** that we generally lack third and higher order beliefs: insight does not show us all our inner states. But even first order subjective probabilities are controversial. One may admit that beliefs vary roughly in strength and still resist the full panoply of subjective probability. First order beliefs do not obviously come in such a finely graded range of strengths, and the second order range is still less obvious. The whole apparatus may reasonably be suspected of Scandinavian fantasy, of the heroic but unrealistic model building that seems to have superseded the saga-making of old.

Kyburg has recently marshalled a notable attack on subjective probability (1978), and one can readily imagine his reaction to iterating it as I have done. But his attack seems to me mostly misdirected, and the rest of it can be met with the aid of the present theory of assent. With it we can in particular remove from the concept of subjective probability a pernicious equivocation of which Kyburg rightly complains.

Subjective probability is mostly presented as measuring how strong people's beliefs actually are. But there is evidence, which Kyburg adduces, purporting to show that the strength of people's beliefs does not in fact satisfy this measure. Faced with this evidence, subjectivists have been apt to claim only to be prescribing the measure on grounds of rationality, *i.e.* to say not that people do have probabilistic degrees of belief, but that they are irrational if they don't. But subjectivists who say that cannot also claim to be doing psychology. In particular they cannot claim to explain away people's actual agreement on objective probabilities as being merely the result of their conditionalising their subjective probabilities in response to shared evidence. Moreover, reference to rationality at this stage seriously confuses the question of what people's degrees of belief actually are with the question of what they ought to be, given knowledge of chances or of other inductive evidence for or against their truth. So it is important on several counts to decide whether subjective probability is supposed to be a theory of real or merely of rational degrees of belief. The theory of assent will enable us to do just that.

I must emphasise that in what follows I shall not be arguing for the full-blooded subjective view of probability. I do not believe for a moment that one man's degree of belief is as good as another's, nor that conditionalisation does in fact explain away the phenomenon of agreement on values of objective chance. It is true that my view fits Kyburg's definition of 'subjective probability', since I do think "the assignment of a numerical probability . . . [need] not reflect any known or hypothetical frequencies". But Kyburg's is an unreasonably broad definition: one can quite well be an objectivist without being a frequentist. On the other hand, I do wish to characterise objective probability by the constraints it prescribes for degrees of belief, so I have some interest in defending subjective probability: namely, that the statement of my views will be somewhat simplified if degrees of belief have a probability measure.

11 Kyburg does not deny that we think of belief as coming in rough and comparative degrees. He would not dispute the examples I have given, and I need not therefore multiply or defend them. But it is still worth emphasising how deeply the concept is rooted in our everyday judgements. Subjective probability is not a radical innovation of theoretical psychology such as Freudian theories, for example, have proposed. It is no more than a quantitative development of a perfectly familiar state of mind which we freely and uncontentiously attribute to ourselves and other people all the time. The only question is why one should jib at such a development.

Let us compare it, as Ramsey (1926: 75) did, with Newtonian

mechanics. That is a quantitative development of rough and comparative ideas of force and mass, *i.e.* of what sets things moving and of how hard things are to move. No one jibs at this development and, though I admit it is often easier to measure forces than beliefs, the case for each is much the same. In each case we have a theory that postulates a continuum of degrees of a state whose rough gradation is a commonplace. Each postulation is supported by quantitative applications which link the quantity proposed with its causes and effects. Perception produces beliefs of various strengths which in turn combine with desires *ditto* to produce definite action even in conditions of uncertainty. Similarly, gravity and other causes produce forces of various strengths, which in turn combine with masses *ditto* to produce definite accelerations. Force and mass are quantitative quasi-dispositions to yield the behaviour they explain, just as belief and desire are. And the range of behaviour explained by the theory that invokes each of these pairs of states is what gives us reason to believe in their existence.

The reason may look more impressive in the case of force and mass, but the difference is only one of degree, and the degree should not be exaggerated. One could easily level at Newtonian mechanics most of the criticisms brought against subjective probability. One could object especially to the factual underdetermination of Newton's theory. Its apparatus can easily be made to appear grossly disproportionate to the data which it is based on and which it is used to explain. A thing's mass, for instance, is an infinite conjunction of the dispositions it has to accelerate under forces of different strength. Only one of these dispositions is ever displayed at any one time, and an infinite number will never be displayed at all. One might well ask what the point can be of attributing to a thing so extravagant a profusion of dispositions, and how one could possibly claim to know the truth of such attributions.

The second, epistemological, question I shall not try to answer. The answer to the first question can only be that these Newtonian dispositions are supposed to be present, whether they are displayed or not, in order to be available to explain any of an infinite number of possible interactions with other things. That is, we suppose it to be true of the thing now that it would accelerate at definite rates under all these definite forces, whether or not it will ever be exposed to them. Well, it may in the same way be true of me now that I would behave in definite ways in an infinite range of definite circumstances, whether I am ever in them or not. I may have a quite precise degree of belief, even though it will only show up in actions which, given my desires and other beliefs, a slightly weaker (or slightly stronger) belief would make me forgo. The degrees of most of my beliefs never will show up in action. But that will be no reason to deny their existence unless I am also to be denied Newtonian mass.

Now I am not in fact claiming precise degrees for my beliefs, any more than I would claim to have a precise mass. Nor does the theory of subjective probability entail so rash a claim. Its mathematics indeed makes sense of indefinitely precise degrees of belief, just as Newtonian mechanics does of precise degrees of force and mass. That is because it is not for the mathematics to limit *a priori* the precision of these states. Their precision of course is limited, as that of all quantitative states is (see Mellor 1967), but only *a posteriori*, by the several natures of the kinds of things involved. It is nonsense, for example, to give the mass of Everest to the nearest gram; but that does not prevent Newtonian mechanics applying to the Himalayas. Similarly, subjective probability is not seriously impugned by the obvious fact that most of our beliefs have imprecise degrees, and are more properly represented by intervals than by precise values of subjective probability (*cf.* Levi 1974).

Imprecision is not a feature peculiar to degrees of belief, and its significance should not be exaggerated. Nor should its extent. We may quite easily have more precise degrees of belief than we think we have. Assent, we have seen, is a product of insight, and insight is no more precise a sense than eyesight is. My unselfconscious choices might well display more definiteness in my first order doubts that I can in advance be consciously aware of. I may be conscious only of thinking something probable, *i.e.* that my degree of belief in it lies in the interval $(0.5, 1)$, when my first order degree of belief actually only spans the narrower interval $(0.7, 0.8)$. No one may know this, just as no one knows the mass of most things; yet, it may be so.

12 All this, however, is still only a preface to the main dispute. Kyburg's chief complaint is not that subjective probabilities are too inactive, too numerous or too precise for the behavioural data they purport to explain. His complaint is that the Dutch book argument he considers fails to show that degrees of belief are subjective probabilities at all; and that, on the contrary, real betting behaviour shows them not to be. And to answer this complaint, the relation of betting to belief needs to be examined more closely than it usually is.

We do not normally learn the strength of people's beliefs by making them choose odds for bets, any more than we normally measure their masses by their accelerations under unit forces. We infer beliefs and masses alike from behaviour which is also affected by many other factors. Such inferences of course need knowledge of what the other factors are, and of how they interact with belief and mass respectively to produce the behaviour we observe. Moreover, we need this knowledge even to discuss how in principle these quantities could be directly and unequivocally measured: because, to measure them, we have to try and specify a situation in which the influence of the other factors we know of can be either eliminated or allowed for. Then we can take behaviour in that situation to be an explicit measure of belief, mass, or whatever else concerns us. That our specification will succeed, that the measure will be of the very quantity we want, cannot be guaranteed *a priori* or independently of theories in which the quantity already figures, and which tell us what other factors interact with it. It is not a matter of an arbitrary specification stipulating what we are to mean by degree of belief or mass: we already know most of what we mean, and our specification must accommodate itself to what we know. It is not, for example, by stipulation that IQ tests measure intelligence. If they do, it is because we already know that intelligence is one of the factors that affect their results, and that the other mental factors which might do so have, as a matter of fact, had their effects eliminated or allowed for. What these other factors are, and how their effects may be eliminated, is for our psychology to say; the information is not given us either by pure reason or by raw uninterpreted experience.

So it is with the betting measure of belief. We know a belief's strength affects its owner's choice of odds, or quotient, for a bet on its truth. But we also know that this is not the only mental factor which affects the choice. So we must constrain the betting situation in order to eliminate or allow for the effects of these other factors. In chapter 2 of *The Matter of Chance* (1971) I proposed constraints to that end: the bet was to be compulsory, with the opponent choosing its direction and the stake after the quotient is fixed. The point of these constraints is to prevent the quotient being directly affected by a preference for particular stakes, by desire for a particular outcome, or by a like or dislike of the process of betting. The constraints moreover do this in a way that was explicitly designed to meet objections Kyburg has now resurrected against the inept Dutch book argument which is unfortunately the only one he considers. That argument tries to use the least odds a man would accept for a bet on h's truth in order to measure his degree of belief in h – and this, as Kyburg reminds us, is nonsense if the man is to be made to bet, as he must be for a Dutch book to be made against him. "No odds can be unacceptable to a man who is compelled to bet in any case" (Mellor 1971: 36). But it makes perfect sense for a man to say what odds he would choose if he had to bet on h with his opponent deciding subsequently which of them will win if h turns out to be true. That is a very plausible measure of his degree of belief in h, if he has one, whether he is willing to bet or not.

It must be emphasised that the justification for placing these constraints on the betting situation has nothing whatever to do with making degrees of belief satisfy the probability calculus. The constraints are there simply to prevent the quotient being affected by factors other than the degree of belief it is supposed to measure. They may not, as a matter of fact, suffice to make the quotient measure nothing but degree of belief, but they are clearly at least necessary to that end. And they do suffice to set up a valid Dutch book argument. The only way a man who is compelled to bet, at stakes and in directions subsequently determined by his opponent, can prevent certain loss is by choosing "coherent" quotients, i.e. quotients which are probabilities. That the loss would otherwise be certain follows from the fact that his opponent is also trying to win the bet: if he weren't, it wouldn't be a bet at all. But nor would it be a bet if one party were certain to lose; it would only be a pointlessly complex method of giving goods away.

It is irrelevant to remark as Kyburg does (1978: 162) that professional gamblers make money quite rationally by offering nonprobabilistic betting quotients. So they do, but they would not do so in situations constrained to reflect only their degrees of belief and not their greed. They would be coherent all right in the situation I have specified.

The experiments Kyburg cites (1978: 165), in which actual quotients close to 1 and 0 were not coherent, are equally inconclusive.

His description of the experiments makes it clear that they did not satisfy the constraints needed for the quotients to measure only degrees of belief. The choice of quotients was clearly open to influence by some of the other factors I have mentioned, factors which would be especially likely to affect values close to 1 and 0, since these values greatly increase the possible gain and loss. Those experiments no more falsify subjective probability theory than a car's needing an engine to keep going on the flat falsifies Newton's first law of motion.

13 Still, it may be urged, even in the betting situation I have specified, a man could choose incoherent betting quotients. He will lose money, but he need not have had that intention; and if he did not, that intention cannot have been the cause of his behaviour. Lacking any other cause, then, we can only attribute it to his having non-probabilistic degrees of belief. We may of course suspect other unknown causes – but, after all, there may not be any. To insist *a priori* that there must be would simply beg the question in favour of subjective probability.

I remarked in **10** that many subjectivists admit that people may have non-probabilistic degrees of belief, and use the Dutch book argument only to show that such people are irrational. And that much the argument certainly shows: a man who has no desire to give away his goods should certainly not choose betting quotients which he knows will inevitably have that effect. But we can do better than this. With the aid of the theory of assent developed in Part **I**, we can show that degrees of belief really are probabilities, not just that they ought to be.

First we should observe that the argument just given for the possibility of incoherent quotients only shows that degrees of belief might not be probabilities, not that they are not. It would only defeat an *a priori* argument for a probability measure, and although I hope my argument will prove compelling, I do not mean it to be *a priori*. The facts it appeals to, about assent and the psychology of betting, are entirely contingent. It could be defeated by an experimental proof that degrees of belief are not probabilities; but Kyburg, we saw in **12**, has provided no such thing.

Next, I have to say that the significance of betting for the measurement of belief has been uniformly misconceived in the literature, a misconception with which I have so far gone along. It is actually not at all like measuring masses by accelerating them, or even by weighing them. We cannot directly discover degrees of belief by observing quotients chosen for actual bets. The most we could discover directly in this way are degrees of assent, not degrees of first order belief. Choosing odds is a selfconscious activity, as I remarked in **5**. What it reveals is what the chooser believes the degree of his first order beliefs to be. Usually he is right, for the reasons discussed in **8**: insight is a generally reliable sense. But right or not, a gambler's choice of odds does no more than report the result of his internal observation of the degree of his first order beliefs; an observation he can make without going on to gamble at all.

This is why there is no point in making people bet in order to determine the degree of their beliefs. Thinking of odds or quotients is just a way of providing a uniform scale for reporting the deliverances of insight. It is like training people to report their feelings of warmth in degrees Celsius, or their visual sensations of colour in Angstrom units. Such a training has the virtue of sharpening our senses by providing an indefinitely precise and extendable vocabulary for stating our observations in. That such a vocabulary does have this virtue may be only a contingent fact, but it is a very familiar and important one. My ability to discriminate different degrees in one of my beliefs is undoubtedly improved by my habit of thinking what odds I should choose if I had no other reason for my choice. And not only different degrees of the same belief: the vocabulary of odds enables me to compare the strength of beliefs with widely different contents. Without this vocabulary, our perception of these inner states would certainly be much less precise. And because of the causal links between first and second order beliefs (see **9** above), the degrees of our first order beliefs might then well be less precise themselves.

But what is the relevance of betting, if there is no point in actually doing it? How does the vocabulary of betting quotients acquire its virtue? Suppose I am thinking what quotients I should choose if I had no reason for my choice other than my degree of belief. I must still conceive myself to be choosing for a bet, albeit one constrained as specified in **12**. If there were no bet, then even my degree of belief would give me no occasion for choosing one quotient rather than any other. And the occasion the bet supplies is simply one of possible but uncertain gain or loss. If either gain or loss were certain,

I should again have no occasion to choose a particular quotient: my insight would be given no basis on which to answer my hypothetical question. So what I must suppose is that neither gain nor loss is certain in the circumstances; which means that the quotients must be supposed to be coherent, and therefore probabilities.

I might of course sincerely produce incoherent betting quotients in reporting the degrees of my beliefs. But if I did, I should not be rightly reporting an irrational state of mind. Irrationality only lies in actually betting at such quotients in situations so constrained as to measure belief, and I am not actually doing that. But it is just because all such quotients would be equally irrational that they make no psychological sense as measures of my particular degree of belief. So the fact that I produce them shows, not that I am being irrational, but that, in introspecting my degrees of belief, I have made some error of measurement. It is as if I had insight also into my mass, and felt myself to be more or less massive than my acceleration under Newtonian forces showed me to be. Newtonian mechanics tells me my introspection must have deceived me; and it will not do to retort that Newtonian mechanics might be wrong. So it is, but it was not that lightly overthrown; nor is subjective probability overthrown by the exactly analogous experiments that Kyburg cites.

Even if the inept design of these experiments had not made them inconclusive, therefore, even as introspections of degrees of belief, they would still have been completely insignificant. But what then would overthrow subjective probability, if not experiments of some such kind? I am not advocating subjective probability *a priori*, so something should be able to show if it is wrong. Well, consider what would show Newtonian mechanics to be wrong. Suppose certain bodies did not always accelerate as Newton requires under all forces. As a matter of fact, they don't exactly, and not only for relativistic reasons. Different motions strip off different numbers of their surface molecules, and carry different amounts of air along with them. So the accelerations produced by different Newtonian forces are not, even at low speeds, related to each other by any one precise value of inertial mass. The utility, and the truth, of Newton's theory consists in the accelerations being almost always related by values lying within some narrow interval (*cf.* Mellor 1967). If that interval became too wide for useful prediction, the concept of mass would eventually be discarded: Newtonian mechanics would have been falsified. But whilst we retain the concept at all, we retain the laws of motion by which its values, however imprecise, are determined.

And so it is with degrees of belief. Our unselfconscious behaviour no doubt exhibits some quantitative inconsistency. I dare say I should not exhibit precisely the same degree of first order belief in imminent rain (say) in all the diverse unselfconscious actions which some degree of that belief might serve to explain. The best that can truly be said of me is that the degrees of this first order belief which would be exhibited in most of these actions lie within a certain interval of subjective probability. The wider the interval, the less useful the concept, and it is an entirely contingent matter that it has any use at all. My unselfconscious behaviour could be so erratic as to falsify the claim that I had any definite degree whatever of some particular belief. This is likely to be true, for example, of beliefs expressible only in languages I do not understand, such as the mathematical languages of most microphysics. I know I have no determinate degree of belief on those matters, *i.e.* that my unselfconscious actions are in no way affected by any such state of mind. Consequently, although I could indeed be forced to choose precise odds for a compulsory bet on the truth of some such microphysical proposition, I know it would manifest no insight into the degree of any first order belief I have.

But on matters I understand, my insight does tell me to avoid quotients outside certain intervals. There is a significantly narrow interval of subjective probability values within which I believe, with high second order subjective probability, my first order degree of belief to be confined. On that basis I can predict, and generally claim to know, what my behaviour would be under quite a wide range of circumstances. Where that is the case, we have the same justification for applying the theory by which degrees of belief may, however imprecisely, be measured as we have in the case of mass for employing Newton's laws of motion.

As a matter of fact, therefore, many of our beliefs have usefully precise degrees. Of those that do, the Dutch book argument shows there to be a probabilistic measure. It is not a matter of rationality, but a matter of a theoretically based scale of measurement. Rationality comes in only later, in considering what degrees people should have of various beliefs in various circumstances. (And even that is mostly a matter not of rationality, but of chance.)

III

14 Parts **I** and **II** have given reasons for thinking that assent is second order belief, that first and second order beliefs come more or less precisely by degrees, and that these degrees are subjective probabilities. I have not proved any of these propositions; I only incline to believe them because they enable us to explain sundry psychological phenomena. But that of course is not enough. I need also to check that their other consequences are equally acceptable.

Some of the other consequences are both familiar and attractive. One is the explanation they provide of how we can fail to believe consequences of our beliefs. The explanation runs briefly as follows. Clearly no one believes any contingent proposition *h* to degree 1, *i.e.* no one behaves as if he would risk unlimited loss should *h* prove false for a penny gain should *h* prove true. So the qualitative state of full belief can only call for some high degree of belief, short of 1. The degree will no doubt be determined by the context: roughly, the least degree such that, in the context, no higher degree would affect anything the believer would be at all likely to do. The details are both tricky and important, but all that matters here is that the degree of a full belief can be less than 1. For then I can believe two things without believing their conjunction. Let $p(k)$ be the probabilistic degree of my belief in any proposition k, and suppose there are two particular propositions *h* and *i* such that

(2) $p(h) = p(i) = 0.95$.

Suppose I also believe *h* and *i* to be independent, *i.e.*

(3) $p(h\&i) = p(h)p(i) < 0.91$.

Suppose further that, (4), in the circumstances, the degree requisite to a full belief lies between 0.91 and 0.95. Then I believe *h* and believe *i*, but I do not believe *h&i*.

As for belief, so for assent, if

(1) $A = BB^*$

is true. Suppose I have virtually perfect insight into my beliefs about *h* and *i*, *i.e.* I believe (2), (3) and (4) to a degree very close to 1. Then I assent to *h* and to *i*, but not to *h&i*.

Given enough more or less independent propositions, I can both assent to each of them individually and dissent from their conjunction, so low can my degree of conscious belief in it be. This is a most attractive result, because it so naturally resolves the paradoxes of the lottery and the preface. I can consciously believe that some ticket will win a lottery while also consciously believing of each ticket that it will not win. I can sincerely apologise in my preface for mistakes which I am sure my book contains, while assenting to every single sentence in it.

So far so good. However, our theories have other, less agreeable consequences. If I believe h to a probabilistic degree x, I must believe its negation, $\sim h$, to degree $1-x$, and therefore the disjunction, $h \vee \sim h$, to degree 1. That is,

$$(5) \qquad (\exists x)(p(h) = x) \vdash (p(h \vee \sim h) = 1).$$

In other words, however high the degree required for full belief, $p(h \vee \sim h)$ will exceed it. So, whatever the context, I believe $h \vee \sim h$. This is a rather disconcerting result. Recall that I am taking subjective probability to measure my actual degrees of belief, not just those I ought to have. Perhaps I ought to believe $h \vee \sim h$ to degree 1, since as a tautology it cannot be false – so that a bet on its truth, whatever the stakes, runs no risk of being lost. But (5) says that I actually do believe $h \vee \sim h$ to this degree, not just that I ought to. Yet it seems possible *prima facie* to doubt even a tautology.

One might on reflection be willing to accept (5), since $h \vee \sim h$ is a very simple and obvious tautology, and yet not to accept that one believed all tautologies, however complex, to degree 1. Unfortunately, it can be proved (Field 1977) that all tautologies, indeed all theorems of the predicate calculus, have probability 1, and *a fortiori* have subjective probability 1. The same result seems to follow also from the betting considerations of **13**. Quotients that would be irrational in the betting situation specified in **12** cannot be measures of one's actual degree of belief. But in that situation the only rational betting quotient on any knowably necessary proposition would seem to be 1, since otherwise the opponent can arrange to win as much as he likes on it with no risk of loss. So 1 is indeed the probabilistic degree of my belief in all knowably necessary propositions, however complex.

This conclusion, in (5) at least, is derived from the assumption that I do have some degree of belief in h itself. Now I suggested in **13** that there might be some contingent propositions I have no degree of first order belief in at all, and perhaps I do not believe to degree 1 tautologies whose contingent constituents are all of this kind. But this, even if true, would be small comfort. In particular, it would not mean that imprecision in my degrees of belief could be relied on to prevent me believing tautologies to degree 1. However erratic my behaviour, and hence imprecise my degree of belief in h and therefore in $\sim h$, there will be nothing imprecise about their sum. Uncertainty about the right quotient for a bet on h is not going to make me think I could win a bet on the falsity of $h \vee \sim h$.

Believing at least most necessary truths to degree 1 seems to be an inevitable consequence of our theories. But this seems at second sight a defensible, if not an attractive, result. For it only concerns first order belief, not assent. It does not mean we consciously believe most necessary truths. All it really means is that none of our unselfconscious actions can display, or be explained by, our failing to believe them. Only our speech would do that, and what that displays is lack of assent, not lack of first order belief. First order belief in necessary truth need not affect anything we do; so why not accept it as the innocuous extreme end of our range of quasi-dispositions to action? It does not commit us to being able consciously to recognise every complex instance of necessity that our actions trivially show us to believe.

15 Unfortunately, giving necessary truths subjective probability 1 has further and far less digestable consequences. Suppose I have some degree of belief in contingent propositions h and i such that i follows from h, *i.e.*

(6) $h \vdash i$.

That is, $h \supset i$ is necessary, so I believe it to degree 1. It follows from the probability calculus that I believe i at least as strongly as I believe h, *i.e.*

(7) $p(h) \le p(i).$[1]

[1] For all propositions h and i,
$$p(h\&i) \le p(i),$$
$$p(h) = p(h\&i) + p(h\&\sim i),$$
and $h \supset i \vdash \sim(h\&\sim i).$
So $(p(h \supset i) = 1) \vdash (p(h\&\sim i) = 0).$
So if $h \vdash i$, $p(h) = p(h\&i) \le p(i).$

Now suppose p_1 is the subjective probability I need in the circumstances for full belief. Then, whatever p_1 is,

(8) $(p(h) > p_1) \vdash (p(i) > p_1)$.

That is, if I believe h, I must believe i:

(9) $Bh \vdash Bi$.

In other words, I must believe every consequence of each proposition I believe.

This again, although not an attractive result, could be defended in the same way as its predecessor. It is not a matter of assent, only of first order belief construed as a quasi-disposition to unselfconscious action. My actions could of course show that I have changed my mind from believing h at one time to not believing i at another, or display the sort of inconsistency which makes my degrees of belief in h and i imprecise. Granting that, one could argue that no single action could reveal both that I definitely believe something and at the same time that I definitely fail to believe its logical consequences. So (9) might perhaps be accepted, albeit reluctantly and with foreboding.

The foreboding is well justified. Consider our second order beliefs in h and i. 'Bh' and 'Bi' in (9) are of course abbreviations, as explained in **6**, the reference to the common time and believer being left out. The abbreviation is all right because (9) is a necessary truth: it holds of all believers at all times. So it holds in particular of myself at the present time, whatever time that is and whoever I am. That is, it holds of the indexical states B^*h and B^*i:

(10) $B^*h \vdash B^*i$.

That is, $B^*h \supset B^*i$ is necessary, so I believe it to degree 1. It follows that I believe B^*i at least as strongly as I believe B^*h, i.e.

(11) $p(B^*h) \leq p(B^*i)$.

Now suppose p_2 is the subjective probability I need in the circumstances for full second order beliefs. Then, whatever p_2 is,

(12) $(p(B^*h) > p_2) \vdash (p(B^*i) > p_2)$.

That is, if at any time I believe I now believe h, I must at the same time believe I now believe i:

(13) $BB^*h \vdash BB^*i$.

But that, given (1), entails

(14) $Ah \vdash Ai.$

In other words, if I assent to h, I must assent to i. We are being required to assent simultaneously to every logical consequence of any single proposition we assent to.

This result cannot possibly be accepted. It is a result about conscious belief, not just about unconscious quasi-dispositions to action. No amount of theory could defend it against our consciousness of almost never consciously believing all the consequences of one of our conscious beliefs. So unless there is a flaw in the argument leading to (14), one or other of its premisses will have to go. Either assent is not believing one believes, or belief does not come by degrees of subjective probability. Let us survey the options.

16 There are two reasons for trying to keep the theory (1), that assent is believing one believes. One is that without it we shall have no theory of assent; nor, I suggest, of second order belief either. If believing one believes is not assenting, I cannot imagine what it is. But whatever it is, (13) seems to me barely more believable than (14). Believing one believes a proposition does not seem to entail believing one believes all its consequences, since something might be a consequence without one believing one believed it was. And that is the other reason for keeping (1): giving it up generates other problems without solving this one. The real trouble with (14) is (13), not (1).

Perhaps the trouble with (13) is (12), *i.e.* lies in the theory of subjective probability. If so, it is not that our argument has credited beliefs with implausibly precise degrees. It nowhere depends on two contingent beliefs being of precisely the same strength. So long as my beliefs in h, i and in my first order beliefs in h and i are strong enough to be full beliefs, (12) follows. And imprecision in belief will not generally stop it being full belief. It might for propositions like those referred to in **13**, expressible only in languages I barely understand. Perhaps there are some propositions of physics I understand so little I can neither fully believe nor fully disbelieve them. But (14) is no better when h and i are propositions so plain I must be able to believe them: *e.g.* h, that John was born in 1948; i, that he was born in a leap year. I can easily assent to h without thinking about i at all.

And that is the clue: the trouble with (12) is in fact (11), or rather a condition on which (11) depends, namely that I have some degree of belief in B^*i. But on our theory of assent I have no such degree of belief unless I am (to some extent) consciously believing i to some degree – which usually I am not. Moreover, quite independently of considerations of assent, we must be able to avoid having higher order degrees of belief, however hard it may be to avoid having first order ones. Otherwise there would be a psychologically quite incredible regress of beliefs about one's beliefs about one's beliefs . . .

So the condition on which (11) follows from (10) is contingent. (11) follows only if read hypothetically, as relating $p(B^*h)$ and $p(B^*i)$ *provided* they exist; and the same goes for (12). (13) and (14), on the other hand, are clearly not hypothetical. If a high enough $p(B^*h)$ can exist without any $p(B^*i)$, (13) is false. But a high $p(B^*h)$ can easily exist without any $p(B^*i)$: nothing prevents me thinking of h and not of i. So (13) and (14) do not follow from (11) and (12). They only follow if (11) and (12) are construed categorically, and then (11) and (12) do not follow from (10). So either way (13) and (14) can be rejected without impugning either the theory of assent or the theory of subjective probability.

17 This result is some relief, but not enough. Provided I *am* thinking of h and i together, I do still have to assent to i if I assent to h – basically because if $h \supset i$ is necessary, so will $B^*h \supset B^*i$ be, and I must therefore believe that also to degree 1. Yet I could surely fail to assent to i, even while thinking about it and assenting to h, by not assenting to $h \supset i$, *i.e.* by failing to assent to a truth of which I am conscious and which is in fact necessary.

The problem therefore boils down to this. The subjective probability of necessary propositions has to be 1. So if subjective probability measures degree of belief, and assent is believing one believes, necessary truths cannot be consciously doubted. Yet obviously they can. I can consciously doubt that $h \supset i$, or that $10^{23}+1$ is a prime number, even if these propositions are necessary. Given this evident possibility, is there any defensible alternative to giving up the theory of assent or the theory of subjective probability?

One reason for seeking an alternative is that, as I remarked in **16**, giving up these theories may generate other problems without really solving this one. Giving up the theory of assent, for example, still leaves us with second order subjective probabilities of 1 in necessary propositions. And I can make no sense of my having to be believing I believe that $10^{23}+1$ is prime even when I am consciously doubting, or even dissenting from, that proposition. So some of subjective probability theory will have to go. But we cannot hope to escape just by tinkering with the theory, nor by taking it after all to measure rational rather than actual degrees of belief. For instance, it will not help to let the subjective probability of necessary propositions fall a little short of 1: if I can doubt them at all, I can disbelieve them entirely. And if that is possible, I see nothing irrational in believing that $10^{23}+1$ is prime to degree 0.3 – on the grounds, say, that 0.3 is the proportion of primes so far found among other numbers of the form $10^{n}+1$. If subjective probability has to go, I reckon it will all have to go, whether as a theory of actual or merely of rational degrees of belief. That is a high price to pay for solving this problem. Before paying it, therefore, we should make sure both that it would deliver the goods and that we can't get them more cheaply in some other way.

The problem stems from our thinking that there is no way of losing a bet on the truth of a belief which is in fact necessarily true. This is because to think the content of a belief to be a necessary truth is, I take it, to have a conception of truth conditions – *e.g.* possible worlds – on which a belief with that content would come out true under all such conditions. On that conception there will similarly be no way of both winning a bet on the truth of a belief whose content is h and losing one on the truth of a belief whose content is any logical consequence of h, such as i. If $h \supset i$ is necessary, there are no conditions under which it would be false, *i.e.* all conditions under which h would be true are conditions under which i would be true. This is why the probabilistic degree of belief in necessary truths has to be 1, and that of my belief in any proposition has to be no greater than that of my beliefs in its logical consequences. These incredible subjective probabilities result, therefore, from assuming that the content of a belief in a necessary truth is sufficient to make its truth conditions differ in this way from those of contingent and false beliefs. But is it?

It looks a very innocuous assumption: it is, after all, only a special case of the almost invariable assumption that the contents of beliefs suffice to fix their truth conditions. In other words, if two beliefs have different truth conditions, they have different contents. And this assumption is indeed innocuous enough for contingent beliefs. In particular, the content of a contingent belief can fix its truth conditions and still be the same content whether the belief is true or false, since the same truth conditions will allow it to be either. But this is not so for beliefs that are necessarily true if they are true at all. Consider the belief that $10^{23}+1$ is prime. Suppose I am convinced that this belief is, if true, necessary. That means I am convinced that its truth conditions depend on its truth value in a way in which those of contingent beliefs do not. For, if it is true, its truth conditions are, I believe, such as to forbid its falsity; so if it *is* false, I must suppose them to be something different. If therefore I thought the content of this belief fixed its truth conditions, I should have to think the content also depended on its truth value. But of course I think no such thing. I do not for a moment suppose that my being uncertain of its truth makes me uncertain of its content. I take the content of the belief that $10^{23}+1$ is prime to be the same whether it turns out true or false. Indeed, what I want to find out, when I am uncertain of it, is just which truth value *it*, namely the belief state with that definite content, has.

The content of a belief which is, if true, necessary does not, therefore, suffice to make its truth conditions such that it cannot be false. If we use the philosopher's term of art, 'proposition', for a belief content which does determine its truth conditions, we can put this by saying that these beliefs at least are in something less definite than propositions; and perhaps all beliefs are. But however we put it, it follows that these beliefs need not have subjective probability 1. I can have any degree of belief I like in the prospect of winning a bet on $10^{23}+1$ being prime, even while believing that, if I do win, I could not have lost. And the same goes for my degree of belief in $h \supset i$; so my degree of belief in i can be less than my degree of belief in h, even though, if $h \supset i, h \vdash i$. Therefore I need not, after all, when I assent to something, assent to all the consequences of it that come to mind.

It is, unfortunately, not easy to say what the content of a belief is, if not a definite proposition, *i.e.* something that fixes the belief's truth conditions. So the assumption that we believe definite propositions continues to be made *faute de mieux*. Mostly it gives no trouble, especially not with contingent beliefs. But occasionally it delivers spectacular falsehoods, in this case through the medium of our theories of assent and of subjective probability. When that happens, one should take care not to blame the medium for the message. Perhaps a more realistic account of the content of beliefs will produce further objections to our theories; but until it does, I believe we can continue to assent to them with a clear conscience.

University of Cambridge

REFERENCES

Armstrong, D. M. 1973. *Belief, Truth and Knowledge.* Cambridge.
Braithwaite, R. B. 1933. The nature of believing. In *Knowledge and Belief*, ed. A. Phillips Griffiths, pp. 28–40. 1967. London.
Field, H. H. 1977. Logic, meaning and conceptual role. *Journal of Philosophy* **74**, 379–409.
Hume, D. 1739. *A Treatise of Human Nature*, ed. L. A. Selby-Bigge. 1888. Oxford.
Jeffrey, R. C. 1965. *The Logic of Decision.* New York.
Kyburg, H. 1978. Subjective probability: criticisms, reflections, and problems. *Journal of Philosophical Logic* **7**, 157–80.
Levi, I. 1974. On indeterminate probabilities. *Journal of Philosophy* **71**, 391–418.
Mellor, D. H. 1967. Imprecision and explanation. *Philosophy of Science* **34**, 1–9.
Mellor, D. H. 1971. *The Matter of Chance.* Cambridge.
Mellor, D. H. 1974. In defense of dispositions. *Philosophical Review* **83**, 157–81.
Mellor, D. H. 1978. Conscious belief. *Proceedings of the Aristotelian Society* **78**, 87–101.
Perry, J. 1979. The problem of the essential indexical. *Noûs* **13**, 3–21.
Price, H. H. 1969. *Belief.* London.
Ramsey, F. P. 1926. Truth and probability. In his *Foundations*, ed. D. H. Mellor, pp. 58–100. 1978. London.
Ramsey, F. P. 1929. Knowledge. In his *Foundations*, ed. D. H. Mellor, pp. 126–7. 1978. London.

8   *Opinions and chances*

SIMON BLACKBURN

I Ramsey was one of the few philosophers who have fully appreciated the fundamental picture of metaphysics which was originally sketched by Hume. In this picture the world – that which makes proper judgement true or false – impinges on the human mind. This, in turn, has various reactions: we form habits of judgement, and attitudes, and modify our theories, and perhaps do other things. But then, and this is the crucial mechanism, the mind can express such a reaction by "spreading itself on the world". That is, we regard the world as richer or fuller through possessing properties and things which are in fact mere projections of the mind's own reactions: there is no reason for the world to contain a fact corresponding to any given projection. So the world, on such a metaphysic, might be much thinner than commonsense supposes it. Evidently the picture invites us to frame a debate: how are we going to tell where Hume's mechanism operates? Perhaps everywhere; drawing us to idealism, leaving the world entirely noumenal; or perhaps just somewhere; or nowhere. Hume's most famous applications of his mechanism, to values and causes, are extended by Ramsey to general propositions, which to him represented not judgements but projections of our habits of singular belief, and also to judgements of probability, which are projections of our degrees of confidence in singular beliefs.

If we are to assess his views we must be sure of what counts as an argument for or against this projectivist picture. (I am apologetic about using the new term, but the word 'subjectivist', which is often used, has connotations which, I shall try to show, are damaging and not essential to faith in Hume's mechanism.) The main burden of my paper is that most ways of framing the debate

175

underestimate the resources available to the projectivist. I think it is also clear, particularly from his 1929 paper 'General propositions and causality' that Ramsey himself was optimistic about those resources, in a way that has not been widely recognised.

The usual way of attacking the projectivist is this. He is saddled with a particular view of the meaning of remarks made in the area in question. This view is then shown not to correspond with some feature of the meaning which we actually give to those remarks. It is triumphantly concluded that projectivism is inadequate, and that we must adopt a realistic theory, seeing the remarks as straight-forward descriptions of a part of the world which we are (some-how) able to cognise. This kind of attack is clearly worthless unless it is clear that the projectivist is indeed committed to the theory of meaning attributed to him. Yet, I shall argue, the theory of meaning to be linked with Hume's picture is variable, subtle, and obscure: if, as I suspect, it is as yet unclear what resources the projectivist has in this matter it follows that all such attacks so far made are unsuccessful.

A couple of examples may help. It used to be thought that a subjective theory of value entailed identifying the assertion that X is good, with the assertion that the speaker himself liked X. This is properly refuted by pointing out that the two have entirely different truth-conditions (or assent-conditions), and the subjectivist is dis-comfited. But it is now widely recognised that only a very naive subjective theory of value commits this howler: a theory of value as a projection of our attitudes can adopt a much better theory of what then is said by attributions of value – primarily in terms of expres-sion of such attitudes. Again, it used to be thought (perhaps it sometimes still is) that someone who, like Hume, thinks of the world as a succession of distinct events, and who accords no real distinct existence to necessary connections between those events, must think that we mean no more than regular succession when we talk of cause. But there is no reason for saying that this is what we *must* mean when we project a certain habit of reliance on a regular-ity, or some other attitude towards it, onto the world. Perhaps, for example, we express some special attitude to the regularity or dignify it in a certain way, and then many stock objections to regularity theories (factory whistles blowing at the same time and so on) are entirely irrelevant. They simply draw attention to reg-ularities which, for some reason yet to be explored, we do not dignify.

But expressive theories of meaning are themselves attacked. It is probably necessary at present to distinguish two kinds of rejection. One, which I shall be coming to, joins issue over some particular aspect of meaning, such as the occurrence of the disputed remarks in subordinate clauses, to which the theory is supposed to be inadequate. The other is hostile to the whole idea of there being a debate. I have in mind the conservative, pessimistic, and perhaps Wittgensteinian view that we cannot do much with our language except speak it, or at best put down rules for the building up of meanings in terms of rules governing the components of sentences with those meanings. But if that enterprise leaves us with such things as the placid truths that 'good' is satisfied by good things, 'chance' refers to chance, and that A, B satisfy 'x causes y' just when A causes B, then we should just rest and be thankful. Sometimes, indeed, it is felt that the very endeavour to find semantic structure in a rule-governed way rules out Hume's kind of theory by committing us to a *correspondence* theory of truth, as if a coherence theorist, or a pragmatist, or the projectivists I am interested in, have to half-wittedly deny that 'London' refers to London, and so on. In fact, of course, in constructing such a theory of semantic contribution we simply use our language to describe itself, and leave perfectly untouched the question of which metaphysics is appropriate to that use. It is puzzling to think why people still associate the creation of a formal truth-theory for a language with particular views of truth (*e.g.* Platts 1979: 35). To exorcise this temptation imagine a formal theory of Arabic numerals enabling us to deduce which number a sequence of digits refers to, given axioms saying to what individual digits refer – the one essential rule merely captures the way the position of a digit indicates the power of ten by which it is multiplied. Does such a theory, or the interest of creating it, tell us what it is to refer to a number, or commit us to a correspondence theory of such a thing? Of course not. It is entirely silent on the issue, and merely uses the notion, while telling us nothing about it.

I think the argument to the contrary which confuses people goes: a correspondence theory of truth needs to identify some fundamental word-to-world relations; Tarski's style of theory can be taken to offer the relations of reference and satisfaction for this job; hence Tarski's style of theory is, or at least helps, a correspondence theory. This would be fine if there were independent argument that *what it is* for words to refer to things, or things to satisfy predicates, is well thought of in terms of correspondence. But it might just as well be thought of in terms of the predicates taking part in a coherent system; or being used in promoting certain ends; or in terms of the things having the reactions of the mind projected onto them. In other words, we might just as well argue that a coherence, pragmatist, or subjective theory needs to identify some fundamental word-to-world relations, hence Tarski's style of theory helps them too. Which shows its irrelevance to this issue. Yet, although it gains nothing from truth-theories, we cannot dismiss the view that Hume's theory is not debatable. The difficulty that perplexes me is that if, as I shall suggest, the projectivist can make perfect sense of apparently realistic practice, it is not clear what intellectual quirks mark him off; nor what is left to fight over except harmless images and metaphors. The interest, at any rate, comes in seeing what he can do by way of incorporating apparently realistic practice: this is a programme which can be called 'quasi-realism', and I see Ramsey as one if its patrons.

Specific charges against projectivist theories will concentrate upon ways in which our thinking about the area in question appears to accord an objective or independent standing to the things allegedly projected. Primarily, chances, laws and causes (not to mention values and Gods) are all things about which, we say, we can be ignorant. Our opinions about them can be wrong, defective, in various ways. We allow the possibility that we think of them as existing when they really don't and that we are unaware that they exist when they really do. We acknowledge experts, so that some persons' views of, say, probabilities, become authoritative enough to count as knowledge, to enter into books as physical constants like values of masses and densities (and other persons' opinions are often not worth a straw). Yet even the experts might be wrong: it is not their opinion which defines laws and chances: the laws and chances would have been what they are regardless of whether people had known about them.

Ramsey is usually thought of as one of the fathers of a "subjective" theory of probability which denies or at best struggles with such facts. On that theory a distribution of confidence across any totality of propositions is coherent if it satisfies some very weak constraints. But those constraints allow for the most bizarre confidences and agnosticisms. Yet coherence is all that there is. As Kyburg and Smokler put it in the introduction to their 1964 collection (p. 7), for subjectivism and degree of belief in any statement is permissible, but there are restrictions placed on the distribution of degrees of belief among sets of related statements. Since there is nothing to be wrong about, the view has been summarised as claiming that "sincerity is enough". On the more modern version which I discuss in part **III**, it is also mandatory to stick by opinions through time and as various kinds of observation are made. However, even this gives us no title to say that a man who announces a quite outrageous set of confidences is "wrong": the only vice he could display would be a kind of fickleness as time goes by. It is easy to see why this implausible theory is fostered onto a projectivist. In probability, as in the theory of value, if projection is all that there is, there is surely nothing to be wrong *about*. But all this flies in the face of the objectivity of our usage and renders the theory an easy prey to criticism.

But Ramsey was well aware of the shortcomings of a purely subjective theory of laws and chances. He explicitly denies, for instance, that chances correspond to anyone's actual degrees of belief (1931: 206); he knows that we believe in unknown laws (and he would have said the same about chances) (1978: 139, 150); he knows that some opinions about chances are much better than others (1978: 95ff). His effort is to show that these phenomena do not refute an anti-realist, projectivist, theory of chances and laws, but are actually explicable given it: it is the fact that he made this quasi-realist attempt which seems to me to show that Ramsey was much better aware of the resources of projectivism than many of his apparent followers (Carnap (1962: 16ff) being an honourable exception). How far can his programme succeed?

II Hume forged the essential tool for the projectivist to use as he attempts to reconcile his theory with the objectivity of usage. In his great essay 'On the standard of taste' he points out, in effect, that it is no part of a projectivist metaphysic to claim that one projection is as good as another. Some may be inferior, some superior, and even the best may, in principle, be capable of improvement. Thus, let us take the difficult case of moral evaluations. If values are projections of a habit of forming some kind of attitude to some kinds of thing, how can I be aware that my *own* attitudes might be defective, and capable of improvement (if we prefer societies to individuals the question becomes: how can *we* be aware that *ours* are?) The answer is that I know that people are capable of habits of projection which from my own standpoint are deplorable: they judge things of which they are ignorant, their views are the function of fears and fantasies, blind traditions, prejudice, and so on. But then: who am I to be sure that I am free of these defects? This thought is quite sufficient to enable me to understand the possibility of my attitudes improving. They ought to be formed from qualities I admire – the proper use of knowledge, real capacity for sympathy, and so on. If they are not, and if the use of those capacities and the avoidance of the inferior determinants of opinion would lead me to change, then the resulting attitudes would be not only different, but better. It is true that in saying this I am presupposing one kind of evaluation in giving sense to the possible deficiencies of the other. An attitude to the processes of attitude formation is used to give sense to the possibility not merely of change but of improvement in moral judgement. But this gives nothing an axiomatic status: at the end of a process of re-evaluation, everything may have changed. The right analogy is with the re-building of Neurath's boat, and we know that in principle the result of that might be an improved boat. Equally we can understand and fear the possibility of deterioration. It follows that a projectivist picture of values need have little to do with the frivolities of traditional moral subjectivism ("one opinion is as good as another" and so forth). By pursuing the point we might begin to see how a projectivist can incorporate notions of truth and knowledge.

In the case of empirical judgements of chance the matter is much easier in two respects.

The first is not my main concern in this paper, but it is worth noticing. Projectivism in moral philosophy is open to attack on the grounds that the reaction of the mind which is supposedly projected is itself only identifiable as a reaction to a cognised *moral* feature of the world. The specific attitudes and emotions (approval, indignation, guilt and so on) can, it is argued, only be understood in terms of perception of right and wrong, obligations, rights, *etc.*, which therefore cannot be reflections of them. Myself, I do not think that this is true, nor, if it were true, do I think that it would refute projectivism. For it is not surprising that our best vocabulary for identifying the reaction should be the familiar one using the predicates we apply to the world we have spread. Thus, to take a parallel, many people would favour a projectivist view of the comic, and they may well be right even if our best way of describing the reaction which we are projecting onto a situation we describe as comic is just that it is that reaction we have when we find something funny. I don't think a behaviourist analysis is either required or helpful, for obviously the behaviour, to someone with no sense of humour, would be incomprehensible.

In any case, a projectivist theory of probability meets no such objection. For it is easy to identify the main conponent projected when we attribute a good chance to an event or a high probability to a judgement: it is, of course, simply a degree of confidence.

Degrees of confidence in propositions are "intervening variables" in psychological theory. We can know about them through interpreting the behaviour which, supposedly, they explain. The measurement of degrees of confidence is not necessarily straightforward, but this does not make the notion improper – as Mellor argues in chapter 7 against Kyburg (1978). It may even be indeterminate, very often, what a person's degree of confidence in a proposition actually is, or whether indeed he has one. But in the same way it is often not straightforward to know what a person's belief is, and it may be indeterminate what his belief about some matter is, and even indeterminate whether he has one. Yet the notion of a belief is a proper theoretical concept in psychological explanation. Here we should notice that a projectivist needs no more degrees of confidence than a person has beliefs about chances: it is no part of his view that, for instance, a real number should be in principle assigned to every proposition an agent has ever thought of, representing his degree of belief in it. We need no such extravagance: often we express ourselves by saying that we have no idea what the chance is – and this attitude need not co-exist with a particular confidence in a proposition. We shall see how to interpret it on a projectivist picture later. If the whole notion of a degree of confidence were suspect, as some authors claim, then we would need at least to indicate another projected psychological state. I am inclined to suggest that it would not be fatal if, as in the moral or even causal example, our success in doing this without using the vocabulary of chance were only partial. But, in fact, I doubt whether it would be too difficult.

The second respect in which things are easier for probability is the backing we can give to our standards for evaluating projections. We need standards for assessing projections of degrees of confi-

dence, enabling us to say that some are better than others, that even
the best may be capable of improvement, that some are worthless.
But there are obvious sources for such standards: an opinion might
be formed in the light of experience of observed frequencies or fit
into an otherwise successful scheme of projections, and most fun-
damentally it might give its possessor the habit of belief in what
happens, and disbelief in what does not. And it is this which is the
lynchpin of Ramsey's theory. We could say that it imports a pragmatic standard for evaluating projections, but this might be misleading. For it is not as though the standard is in any way optional or
avoidable if we adopt different goals or purposes. It is necessary that
truth counts as success in judgement, and that the proportion of
successes achieved by a habit of making judgements is a measure of
the confidence which ought to be felt in the beliefs to which it leads
one. The standard is mandatory.

For, suppose we have a thin, Humean view of the world. What is
our purpose in projecting onto it chances and probabilities? Ramsey
writes that we "judge mental habits by whether they work, *i.e.*
whether the opinions they lead to are for the most part true, or more
often true than those which alternative habits would lead to". The
opinions he is talking about are of course not opinions about
probabilities, for that would get nowhere, but the opinions of
particular matters of fact which judgements of probability will lead
us to form. Fortunately the world displays patterns allowing us to
have successful habits of particular belief: faced with partial or
complete regularities we can form partial or complete confidence in
new cases, and the world grants us success if we are careful. As
Ramsey writes, the best habit of belief formation will have us
forming confidence of a strength proportionate to the ratio of
particular truths to falsities which the habit leads us to believe in.
(For why, see below p. 184.)

So it seems that Ramsey is going beyond mere coherence of sets
of belief, in a thoroughly sensible and necessary way. That standard
is too permissive since, on the face of it, a set of beliefs may possess
the virtue of coherence while having the disadvantage of enjoining
confidence that things happen which never do or that things don't
happen which often do. Pragmatism must supplement coherence.
But this charge ignores the work that has recently been done on the
relation between subjectivism and "learning from experience".
This work makes it plausible to believe that a subjective theory of

probability, relying only on the constraint of coherence, can show that the process called conditionalization is obligatory. It may then seem as though conditionalizing is itself a process which forces opinions to converge, and that what they converge upon is a value for probabilities in accord with observed frequencies. If all this is true then the constraint of coherence would be *sufficient* to give the standard of evaluation which Ramsey wants. In the next section I assess this argument, and in the last I go on to develop a projective theory in more detail.

III In the succeeding sections I shall use the standard terminology, in which a *chance set-up* exists, and there is an actual or hypothetical series of *trials* which yield a stable frequency of various outcomes. The set of trials we can call A, and the outcome in which we are interested, B. There is a slight strain in adapting this terminology to, say, the chance of a person being a gin-drinker, but for the moment we are not interested in any problems caused by extending the notions.

We now suppose that we have conducted a reasonably extended investigation, and in a large number of trials the proportion of Bs is tending to stabilize around some figure, p. Our problem is to give a projectivist account of the natural judgement which such evidence (in the absence of other evidence) would lead to: 'the chance of an A being B is p'. But this way of putting it blurs a vital distinction. There are two sorts of chance judgement which could be made. One is local, and concerns only the chance of one of the trials being B in the set which makes our evidence. The other is not: it is a judgement which concerns other trials and has implications for our confidence in future cases. It is one thing to say: the chance was p of one of the examples of A we have considered having been B. It is quite another to say: the chance is p of any A, including ones yet to be realized, being B. The first judgement is local or restricted to the class of trials in which we already know the frequency. The second involves a prediction, or more accurately, a commitment to a particular kind of confidence in situations not yet brought about. It involves an apparently inductive step. Yet, although it will evidently be more complex to identify the thoughts which license it, I shall consider it first.

It is not surprising that a man observing and recording results from a process which generates a certain frequency of outcomes B

among events A, with no discernible pattern, should come to have a degree of confidence proportionate to the frequency of Bs among As that an arbitrary A, such as the next one, will be B. But why *should* he? The simplest answer has two stages. Firstly, the man has the inductive habit: he expects the process to go on generating roughly the frequency it has done so far. Secondly, given that this is so, he will be right to have the degree of confidence in a particular outcome identical with its relative frequency, because that is the standard for rationality. There is nothing mysterious about this second point. If the inductive expectation is right, then the relative frequency remains stable. If that is so then a habit of adopting and acting upon any *other* degree of confidence in particular expectations would lay you open to certain loss if you are required to act out your confidence by buying or selling bets at the corresponding rate, given that your partner is someone more straightforward. It would be like having confidence other than $\frac{1}{4}$ that a card from a shuffled pack is a heart: a hopeless position if you are required to buy or sell bets at a corresponding rate. Nor should we worry that there is anything unrealistic (undemocratic, as it were) in criticising someone for having a set of confidences which would lead to loss if he were *required* to post odds on which he could be *required* to buy or sell bets: it is not a satisfactory defence to reply that we are not often required to gamble. The defective degrees of confidence are like bad dispositions which may nevertheless remain unrealised. They can still be criticised by pointing out what would happen if they were to be acted upon.

The two stage answer relies on induction, and the rationality of that is left dangling. It is tempting, therefore, to hope that work on conditionalising achieves an answer without relying on specifically inductive habits. It is not, indeed, likely that this could be so, since induction appears to be a necessary component of any answer, in that if there were no reason for expecting the process to generate the same frequency as hitherto there would indeed be no reason for expecting the next A to be a B with any particular confidence. So unless work on conditionalisation provided some justification of induction, it could not provide the requisite standard.

The central argument in this area is credited variously to David Lewis and Patrick Suppes. It is, in effect, an extension of the standard Dutch book argument for coherence to an agent's probability distributions through time. The standard argument makes coherence at any one time a necessary condition of a rational distribution of confidence. The new argument, which we can call the dynamic Dutch book argument, or DDB, extends this to force a rational agent not to wipe his slate clean at any time and form whatever new confidences he fancies (although until Ian Hacking (1967) first made it clear it was not widely recognised that one might do this, so that subjectivists had happily helped themselves to conditionalisation anyhow). The new argument is designed to prove the connection between rationality and conditionalisation. Following Paul Teller (1973) we can see the DDB like this. We imagine an agent with a set of beliefs at time 0, described by a function P_o giving the confidence with which every proposition in the domain is believed. A change in belief in A is described as conditionalised upon evidence E if, at time n, after E becomes known (so that $P_n(E) = 1$), $P_n(A)$ is equal to $P_o(A \& E)/P_o(E)$. That is, at time n the new confidence in A is equal to the old conditional probability of A upon E. As Teller shows, we can generalise everything to the case where E merely changes probability, but this does not matter.

Now it is quite clear that, sometimes, changes of belief that are not conditionalisations are legitimate. One may rethink a problem afresh, and come to regret one's old confidences. One may think up new alternatives. But we can avoid objections based on this by restricting ourselves to cases where nothing of this sort occurs, but where someone has *in advance*, at time 0, a settled policy or habit of not conditionalising. In other words, one has a policy or habit which, should E come about, will lead him to some confidence in A greater or less than his present confidence of A upon E. The DDB shows that a man known to have such a plan, and required to buy and sell bets according to his confidences, can be made to buy and sell bets on which he has a net loss whatever happens by an opponent who knows no more than him (except, perhaps, that he has the habit or policy). The general proof is complex, but its principle is quite easy to grasp. Suppose I am following a plan, or have a habit, which means that I now have a large confidence that A will occur if E does, but which enjoins that if E does occur I will only have small confidence in A. Suppose I think there is a 60% chance that John will play a spade, and a 90% chance that if he does so he will be left with a court card. But, flouting conditionalisation, I am settled that I will only have 30% confidence that John will have a court card after he has played a spade. The nub of your strategy for profit is this. You sell *to* me a bet to yield (say) 1 if he plays a spade and has a court card, 0 otherwise. I will pay a relatively large amount for that (0.54, in fact). You plan that *if* he plays a spade you will cover that bet by buying *from* me a bet to yield you 1 if he has a court card, 0 otherwise, and you know you will be able to do that cheaply, for since I will then have little confidence in the court card, I will want little for such a bet (0.3, in fact). You then only need to arrange side bets to give you a modest profit if he does *not* play a spade, and you will profit in any event. If you can sell me bets when I am confident, and buy when I am less so, you profit. Conversely, if I had announced that although now I regard it as only 30% probable that if he plays a spade he will have a court card, yet, I agree, if he does play a spade I will be very confident that he has a court card (I know I get excited), you buy *from* me a bet on both things now, and sell *to* me a bet on the court card later, if he plays a spade. Again, arranging side bets to cover him not playing a spade, you profit whatever happens. I ask little now for the first bet, and am prepared to pay a lot later for the bet which covers it.

It is not quite right to say that this gives an effective method of profiting from a non-conditionalising agent. The direction of his departure from the present value of conditional probabilities (the probability of A upon E, now) must be known. If we know that he will inflate his confidence in A we can profit, and if we know that he will deflate it we can profit, but it does not follow, and it is not true, that if we know that he will do one or the other we can profit. We have to know the direction of his aberration before we know whether to buy or sell bets, but of course a general tendency in an agent one way or another could also be exploited over time.

What does this argument show? It shows that an agent known to plan a definite confidence in some proposition, if certain evidence comes in, which is either higher, or lower, than the value he now attaches to the conditional probability of the proposition on the evidence, can be made to lose whatever happens if he is required to act out those confidences. Let us agree that such a plan is irrational. Does it follow that we should expect rational confidence to converge upon frequencies, thereby by-passing the apparently inductive step? The feeling that it may have something to do with it comes like this. Suppose we antecedently hand people a number of hypotheses about the chance of an A being a B, and invite them to form a distribution of confidence among them avoiding the pathological values 0 or 1. We then amass frequencies, and since the agents must conditionalise, the posterior probabilities gradually increase for hypotheses giving the chance a value near the observed frequency, and fall away for the others. Eventually opinion converges upon a high probability for the chance being as near as possible to the observed frequency. And the value given the chance dictates our confidence in the next A being a B.

As an attempt to either by-pass or cast light upon the inductive step, this argument clearly fails. It falls to a dilemma. Either the original hypotheses are consistent with changes in chances over time, or they are not, but relate solely to the trials already conducted. They are local in my sense of the term. If they are, then whatever our confidence that the chance of an A being a B took a certain value in generating the frequencies we have so far observed, we need inductive confidence to transpose that confidence to the future. It is no easier to argue that since the chances of an A being B have always been good, they will continue to be, than it is to argue that since nature has always been ordered, it will continue to be so. On the other hand, if the original hypotheses describe eternal chances, so that in accepting a hypothesis concerning chance I would indeed be committing myself to a uniformity – to the probability that a stable observed frequency of As among Bs can be extended indefinitely with a similar value – then the induction is presupposed in setting up the request: it is only if we have an inductive faith in such uniformities that we should be inclined to distribute confidence over the initial finite selection of hypotheses. Otherwise we should simply point out the many many other things that nature might do instead of giving a uniform chance for an A being a B.

This is easily seen if we imagine a concourse of souls in an antecedent heaven, each of whom is handed a ticket describing a different course that nature might take in the world they are about to enter. Some give eternal constancy to the relation between As and Bs, some see it as altering over time, so that although up until a certain time a certain degree of confidence in an A being a B accords with frequencies, after that time a different one does. These souls may dream up conditional probabilities for themselves, giving the world an $x\%$ chance of continuing to conform to their ticket, if it does so until a certain time. But unless they have an *a priori* reason for expecting the world they are to enter to favour uniformities, there is no reason for x to be different for those with straight tickets and for those with bent ones. And if all possible hypotheses are ticketed, then x must be vanishingly small, corresponding to the fact that at any time there will be an indefinite number of tickets conforming to the world up until that time, but subsequently divergent. Of course, I am not here denying that we may be able to think of a reason why x should be placed higher for those with straight tickets: that is solving the problem of induction. But it is quite clear that if this can be done, it is not by simply proving the virtue of conditionalising. For *that* is something which the bent can do with the straight. In a nutshell, conditionalising appears interesting only if we pose the problem in a way that presupposes inductive good sense. (Philosophers of a sociological and Popperean bent are liable to point out that only hypotheses about stable chances would be of interest to scientists, who would regard the others as crazy. This is true. It is true because scientists, like the rest of us, possess inductive good sense.)

It appears, then, that hypotheses about chances which carry implications for future distributions of confidence are not automatically the outcome of conditionalising changes of opinion. Induction is needed, as indeed we might have expected. Furthermore, we can escape the unrealistic element of seeing learning from experience in terms of conditionalising, namely the nebulous nature of the prior distributions of confidence needed. It is usually much more natural to see our experience as putting us in mind of some hypothesis about chance, rather than merely modifying the degree of confidence with which we used to hold one. The rational man does not have to spring fully-armed from the womb, with an infantile probability distribution across all the hypotheses which experience teaches him to believe. But if we now turn to purely local assessments of chance things may appear easier. Here we merely want to say that the chance of an A being B on the trials we have conducted was p. Whether it remains so can be, so far as that judgement goes, entirely up to the gods, and depending on our opinion of them we can expect what we like about the next A. What is the rationale for such local judgements?

The connection between judgements of chance and confidence which we have relied upon has been very simple. We have imagined judgements of chance dictating a corresponding degree of confidence: the reason why that must conform to relative frequency is evident if we demand that the confidence could be acted upon in willingness to buy and sell bets. If we imagine a closed set, like a pack of cards, any confidence in an outcome (*e.g.* a card being a heart) with a known frequency must conform to that frequency, for otherwise, if the confidence were acted out, loss would be certain. So it might seem as though everything ought to be very simple for local judgements of chance. We know the frequency of *A*s in our set being *B*s: the right confidence to have that an arbitrary member of the set is a *B* must conform to it, so the right chance judgement must be one which expresses that degree of confidence, *i.e.* the judgement that the chance is identical with the frequency. But the trouble is that although this may be right in the sense that if we know nothing else it would be the proper estimate of the chance for us to make, it does not follow that we regard it as true.

For there is actually no compulsion on us to identify local chances with local frequencies: we all know that there is a chance that in any finite set of trials the frequency with which an outcome occurred differs markedly from the chance of occurring which it actually had. The chance of getting a *B* might have been q, even if the obtained relative frequency of *B*s was p. Here realism seems to triumph: what kind of account can a projectivist give of this modal claim? Equally we may persist in actually believing that the *A*s in our set had a chance q of being *B*, although we know that the relative frequency was p, so if we were told to bet on whether an arbitrary *A* had been *B*, p would be the right figure to act upon. Again, what account can a projectivist give of the belief about chance, when, as in this case, it appears to diverge from the right degree of confidence to have about arbitrary members of the set?

The answer can only come from seeing the part which induction and science play. If we think the chance of an *A* being *B* was actually q, we think that q would have been the right betting rate antecedently to the set of trials. We can believe this because we can believe that there was or could have been a longer set of trials in which the proportion of *B*s tended to stabilize on the correct figure, q, *and* we believe that none of the things which affect such frequencies was different on our actual trials. This last is a scientific belief, in the sense that our causal theories of the world are what tell us whether particular factors which do influence the frequency of *B*s were or were not present. Of course, if the figure p arose from a sufficiently long series, this in itself will be evidence that such a factor was present, whatever it may have been. But the point is that we may not be forced to think that, and it may be easier to believe the reverse. The judgement of local chance, when it diverges from actual frequency, is then an expression of the confidence which should be felt in a hypothetical situation: a situation where none of the things which, we believe, affect frequencies of Bs among As would be different from that which obtained on our trials. Similarly the modal claim expresses our fear that the hypothetical series might exhibit the different frequency q, and our actual set of trials may be a very poor indication of it. However, there is no reason to be depressed by these possibilities, for induction works, and what produces a frequency of outcomes one day is very likely to do substantially the same the next.

It seems to me that this is an account of our apparently realistic talk (in this case, modal claims and claims apparently divorcing local judgements from expressions of confidence) which yet concedes nothing to realism. Chances have not entered as real facts, capable of explaining or causing events. They remain projections, even if we are interested in spreading them not only over the actual events which have confronted us or which will confront us, but over events which could have happened as well.

In my last section I want to take up another problem which may tempt us to realism: the problem of our willingness to talk about knowledge of chance, and our subtlety in so doing.

IV Let us suppose that the best evidence is that the frequency of Bs among As indeed approximates to p, and will keep doing so. Clearly, then, a man with the degree of confidence p has the habit of singular belief which meets Ramsey's standard: he has a degree of confidence proportionate to the number of times he is right. But there is another standard needed. For it does not follow that we should endorse this confidence, nor this judgement of chance. Consider that we may be able effectively to divide the As into two classes, and rightly predict a high ratio of Bs among the CAs and a low ratio among the others. I shall call this effecting a partition of the As. If this were done we would be in a better position than him in this very straightforward sense. Using our knowledge we can gamble with him and consistently win, by buying bets at a rate corresponding to p on CAs being B, and selling on $\sim$ CAs. And in a variety of less mercenary ways we can see that our habit is more useful than his. It is more accurate, more efficient. It is not necessarily incorrect to say that the chance of an *A* being *B* is *p*, even when effective partitions exist. We can, after all, talk of the chance of an animal being a carnivore, or of a human baby being Chinese. But if an acceptable practical application is to be made of such a remark, then the context must be one in which the participants themselves cannot easily put the subject matter into one or other partition. If they could, then there would be something deficient about the distribution of confidence: it could effectively be improved. We might express this by saying that there is no case of an *A*, neither those which are *C* nor those which are not, on which we should accept such an estimate of the chance of it being a *B*. But if an acceptable single case judgement is to follow from such a remark, then the conversational context will be one in which the participants cannot easily put the subject into one or other of the partitions. It remains true that if this can be done, the judgement of chance is deficient. (Of course, there is no implication here about negligence or otherwise in being ignorant about *C*.)

We here have the beginnings of a reasonably clear view of two topics that sometimes perplex analyses of probability: the rationality of seeking the narrowest reference class when we want single case judgements, and the propriety of restricting the terminology of chance to phenomena which satisfy von Mises' second condition for an empirical collective, namely that there should be no effective selection procedure for singling out a subset of the members with a different overall frequency of the relevant property. (This is felicitously called the requirement of excluded gambling systems.) To take the second issue first. If we believe that a selection procedure (corresponding to the property *C* in the last paragraphs) can *easily* be found, then it follows that we believe that our distribution of confidence can *easily* be improved, by the standards we have seen. While we believe such a thing we are obviously in a deficient position, and, depending on the consequences of a judgement, and the degree of ease of improving our knowledge, we may wish to attach no weight to our judgement – to suspend it in fact. The projectivist thus has excellent pragmatic reasons for confining our judgements of chance of an *A* being a *B* to reference classes of which we do not expect there to be an easy method of partition. There is no metaphysics of randomness required. It is just that if we cannot effect a partition, a judgement of chance leads to our best possible habit. If we can, it does not.

The single case problem is in effect the same. If you want to have a degree of confidence in the judgement, of a particular philosopher that he drinks gin, the statistic of the proportion of men who drink gin helps. But that statistic can easily be refined: middle class people, academics, academics in arts subjects, of a certain age . . . The pragmatic motive for seeking the narrowest reference class is just the same as before: a degree of confidence based solely on the wider statistic leaves its possessor in an inferior position vis-à-vis someone who can partition the class of men, and attach different degrees of confidence to singular judgements depending upon the sub-class in which the subject is found. Again, of course, the extent to which it is worth seeking statistics for narrower reference classes depends upon the expected benefit of the more discriminating judgement, and the expected homogeneity or otherwise of the reference class. If nothing much hangs on it and if our prior judgement is that gin drinking is not likely to be much different in any subsets we can think of, it may not be worth a research programme to find out. Nevertheless the point remains that unless we make our evidence as weighty, in Keynes' sense, as we can, by considering possible partitions of our class, we cannot be sure that we are properly serving the purposes of judgement, and the right thing to do may be to form no opinion. A good example of such reticence comes from legal suspicion of a "mere" statistic putting a defendant into a class with a high frequency of guilt. Unless the class is as weighty as it can be made, it would be impermissible to be confident that the defendant is guilty (see Cohen 1977: especially ch. 7).

It seems to me that this pragmatic perspective on these issues has a clear advantage over a realist metaphysics. Notoriously, in trying to give sense to the single case judgement, a realist metaphysic of chance becomes tangled in the issue of determinism. If it is determined now that I will, or will not catch a cold next winter it is hard to see what sense to make of talk of my propensity to do so or not, just as, if I did not die before I was thirty, it is very unclear what could be meant by saying that I had a propensity to do so. Yet I had a chance of doing so. Equally, only if a chance set-up is indeterministic will it be, for a realist, true that trials on it form a collective. Otherwise, it is in principle possible to select trials with a different long run frequency of outcomes. For the projectivist this becomes simply irrelevant. Our purpose in making judgements of chance, and the standards to use in following out those purposes, are perfectly indifferent to whatever secret springs and principles lie behind the empirical collectives which form the subjects of those judgements. At a time at which our best judgement is that we should treat the trials on some set-up as forming a collective, we are entitled to project a chance and form confidence accordingly; at a time at which we suspect that we can find a partition, we should not. But there need have been nothing wrong with us if we have treated something as a collective, but at some improved state of knowledge a partition is found. Not all ignorance is culpable.

The realist is apt to be impatient with such *laissez-aller* attitudes. True, he will say, you can tell us when we talk of empirical chance, and perhaps you can give some pragmatic understanding of why we do. But for all that we may be *wrong* to do so in some cases even when we are not culpable. Warranted assertibility is not truth. A later discovery that a trial on a chance set-up A fell into a sub-class with a different ratio of Bs from that shown overall would show that we had spoken falsely; but what made our remark false was not the discovery but the fact about the trial. Unless indeterminism is true, there are always such facts, in principle, forcing falsity on all attributions of chance other than 0 or 1. This argument is all the more persuasive because it cannot be avoided by mentioning warranted assertibility in the long run, the usual pragmatist substitute for truth. Once we admit that there are facts determining whether a particular outcome will occur or not, we cannot very well claim that a long run of improving investigation would not find them; and in that case determinism will entail that all chances of particular events are 0 or 1, even on this definition.

But it is the definition which is at fault. A projectivist need have no use for truth, about the chance of a single case, as the limit of the degree of confidence to which progressive omniscience would tend. He *does* need a proper account of fallibility, enabling him to admit that a particular estimate of chance might in principle be improved. This we have provided him, without any involvement in the metaphysics of determinism. This means that along with a judgement he has the concept of a standpoint yielding a possibly improved judgement. It does *not* mean that he needs the concept of a standpoint from which *all* other judgement is seen to be wrong, and this is what the unnecessary notion of the limit is attempting to import.

In practice this means that although we have plenty of use of warranted, defensible, careful, estimates of chances of particular events, we have less use for claims that we know such chances. The claim to knowledge entails, I think, the claim that no improved standpoint, yielding a revised estimate, is possible. To know something is to know that no judgement contradicting one's own could be really preferable. To know that the chance of an outcome on a single trial is p we would need theoretical knowledge that no partition exists. Thus we are entitled to say that we know the chance of an individual outcome on an individual trial, only if we are entitled to say that we know that the chance set-up admits of no partition. Now we can adopt different standards for saying this. The clearest case (where, as it were, even God cannot partition the trials) is one where we know that the system is indeterministic. Yet our standards need not be so absolute. We may know that whatever God could do, there could be no practicable project of partitioning the trials. The systems on which people gamble are designed so that this is so. In such a system we have effectively ruled out the possibility of an improved judgement about any single trial, and we can properly express belief that we have succeeded in doing this by claiming knowledge of the chance. In other cases, responsible judgement is all that we want or need.

How far can our quasi-realism, our attempt to found apparently realist practice on a subjective basis, succeed? A possible stumbling block would be talk of chances as explaining events, or as themselves being things which need explanation. This would seem to invest them with some ontological standing, with a real influence on the world, which fits ill with the projectivist picture. But perhaps the appearance is deceptive: for everything will depend on the interpretation we make of such explanatory claims. Clearly if we have a generalised anti-realist attitude towards science, then chances could be as honest inhabitants of theory as any other. But even without this, once we have incorporated the notion of truth, or right opinion, there will be natural things to ask and say about why chances are what they are. We can ask what it is about the world which makes it the case that one particular distribution of confidence over propositions about some subject matter is right. And we can, in asking why something is the case, cite that some such distribution is right as part of our answer, even if this looks danger-ously like giving some chances a real, causal, place. It need not be doing so, for instance, because if we endorse one distribution (say, give a 0.5 chance to heads) it will standardly follow that we ought to endorse others (a 0.25 chance of two heads in two trials) and it is no surprise that if asked why this is the chance on two trials, we reply by citing the first "fact". This is not the place to enter into all the moves a projectivist might make in tackling explanatory contexts, but their mere existence is unlikely to be much of a problem for him. The empirical part of science connects frequencies with what-ever factors influence them, and our reaction to this knowledge is our talk of chance. If, in expanding such reactions, we find ourselves talking of chances explaining things and needing explanation, the proper response is to ask what we are projecting onto the world by making these remarks.

A more serious threat is that with its very success quasi-realism takes much of the impetus out of subjectivism. Responsible subjec-tivism is less fun. If, one by one, a quasi-realist programme takes over the things which realists used to think their special private property, then the view that we have real metaphysical options becomes more doubtful. We all thought we knew what we meant by subjectivism, as opposed to propensity theories, frequency theories, and so on. But, if I am right, the intellectual practices supposedly definitive of these different positions can be available to all, so that the old definitions and divisions appear quite artificial. (I expand these ruminations on anti-realism in my 1980.)

In any case, if there is a metaphysical issue, then the subjectivists, so far as we have yet discovered, may have been right about it. But the subjectivism is not the irresponsible and therefore inefficient brand with which Ramsey is wrongly associated. It maintains standards for proper projection, and those standards go beyond coherence and beyond the dynamic coherence which I discussed. They involve a proper respect for frequencies, arising from a proper respect for induction. The main consequence of this responsibility is that subjectivism, as a metaphysic, becomes immune to a large variety of abuse. It also finds itself able to give sense to most of the thoughts which tempt us to realism. However, it maintains what can be seen as clear gains: it avoids the metaphysical problems of indeterminism, since proper single case projections can be made when we are perfectly indifferent to that issue, and by trying to purchase realist practice from a more austere metaphysic we may come to feel more secure in that practice. There would, of course, be much more to be said if we were to expand the quasi-realist programme, particularly to cover the hypotheticals which are involved in the modal claims I discussed. By my instinct is that if there are obstacles on this route, then they afford opportunities for delightful scrambles, rather than excuses for retreat. And I think that was Ramsey's view as well.

Pembroke College, Oxford.

REFERENCES

Blackburn, S. 1980. Truth, realism and the regulation of theory. In *Midwest Studies in Philosophy Vol. 5*, ed. P. A. French *et al.* Minneapolis.

Carnap, R. 1962, *Logical Foundations of Probability*, 2nd. ed. Chicago.

Cohen, L. J. 1977. *The Probable and the Provable*. Oxford.

Hacking, I. 1967. Slightly more realistic personal probability. *Philosophy of Science* **34**, 311–25.

Kyburg, H. 1978. Subjective probability: criticisms, reflections, and problems. *Journal of Philosophical Logic* **7**, 157–80.

Kyburg, H. E. and Smokler, H. E., eds. 1964. *Studies in Subjective Probability*. New York.

Platts, M. 1979. *Ways of Meaning*. London.

Ramsey, F. P. 1931. *Foundations of Mathematics*, ed. R. B. Braithwaite. London.

Ramsey, F. P. 1978. *Foundations*, ed. D. H. Mellor. London.

Teller, P. 1973. Conditionalization and observation. *Synthese* **26**, 218–58.

9   *Ramsey, reliability and knowledge*

RICHARD E. GRANDY

If Ramsey's initial remark in his fragmentary note 'Knowledge' (1929) is to be trusted, he always said that a belief was knowledge if 'it was (i) true, (ii) certain, (iii) obtained by a reliable process'. This analysis attracted little attention for a considerable period but has more recently been developed in several forms. In assessing the progress and prospects for this analysis it will be helpful to begin with a discussion of some of the *prima facie* advantages of the idea in resolving earlier problems about knowledge.

A convenient starting point is Russell's views on knowledge as expressed in *Problems of Philosophy*. Russell begins with an example intended to illustrate that knowledge is not merely true belief, but which, with a very slight emendation shows that knowledge is not justified true belief either:

If a man believes that the late Prime Minister's last name began with a B, he believes what is true, since the late Prime Minister was Sir Henry Camp-bell Bannerman. But if he believes that Mr. Balfour was the late Prime Minister, he will still believe that the late Prime Minister's last name began with a B, yet this belief, though true, would not be thought to constitute knowledge (Russell 1912: 132).

If we add that the man's belief that Balfour was the late Prime Minister was a justified belief, then the example also shows that justified true belief is not always knowledge.

Russell next considers a characterisation of knowledge as 'true belief deduced from true premises'; this fails since the premises

I am indebted to members of the MIT philosophy and linguistics department for helpful comments on an early draft and to Brian McLaughlin for useful discussions about relia-bility.

must be more than merely true. His next suggestion is 'true belief deduced from known premises', which fails because of circularity. Finally, to avoid the circularity he divides knowledge into two types and proposes that *'Derivative* knowledge is what is validly deduced from premises known intuitively' (133). Not every definition of knowledge will be similar to this, but any definition which mentions justification, deduction, inference or similar concepts will encounter the problems about to be discussed.

Leaving aside for our purposes the problems about intuitive knowledge, Russell notes that there remains an objection to the definition that it "unduly limits knowledge" (133).

It constantly happens that people entertain a true belief, which has grown up in them because of some piece of intuitive knowledge from which it is capable of being validly inferred, but from which it has not, as a matter of fact, been inferred by any logical process (133).

This leads Russell to loosen the definition to require only that there must be a discoverable logical inference which runs parallel to the "psychological inference".

The points I wish to illustrate by citing this development of Russell's thought are three:

(1) Any definition of knowledge as 'justified true belief plus an additional factor' will encounter a problem about possible inferences which are not made similar to Russell's concerning psychological inference.

(2) Any such definition which requires that justification be noncircular will require a separate class of statements that are either known in a different way or are self-justifying.

(3) Any such definition which does not require noncircularity will have to appeal to concepts such as coherence of the whole body of beliefs, the best explanation of the body of beliefs, or some similar relation involving a large set of beliefs.

We can now state Russell's problem as a rather general dilemma. Either the justification (including self-justification) requires that the person actually make the inference in the justified way or it does not. If one requires that people explicitly go through the steps which would be required to justify the belief, then it appears that many cases of knowledge will be incorrectly ruled out. Few non-philosophers could give satisfactory statements of the principles of inference, both deductive and inductive, nor could they provide any reasonable account of either self-justification, as required in (2) or of coherence and the related notions required by (3). On the other hand, if one does not require that the person go through the justificatory process, but merely that there be a justification on the basis of other things believed at the time, then too much will be allowed as knowledge. For example, anyone who has true beliefs in the Peano axioms and has any other true belief about number theory will have that belief qualified as knowledge.

One intermediate possibility would be to suggest that what is required is not – what is obviously false – that people make the justificatory steps consciously, but that there are non-conscious processes which parallel the justificatory steps. The difficulty with this suggestion is that unless we are also given some means of determining what non-conscious processes are occurring in a person we have no way of knowing whether the justification is satisfactory. People often make errors in their conscious reasoning. If non-conscious reasoning is similar to conscious reasoning then there must be errors there also and we need a criterion for determining what non-conscious processes are occurring. If non-conscious processes are sufficiently unlike conscious ones so that they cannot be erroneous then we must demand a fuller account of what these processes are like and how they yield justifications. In either case, the invocation of non-conscious processes in relation to justification is appealing only so long as it is left sufficiently vague to lack content. In general, the postulation of non-conscious processes is often a convenient device to enable the postulator to retain those features of conscious reasoning which are desired while ignoring those which are not.

I do not claim to have shown conclusively that all attempts to construe knowledge as justified true belief (possibly with the addition of further elements) must fail because of this dilemma but I hope I have said enough to indicate that there are serious difficulties in constructing any satisfactory theory along these lines. I believe that these difficulties indicate a fundamental incorrectness in the approach which reflects the neo-Cartesian origins of contemporary answers to the question. The attempt to analyse knowledge is still too closely connected to the medieval conception of knowledge as a deductive system consciously developed by the knower.

In order to find a better approach to the analysis of knowledge it is instructive to return briefly to Russell. Russell begins his chapter

'Knowledge, error and probable opinion' by asking a series of questions, the final one being can we ever *know* anything at all, or do we merely sometimes by good luck believe what is true?' (1912: 131). At this point, unfortunately, Russell decides that to answer the question he must determine what knowledge is; he then goes into the complex conditions that I mentioned earlier and turns away from the very natural answer the question suggests.

Knowledge contrasts with belief in two respects. First, knowledge must be *true*, the second requirement is the elusive one we have been discussing. Many writers have assumed that what is sought is an extra condition to be added to justified true belief, but I want to defend the plausibility of Ramsey's suggestion that reliability replace justification in the analysis. Thus we are considering the suggestion that true belief reliably acquired is knowledge. On this view it is the method by which a belief is arrived at which determines whether or not it is knowledge, the question of whether the belief is thought to be justified by the knower or by external commentators or observers is irrelevant, except insofar as justification is connected with reliability. Obviously in some cases justification and reliability will be related; to infer R by explicit deduction from known premises justifies R, and is also a reliable method of arriving at the belief that R. Note, however, that on a reliability analysis we can simply stop with the observation that explicit deduction from known premises is a reliable method of forming beliefs. If one requires that the belief be justified then there is at least one remaining open question, namely how one justifies the use of the deductive rules. The analysis of knowledge in terms of justification is prey in many different forms to regress difficulties whereas the reliability analysis is not. There is always the question whether something is justified if one does not know the justification, whereas there is not the same problem with reliability. Many things may be reliable without our knowing that they are reliable or why they are reliable if they are. Questions of justification require answers in terms of principles or rules, but questions of reliability lead to considerations of the methods by which beliefs are formed. The first leads to a Cartesian scrutiny of what principles can be justified in the absence of any knowledge about ourselves or the world whereas the second leads to consideration of persons as complex organisms in a complex physical world.

For example, consider a typical case of basic beliefs, Smith's belief that there is a purple plastic table in front of him. Suppose that this is true and that the light is normal, Smith is not drugged or affected in other unusual ways, that he is wearing proper glasses and so on. We have a second paradigm case of a reliable method of forming beliefs; to observe a middle sized object of a familiar type under normal circumstances is a reliable method of forming beliefs concerning familiar properties of the object. Is Smith's belief justified? Well, if it is then it is justified because the circumstances are normal, because Smith is not drugged, because human beings have certain abilities to make visual discriminations and so on. Does Smith know any of this – in many cases clearly not, or at least not clearly. The reliability analysis of knowledge leads to questions of why a method is reliable, to empirical questions about how people function and what the world is like; the justificatory analysis of knowing leads to questions of how one knows the principles underlying the justification. Thus the first count on which the reliability theory is preferable is its avoidance of implausible psychological postulation and regress difficulties.

A second argument for the reliability analysis can be constructed from considering historical attributions of knowledge. Presumably scientists knew many things about the world before Bacon and Mill formulated the principles of induction which would justify the claims. Again the reliability theory faces no difficulties on this score – whether or not the methods used by scientists are reliable is independent of whether they could prove that or even of whether they could give suitable descriptions of the method. On a justification view, however, the familiar dilemma recurs – to demand conscious justification is too strong, to allow hypothetical justification from the other beliefs of the scientist is too weak, and to appeal to non-conscious processes paralleling the later justification lacks any content. I would argue that the reason that Mill and other philosophers of science have studied scientific practice is because they recognised that scientists did know many facts about the world and they wanted to analyse what the method was.

The argument may perhaps be sharper in non-scientific cases. Imagine two persons totally ignorant of modern or ancient scientific theory, one of whom predicts rain on the basis of "feelings in her bones" and the other on the basis of his observations of tea leaves. The only justification that either could give of their claim to know that it will rain today would be appeal to past successes. Let us assume that each has only made a few predictions and each has always been correct thus far. It seems clear to me that if there is a reliable connection, for example, between barometric pressure and the feelings in people's bones and if the one predictor is reasonably accurate in observing the feelings then she knows that it will rain. But, assuming no reliable connection between tea leaves and weather, it seems clear that the second predictor does not know. The only way I can see a justificatory theory of knowledge handling this type of example is by claiming that the existence of the elaborate scientific justification is what warrants the claim to knowledge, but this makes it extremely obscure why one would want to say that the person in question knew.

Thus far I have been giving examples where the reliability theory of knowledge seems preferable to the justificatory theories because it can explain attributions of knowledge where they are difficult to explain on the alternative theory. Now let us consider some cases of non-knowledge. It should be indisputable that the method of forming a belief by deducing a statement from others is not reliable when important premises are false. Whether the false premises are believed, justified, very strongly justified or whatever is irrelevant: the method is unreliable. Hence the Gettier cases will all be discounted as cases of not knowing since essential premises are false. In general, I see no difficulties arising from the Gettier examples for the reliability theory since what is in question on this theory is the process by which the belief was arrived at, not beliefs the person may have about the process. In particular, it does not matter that the person believes the premises to be true. Of course it is necessary that if a belief is arrived at by explicit inference from premises that the premises be ones which are themselves known, since inference from capriciously formed beliefs will not be a reliable method either.

A further example of the way in which the reliability approach provides insight into problems and disputes is its application to Goldman's so-called causal theory of knowledge. Goldman (1967) claimed that in cases of knowledge involving empirical knowledge about particulars it is part of the truth conditions for the knowledge claim that the known fact have a causal connection with the knower's state of belief. There are considerable difficulties in both the statement and defense of the doctrine, for the notion of causal connection in general is somewhat obscure, as is the notion of a fact.

Further, in order to allow many ordinary cases of knowledge he must allow that the connection may include non-conscious processes of inference under some conditions. Two restrictions must also be noted in setting out Goldman's theory; he considers the theory to provide only the truth conditions of knowledge statements, not an analysis of their meaning, and he considers the analysis to apply only to empirical statements.

If we assume that the reliability analysis is correct, then we can explain why in many cases there is a requirement of some kind of causal connection for knowledge of particulars. It happens to be true because of facts about human beings and the world that, in many cases, knowledge about past and present states of the world can be reliably obtained only if certain causal relations occur. The anomalous status of inference in Goldman's theory is easily seen to be explicable as another method of (sometimes) forming reliable beliefs. A knowledge claim directly requires reliability, but causal considerations only enter *via* further facts about people and the world. It is not surprising that Goldman's analysis can provide truth conditions but not an analysis of meaning.

On the issues of non-empirical knowledge (assuming that Goldman means to include mathematics), it is easy to show that his own position – that the traditional analysis works in the mathematical realm – is incorrect. I may have formed a true belief about a theorem in topology because I derived it from a theorem in a textbook; I may be justified because the textbook is a well-known and respectable one and I have verified the proof in the book to my satisfaction. Still, the text theorem could be false, and if so my justified true belief in my own theorem would not be knowledge. Benacerraf (1973) has attempted to utilise the requirement of a Goldman type theory for mathematical knowledge as an argument against certain positions in philosophy of mathematics. However, if my analysis of knowledge is correct, this approach is misguided. If knowledge requires reliability, then although reliability may require causal connections for knowledge about protons, poplars, planets and putty, there is no reason to think that reliability requires causal connection when it is the properties of numbers, sets of functions that are in question. I have argued elsewhere that, for example, a Platonistic view of mathematical knowledge is epistemologically bankrupt because of its failure to provide an account of how we reliably acquire mathematical beliefs (Grandy 1977).

Having argued for the plausibility of a reliability analysis (or at least partial analysis) of knowledge, let us now consider the task of making the concept of a reliable process. There are two significantly different ways of understanding this crucial phrase and both paths have been followed. The first post–Ramsey discussion of reliability and knowledge that I am aware of is that of J. Watling (1954). With regard to knowledge of future events Watling allows that someone who reliably has true beliefs has knowledge, regardless of whether they can give any justification. (He does not use the word 'reliable' but the term fits well his conception.) Some of his passages are unclear as to how strict a requirement he intends:

For it is not true that people know facts only when they have made predictions and verified them: they need only the ability to make correct predictions (Watling 1954: 90).

This passage leaves it unclear whether the 'ability to make correct predictions' is to be taken as requiring the ability to *invariably* make correct predictions, or only *occasionally*. But a later discussion of other minds indicates that he requires at most a high percentage:

however right or wrong we may be about the minds of others, or however adequate or inadequate our evidence for our beliefs about them, yet we certainly know that they are often correct in their assertions about our experiences and thoughts. Surely this is sufficient warrant for me to assert that some other people have knowledge of at least one other mind, my own (97).

The alternative stronger requirement was first, so far as I know, proposed by P. Unger (1968), again without reference to Ramsey or use of 'reliability'. Unger's analysis of knowledge is that:

For any sentential value of p, (at a time t) a man knows that p if and only if (at t) it is not at all accidental that the man is right about its being the case that p (Unger 1968: 158).

Unger, and also Armstrong (1973), who is a later, more explicit proponent of a strong reliability analysis, both give the same general form of argument for a strong requirement, as opposed to a statistical one, as follows.

Consider someone confronted with a deck of well-shuffled cards face down. Since the deck is well-shuffled and there is but one ace of spades among the cards, it is very unlikely that the ace of spades is the topmost card, in fact the chances are 1/52. If the subject believes the top card is not the ace of spades and, as a matter of fact, the topmost card is the three of clubs, then unless we set the statistical requirement for reliability higher than 0.98, our subject has reached a true belief by a reliable method. Both Unger and Armstrong find this implausible, not only with the specific numerical probabilities in the case but for any probabilistic argument.

Armstrong gives a further articulation of his reasons for rejecting a probabilistic treatment of reliability as a knowledge condition. It is, he says, highly plausible, given the intuitive concept of knowledge, that if S knows A and knows B, and consciously infers A & B knowing the relevant inference rule, that S then knows A & B. But for any value of $r < 1$ that we choose as the cutoff point, so that a process with higher reliability suffices for knowledge, we will find cases where the inference does not provide knowledge.

While Unger discusses numerous examples in an effort to clarify his key locution 'it is not at all accidental' he never gives a more formal account of how to apply his analysis. Thus we turn to Armstrong who has given the most detailed and extended treatment of a strict reliabilist analysis. He divides the problem into two parts, the analysis of non-inferential knowledge and then an analysis of inferential knowledge. In each case the key ingredient is the requirement that there be a nomic connection between the situation in which the belief is formed and its truth.

More explicitly:

A's non-inferential belief that c is a J is a case of non-inferential *knowledge* if, and only if:

(i) Jc
(ii) $(\exists H)$ [Ha & there is a law-like connection in nature (x) (y) {if Hx, then (if $BxJy$, then Jy)}]. x ranges over beings capable of cognition (1973: 170).

Armstrong adds a further qualification to the effect that it should not follow from Hx alone that Jy and also stipulates that 'H' must not be so detailed that it could not apply in other cases as well. Thus the idea is that 'H' specifies conditions of the believer A (whose logical name apparently is 'a') and of the environment such that under those conditions A would believe something to be J only if it were J.

A pair of examples will help to clarify the initial plausibility of the general approach before we consider some problems about the details of Armstrong's definition. Imagine Adam and Alice each standing ten feet from an oak tree on a clear fall day with bright sun and no other trees, brush or other obstacles between them and the oak. Each forms non-inferentially the belief 'That is an oak tree.' Let us suppose that Alice is a forester who can, with a second's thought, also identify which type of oak is present. And suppose that Adam, so far as we can tell, cannot discriminate an oak from a maple but was apparently lucky in this instance. Clearly we would want to say that Alice knew, and Adam did not, that there was an oak tree there. Armstrong's analysis is intended to capture this intuition by requiring a law-like connection between the situation, believer, and believed statement.

Returning to the details of his analysis we can see that it is essential that the connection be law-like rather than logical. For example, if we let 'H' be 'x has no false non-inferential beliefs about oak trees in his immediate environment', then the fact that Adam satisfies 'H' and believes what he does will imply that his belief is true. Let us therefore understand Armstrong's condition 'law-like' as 'law-like and not logical'.

Notice that because of the logical form of Armstrong's condition, namely the existential quantifier over properties, we cannot be certain that Adam does not have knowledge. It is possible that although Adam has no better than a 50% record at identifying oaks as opposed to maples when presented with specimens of each, some particular subset of oaks have a specific configuration so that he is always correct about those. And our case might, unbeknownst to us, be one instance of the type about which he is reliable. Note how far removed this reliability analysis is from a justification analysis of knowledge – Adam might have knowledge even though no one, including himself, would currently regard his belief as justified.

Having noted the difficulty in disproving the occurrence of knowledge, let us consider whether we can establish that Alice does know by finding a suitable 'H'. We cannot mention as part of the condition that there is an oak tree in the environment, so presumably we must specify such matters as the shape of the leaves and the visual texture and shape of the apparent trunk and branches. However, I doubt that this will do the job. Is it impossible that someone could in principle create a sufficiently clever imitation of an oak tree so that Alice or someone else with the relevant training would be fooled for a brief instant? If it is possible in principle then Alice does not know that there is an oak tree in front of her now.

Armstrong seems by example to accept this point. In discussing whether his analysis might not put too stringent a demand on knowledge he replies:

Our analysis would have no tendency to discredit the statement that I know that there is a piece of paper before me. Or if, as is likely, this knowledge involves an inferential component, then let the example be that I know that there is something white, oblong, more or less flat and with blue horizontal markings before me (1973: 188).

Thus it appears that Armstrong expects at most that his analysis will justify claims to non-inferential knowledge about qualitative features of the environment. This is in itself rather worrying since many of us are in the habit of forming less cautious non-inferential beliefs.

Let us set aside this worry, however, and turn to Armstrong's treatment of inferential knowledge to determine how a suitably cautious non-inferential knower can extend her or his stock of knowledge by inference. To quote in full:

the suggested conditions for A's inferential knowledge that p become:
  (i) A believes that p
 (ii) A knows that q (noninferentially)
(iii) A's belief that q actually functions in A's mind as a conclusive reason
      for believing that p
(iv) A knows the truth of the general principle of his reasoning (199–200).

(ii) is clearly too restrictive, for many cases of inferential knowledge do not depend simply upon one non-inferential item of knowledge. (Recall that even if q and r are each non-inferential q & r need not be.) But the emendation required for (ii) is neither difficult nor exciting, and our attention will focus on (iv).

Armstrong notes that the requirement (iv) threatens to subject his analysis to regress difficulties if the knowledge in it must be inferential. Therefore he adopts the alternative apparent possibility and proposes an account of non-inferential knowledge of general principles.

It is important to see that his notion of a general principle of reasoning is not, as one might have expected, something like *modus ponens* or a straight rule of induction. The examples of general propositions that he discusses are more concrete generalisations such as 'All arsenic is poisonous.' Thus, to give the analysis more specificity, he apparently intends that 'p' would have the form 'c is poisonous' and 'q' the form 'c is arsenic'. I do not elaborate this point, which is left implicit in the text for reasons that will soon become manifest.

Moving on to the next analysis, that of non-inferential knowledge of a general proposition, we are told:

A knows that (x) (if Fx, then Gx) if, and only if:

(i) A believes that (x) (if Fx, then Gx)

(ii) If this disposition (this general belief) is *manifested*, then (x) (if A *knows* that Fx, then A *knows* that Gx)

(iii) $(\exists J) [Ja$ and there is a law-like connection in nature such that (y) [if Jy, then {if conditions (i) and (ii) hold, then $(\exists z)(Fz)$}]] (204).[1]

If we recall the reason that we were led to inquire into the non-inferential knowledge of general propositions, (ii) is troubling. It does not make analysis totally circular, for when we test whether A knows that Gc on the basis of non-inferential knowledge of Fc and of the principle that (x) (if Fx then Gx) we may be able to disprove A's knowledge claim by finding a d such that A knows Fd and does not know Gd, thus falsifying (ii) of this analysis and (iv) of the previous one. But as a positive condition it is circular – for we cannot establish (ii) without establishing that Gc is known by A. Thus Armstrong's analysis is useless for establishing inferential knowledge claims.

An alternative to Armstrong's analysis would be to attempt to give a straightforward account of knowledge of (x) (if Fx then Gx) more exactly parallel to Armstrong's account for singular non-inferential knowledge. The difficulty with this approach is that it is very implausible that the conditions are ever met. What would be required would be a condition H such that anyone who satisfied conditions H and believed a general statement of this form would have a true belief. But however reliable we may be in specified circumstances about perceptual matters, our reliability about truly general statements is virtually non-existent if we make unfailing truth the condition of reliability.

Yet another alternative would be to conceive of the inferences as governed by principles that have the form of inductive rules rather than specific generalisations. This latter is a view that Russell at times espoused (Russell 1912). But inductive principles have their weakness within a *strict* reliability framework: either the principle is true but merely confers probability on the conclusion, or else the

[1] If (iii) is to make any sense we must assume that $a = A$ and that in (iii) the bracketed reference to conditions (i) and (ii) is intended to be a reference to the result of replacing occurrences of 'A' there by occurrences of 'y'.

principle asserts the truth of the conclusion but is itself only a probable instrument. In either case it would be peculiar to relax the sense of stringency attached to reliability here and to insist on the strong requirement for non-inferential knowledge. Thus any alternative seems to end us in a regress, to leave us without much knowledge worth mentioning or to lead back to the probabilistic approach.

What is a pragmatist to do? We have the choice of arguing that knowledge does not (should not?) satisfy the conjunction condition or giving up on knowledge. My own preference is for the latter – knowledge is an epistemological concept whose origins trace back to a time when we had far less detailed or satisfactory theories about the universe, let alone about our own cognition and perception. I suspect that the origins of the *knowledge that* sense of the term stem from a model in which knowledge that q is like acquaintance with a particular. The only difference would be that in the case of knowledge that q one would be acquainted with the state of affairs that q. This is not, or at least was not, a silly view. But acquaintances with states of affairs have no place in our current views of epistemology.

Does this represent capitulation to scepticism? In one sense of scepticism it does. I am suggesting that there is no knowledge, just as there is no absolute space or centre of the universe. But this negative remark about knowledge does not mean that some beliefs are not more reliable than others any more than the corresponding remark about space implies that all bodies are equidistant from each other. I must concede that a major difference between the two examples is that we have thus far only a very poorly developed theory of reliability, but perhaps clearing away the old concepts and terminology will facilitate and motivate development of a positive theory.

Would Ramsey concur with my suggestion? His 'Knowledge' includes a discussion of a problem raised by Russell that is similar to the difficulty that we have seen about conjunction, namely that we may claim to know p, q, r, . . . and yet also claim to know that at least one of these is wrong. In his note Ramsey never resolves this problem but it is not implausible, especially given his interest in probabilistic matters, that he would eventually have moved in this direction.

University of North Carolina at Chapel Hill

REFERENCES

Armstrong, D. 1973. *Belief, Truth and Knowledge*. Cambridge.

Benacerraf, P. 1973. Mathematical truth. *Journal of Philosophy* **70**, 661–79.

Grandy, R. E. 1977. In defense of a modest Platonism, *Philosophical Studies* **30**, 359–69.

Goldman, A. I. 1967. A causal theory of knowing, *Journal of Philosophy* **64**, 357–72.

Ramsey, F. P. 1929. Knowledge. In his *Foundations*, ed. D. H. Mellor, pp. 126–7. 1978. London.

Russell, B. 1912. *The Problems of Philosophy*. Oxford.

Unger, P. 1968. An analysis of factual knowledge, *Journal of Philosophy* **65**, 157–69.

Watling, J. 1954. Inference from the known to the unknown. *Proceedings of the Aristotelian Society* **55**, 83–108.

10 *The problem of natural laws*

L. JONATHAN COHEN

Inseparable from the concept of a law is the contrastability of a law with an accidentally true generalisation. The problem is: how is this contrast possible? In **1** I shall attempt to make the question more precise. In **2** I shall discuss Ramsey's truth-functionalist answer to it. In **3** I shall discuss whether some recent possible-worlds models for modal logic can provide a better answer. And in **4** I shall propose an answer in epistemological rather than meaning-theoretical terms.

1 *A statement of the problem.* The question at issue has an easy answer if the relevant laws are those prescriptive ones that regulate human society. On the one hand there may be a law that makes any trade in rocket-driven lawn-mowers illegal: on the other, every actual commercial transaction in rocket-driven lawn-mowers may turn out to be illegal, for one or another of a variety of different reasons (unlicensed trader, false representation, excessive price, violation of import restrictions, *etc.*). In the former case there has been specific legislation; in the latter, a series of largely unconnected offences. Nor can we readily find a sentence-utterance that is ambiguous between these two interpretations. Law-makers have accustomed us to expect imperative moods, future tenses, or other prescriptive idioms from them, whereas reports of coincidences of the above sort fall more naturally into the indicative mood and past tense of historical discourse.

Difficulties begin to appear as soon as the distinction is transferred from norm-bound human society to the factuality of the physical universe. You might think that at least in the initial stage of this transfer, when a Divine legislator merely replaces a human one, the metaphor would be trouble-free. Not so. If God is assumed to be omniscient, he must be thought of as willing *every* regularity that emerges (except perhaps through human free-will) from his creation of the physical universe. So the distinction can only be preserved if the conception of a Divine legislator is buttressed by some such adjunct as a premiss of Divine Wisdom, as in Leibniz, whereby the laws may be distinguished from the consequential coincidences by being the specifically chosen instrument of this Wisdom. But in secular culture such a theological conception of natural law can hardly be the dominant one. Instead deontic modalities are replaced by alethic ones, and law is identified with necessity. Or at any rate that is what happens in a popular locution like

(1)   Where there's fire there must be heat.

An even more radical step would be to eliminate modality altogether. But there are limits to how far we can go here. These limits are set by the fact that we cannot dispense altogether with the distinction between a law and an accidental uniformity, because they have different deductive potentials.

The point has normally been put by claiming that laws underwrite unfulfilled (counterfactual) conditionals, while accidentally true generalisations do not. This was what Ramsey (1978: 133) claimed, and many others have followed him. For example, Goodman (1954), Rescher (1964), and others have discussed issues that arise about the premisses that are cotenable with a counterfactual condition. And that outcome of those discussions has been the thesis that, when inconsistencies are being eliminated from a set of propositions that are to constitute cotenable premisses, retention of a generalisation in preference to a singular proposition is a sign that the generalisation is functioning as a statement of a law rather than as a statement of a coincidence. Thus given the three premisses

(2)   That dog is one of my dogs [the counterfactual condition],

(3)   All my dogs are white,

and

(4)   That dog is not white,

we may be inclined to preserve consistency by rejecting (3) rather than (4); and this is to be taken as a sign that we are treating (3) as being at best an accidental truth. Conversely, it follows, if we reject (4) rather than (3), as in the inference corresponding to

(5)   If that dog had been one of my dogs, it would have been white,

we must be treating (3) as the statement of a law or of a consequence of one in the relevant circumstances (perhaps the water in my well, which my dogs have to drink, contains a chemical that bleaches every hair of the animals that drink it).

But some caution is necessary here. On another reading of (5), it also matches an inference from (2) and (3), but from (3) as an accidental truth (perhaps you needed to know (5) in order to be convinced that the dog was not mine because you know it to be brown). So it looks as though we can't distinguish laws from accidentally true generalisations just by whether or not they generate counterfactual conditionals, as Ramsey and others have supposed. Pretty well every accidental uniformity turns out to be usable as a help for recognising non-membership of its subject-class, in circumstances where we stand in need of such help; and then the appropriate counterfactual, like (5), is deducible. Admittedly some accidental uniformities look at first sight rather unpromising candidates for this role, like

(6)   All the men in this room are bald.

But if you first tell me that over the telephone, and then later a question arises whether a certain suspect, whom we all know as Mr X, was in your room at that time, I can say to someone else

(7)   If Mr X had been one of those in the room, he would have been bald

whereas we all know him to be hirsute. Here (7) is undoubtedly based on (6).

In order to draw the distinction that Ramsey wanted we have to differentiate between ampliative and non-ampliative counterfactuals. An ampliative counterfactual is one whose antecedent posits the existence of at least one more entity satisfying a specified condition than the actual world contains. A non-ampliative counterfactual is content for its antecedent to envisage a possibility that would not increase the number of entities satisfying the relevant condition. So a statement of natural law like (1) can be said to be a uniformity that generates both ampliative counterfactuals like

(8)   If there had been a fire in this room, it would have been warm

and also non-ampliative ones like

If there had been a fire in this room, instead of in the study, it would have been warm.

But an accidentally true statement, like (6) – on its most plausible reading – only summarises what is actual, and can therefore generate only non-ampliative counterfactuals, like (7).

The problem of natural laws may now be reformulated: how is it that some general statements (when conjoined with whatever co-adjutor premisses are appropriate) entail ampliative counterfactuals? And now we have a secondary problem also: how is it that some general statements (when conjoined with analogous additional premisses) entail only non-ampliative counterfactuals?

2 *Ramsey's solution.* In 1928 Ramsey (1978: 128–32) suggested that causal laws are consequences of those truth-functional propositions which we should take as axioms if we knew everything and organised it as simply as possible in a deductive system. Actually he would need to have added some further constraints on the idea of such a system if his suggestion was to draw an adequate contrast between causal laws and accidentally true generalisations. For in a system that axiomatises everything we know both types of proposition would be derivable, just as in a system created by an omniscient God, as I remarked earlier, every actual uniformity would have been willed. Perhaps Ramsey could have excluded this by requiring the derivation of causal laws to proceed without using as premisses any statements about specified individuals. But in any case he (1978: 138) rejected the theory a year later, in 1929, on the ground that it is impossible to know everything and to organise it in a deductive system. He then developed what he took to be a rather different view. But, if certain *prima facie* inconsistencies and implausibilities in this second theory are ironed out, it comes to look remarkably similar to the first one.

Ramsey's second theory suggested (1978: 137) that "causal laws form the system with which the speaker meets the future". They "are not judgments but rules for judging 'If I meet a φ, I shall regard it as a ψ.' This cannot be *negated* but it can be disagreed with by one who does not adopt it" (Ramsey's italics). Perhaps someone would object that Ramsey's view does not allow us to state the existence of an unknown causal law. Ramsey's answer is that to make such a statement is to claim that there are facts which, if we knew them, would lead us to assert a causal law. This answer obviously makes use of a subjunctive conditional that must itself depend on a law of some kind, but Ramsey denies any circularity. The causal law, he says, in virtue of which the facts would lead us to the generalisation is not itself an unknown law but the known principles "expressing our methods of inductive reasoning" (1978: 141). Again, someone might object that Ramsey's view seems to deprive causal laws of the objectivity that we are inclined to attribute to them. But the only facts, on Ramsey's view, are particular occurrences. Like Hume he refused to take causal necessity as a feature of nature. He admits that people may at present find more than one system of truth-functional generalisations that fits the known facts. But, he says (1978: 149).

we do . . . believe that the system is uniquely determined and that long enough investigation will lead us all to it. This is Peirce's notion of truth as what everyone will believe in the end; it does not apply to the truthful statement of matters of fact, but to the 'true scientific system'.

Now clearly the system with which a particular present-day speaker is prepared to meet the future need not be, nor even be thought by him to be, the system that everyone will believe in the end. So to preserve consistency Ramsey would have had to reformulate his view somewhat. Perhaps Ramsey should rather have said that what a speaker sincerely asserts to be a causal law is a rule of inference about matters of fact that is at least believed by the speaker to be part of the true scientific system that everyone will believe in the end, and also, where its content is specified, part of the system with which the speaker himself meets the future.

But this formulation is open to a number of objections. Not everyone is so optimistic as to believe that intelligent life in the universe will continue long enough, under conditions of free inquiry, for a conclusive scientific consensus to emerge. Scientists might be bludgeoned into unanimous error by oppressive governments, or they might just relapse into premature unanimity through intellectual complacency. Or, even if neither of these disasters occurred, intelligent life might still die out too soon. Peirce's pragmatist conception of truth is acceptable only if you have rather strong convictions about the power of human intelligence to maintain not only life, but also scientific progress, for as long as is needed. But the vicissitudes of past history – both human and geophysical – do not offer much evidence to support such convictions.

The obvious way to rescue Ramsey's analysis from the above objections is to identify the true scientific system as the one that everyone *would* believe in the end *if* free scientific enquiry continued long enough. We might call this 'idealised pragmatism'. It has, of course, an appearance of circularity because it seems to use a subjunctive (and probably counterfactual) conditional in order to elucidate the derivability of such conditionals. But in any case no one could be sure that free scientific inquiry had continued long enough unless he already knew every fact, *i.e.* every observable occurrence. And any free scientific inquiry must surely pay due regard to the various criteria of simplicity that deserve to be respected. Accordingly, the true scientific system is now being identified as the one that we should regard as the simplest axiomatisation of our knowledge if we perceived everything. That is to say, Ramsey's second analysis has had to be reformulated in such a way that it is not seriously distinguishable from his first one. It is therefore open to the objection that he himself made against his first analysis: factual omniscience is impossible and unaxiomatisable.

How fatal is this objection to idealised pragmatism? Omniscience is certainly impossible for human beings: their adaptation for survival does not require it. Their conceptual apparatus permits only certain kinds of discriminations and is open only to a rather gradual and inconclusive self-improvement. Their sensory organs permit only a relatively narrow range of sensation. Even on earth many animals have sensations of a kind that humans do not, and humans may never have any knowledge about the perceptual capacities of extra-terrestrial intelligences, if any exist. Indeed, even on earth most of what happens goes unperceived by intelligent creatures, and however long human observations continue into the future they have certainly missed almost all the past. Moreover the universe is so vast, and intelligent life apparently so rare in it, that most of what happens is bound to go unobserved by anyone at all. But, just so far as we can understand various ways in which recorded human observation falls short of omniscience, we are cut off from arguing that the concept of omniscience is somehow inconsistent or incoherent. Ramsey's own objection to his first analysis (and, by implication, to idealised pragmatism) is therefore rather a weak one.

A different and rather stronger objection is nevertheless available. Why should we accept Ramsey's unargued assumption that what he calls 'the true scientific system' is uniquely determined, even by the observations of an omniscient intelligence? The universe might just be so tantalisingly niggardly with crucial data that some choices between rival scientific theories – or between rival methodologies for choosing between rival scientific theories – remain for ever underdetermined, with some generalisations figuring as laws in one theory but as accidental truths in another. Idealised pragmatism, just like ordinary pragmatism, is acceptable only if you believe that the universe is rather conveniently adapted to the aims of scientific inquiry. But this belief requires underpinning either by an epistemologically oriented conception of Divine Providence or by a thoroughly Kantian metaphysics, neither of which fits in well with Ramsey's other views.

It would, however, be open to Ramsey to reply: 'The belief may be true, nevertheless, and faith in the progress of science requires us to hold it.' I am inclined, therefore, to argue that this point, though a powerful one, is not a decisive objection to Ramsey's account of natural laws. The most serious trouble with that account is something quite different: it lacks any explanatory or elucidatory force. At best it characterises (with the aid of some such constraints on derivation as the one that I suggested earlier) a certain class of generalisations, which it claims to be identical with the extension of the term 'law of nature'. But it says nothing to explain why, when we in our own generation take a supposed subset of this class to provide the rules for our system of material inference, we assume that we can apply such rules not only to situations which actually occur but also to situations which do not actually occur. On Ramsey's account the generalisations are merely consequences of an axiomatised representation of the actual. So, however vast and complete this representation of the actual may be, what entitles us to assume that, if we had it, it would also give us knowledge about the non-actual – knowledge of true ampliative counterfactuals?

The same criticism may be made of other accounts, like those of Carnap (1936), Braithwaite (1953: 297ff), Popper (1959: 62ff and 420ff) and Quine (1969: 131ff), which also offer truth-functional characterisations of the semantic role of terms like 'law of nature'. Generally there are also some difficulties about the details of the characterisation: *cf.* Cohen (1966: 305–11) on Popper and Braithwaite, and Cohen (1977: 325–7) on Quine and Carnap. But even if some such characterisation were adequate it would still not suffice to untie the knot at the heart of the problem: how can such laws generate ampliative counterfactuals? Still less would it explain why some generalisations, that are not entailed by laws, are themselves capable of generating non-ampliative counterfactuals.

3 *Possible worlds solutions.* Many recent approaches to the problem of counterfactuals have abandoned truth-functionalism and have tried instead to exploit the conception of alternative possible worlds in various ways. And though there are general objections, as in Cohen (1977: 242–4), to the use of this conception for philosophical purposes, it would be a mistake to rely on those objections here, since there are other – more specific and more revealing – reasons why theories about alternative possible worlds cannot contribute much towards solving the problem of natural law.

One such approach – that of R. C. Stalnaker (1968), D. Lewis (1973), and others – is via the definition of a special conditional connective as holding between certain statements in virtue of what is the case in some one or more possible but non-actual worlds. So, according to Stalnaker, counterfactual conditionals are "statements about particular counterfactual worlds" (1968: 104). But, of course, if the falsehood of a law of nature is logically possible (as Hume has persuaded most modern philosophers), there are many possible but non-actual worlds in which conterfactuals like (8) would be false because laws like (1) were false. Also most counterfactuals presuppose the truth of certain cotenable statements of initial conditions, alongside that of the appropriate law, and in many possible but non-actual worlds counterfactuals like (8) would be false because some of the required statements of co-occurring initial conditions were false. (8) might not be true if the window had been left open. Accordingly these treatments of the problem need a selection-function that ranges over possible worlds and selects those in which a given counterfactual conditional would be true. But, unfortunately, any feasible definition of the right function, or class of functions, seems inevitably to invoke the concept of a law of nature. Thus Stalnaker (1968: 104) stipulates "that there are no differences between the actual world and the selected world except those that are required, implicitly or explicitly, by the antecedent". But how can we know what differences are *required* by the antecedent? it certainly won't do to restrict these requirements to those of logical implication, since one of the differences required by the antecedent of a counterfactual like (8) is the truth of the consequent, and requirement operates here *via* causal necessitation. Similarly, Lewis defines physical necessity as truth in all worlds "where the actual laws of nature hold true" (1973: 5), and he himself offers (1973: 73) a restatement of Ramsey's first analysis as his definition of the concept of a law of nature. In short this kind of possible-worlds theory does not offer a solution to our present problem. It is capable of elucidating the logic of ampliative counterfactuals on the assumption that you are not at all puzzled about what a law of nature is. But, if you are puzzled about this, it cannot contribute anything towards resolving your puzzlement.

The difficulty here seems to arise just because the class of physically possible worlds is not co-extensive with the class of logically possible ones. If what was physically necessary was true in all logically possible worlds, the need for a selection-function would not arise. The problem about laws of nature would be reduced to that about logical possibility, and the former concept would be elucidated in terms of the latter. Of course, such a solution would have to reject Hume's contention that there is nothing contrary to reason in supposing the falsehood of a law of nature. But Hume's psychologistic treatment of natural necessity was in any case unsatisfactory. It might explain our belief that (8) is derivable from (1), but it could never show how we are entitled to derive (8) from (1). So perhaps we should not allow merely Humean scruples to weigh against the theory that has been advocated by Putnam (1962) and (1973) and Kripke (1972) on semantical grounds. As Kripke puts it, terms for natural kinds, such as 'cow', 'heat' or 'gold', are to be understood as rigid designators, in the sense that precisely the same species or kind of entity is designated, in whatever possible situation the entity is supposed to be present. Membership of the species or kind is an essential property of the entity, by whatever criteria that membership is currently recognised. Consequently, if an identity is asserted between two such natural kinds, as in

(9) Gold has the atomic number 79

or in

(10) Heat is molecular motion,

the identity must hold good in all possible worlds, if it holds in the actual one; and this is true also for non-analytic assertions of a sub-class relationship between natural kinds, as in

(11) Whales are mammals.

Statements like (9), (10) and (11) thus come to express necessary truths, despite the fact that their truth is empirically discovered.

Admittedly people might think that they can imagine a possible world in which heat is not molecular motion. But, says Kripke (p. 325), what they would actually be imagining is a world in which creatures with different nerve endings from ours inhabit the planet and are sensitive to something else, say light, in such a way that they feel the same thing as we feel when we feel heat.

The semantical considerations that have been advanced by Putnam and Kripke in favour of this neo-essentialism are not strong: compare Zemach (1976), Mellor (1977) and Margalit (1979). But refutation of those considerations still leaves open the question whether neo-essentialism may not be acceptable on other grounds. In particular, if neo-essentialism can give an adequate explanation of the necessity that we attribute to laws of nature, we should perhaps try to adjust our semantical doctrines accordingly. But in fact the Putnam–Kripke thesis turns out to be seriously defective as an explanation of nomological necessity. It cannot accommodate at least one important category of natural law, if natural laws are to be characterised, as in 1 above, by the derivability of ampliative counterfactuals.

Specifically, the neo-essentialist thesis does not allow for the derivability of ampliative counterfactuals from statements like

(12)   Gold is yellow

where yellowness is treated as an identifying, not an essential, attribute of gold, as in

(13)   If this ring had been gold, it would have been yellow.

The fact is that neo-essentialism requires the existence of such contingent attributes, to act as the criteria whereby we detect essential ones. There has to be a contrast between statements of discovered essences like (9) and (10), which are both empirical and necessary according to the theory, and other statements about a natural kind, like (12) perhaps, which are empirical but contingent. Kripke states this quite explicitly about heat (1972: 326), when he remarks that "the property by which we identify it originally, that of producing such and such a sensation in us, is not a necessary property but a contingent one". Of course, he goes on, "it might be part of the very nature of human beings that they have the neural structure which is sensitive to heat. Therefore this too could turn out to be necessary if enough investigation showed it." But then human beings would still have to be characterised by some contingent property in order that the referent of the term 'human nature' may be properly identified. If the Kripke–Putnam theory is correct, then even at the stage of our investigations at which we have not yet discovered the essence of a natural kind, and cannot claim knowledge of necessary truth about it, we need nevertheless to feel entitled to formulate ampliative counterfactuals like (13) in order to assist in identifying instances of the natural kind in question. That is, we need to feel entitled to formulate ampliative counterfactuals on the basis of generalisations like (12), for which, according to the theory, we can at that time claim only contingent truth. In short neo-essentialism, so far from solving the problem of natural laws, serves only to shift its location.

It looks therefore as though theories about alternative possible worlds are intrinsically incapable of resolving that problem. Either such a theory assumes that a puzzle-free concept of natural law is already available in order to mark off what is physically possible within the much larger area of what is logically possible. Or it avoids this assumption at the cost of extending the validity of certain natural laws, but not all, to truth in all logically possible worlds and leaving the nomologicality of other natural laws wholly unelucidated.

Nor is it at all easy to see how a theory about alternative possible worlds could contribute much towards solving the other half of the problem. Such a theory seems to be intrinsically handicapped in trying to elucidate how it is that only non-ampliative counterfactuals are deducible from accidentally true generalisations. What kind of selection-function should we use in order to pick out just those possible but non-actual worlds in which (3) is accidentally true? If the function allows us to include worlds in which I own more than my actual number of dogs, then the counterfactuals that it licenses would not all be non-ampliative. But, if the function is appropriately restricted, so as to pick out only those possible but non-actual worlds in which I own just the same number of dogs as I actually do, then the possible worlds model merely restates the circumstances of the problem without contributing anything towards its elucidation. After all, if one hadn't thought at all about the nature of the derivable counterfactual, one might well have expected that no such restriction would be needed. Certainly there are many other possible worlds where I own a different number of dogs but where it is still accidentally true that all my dogs are white.

4 *An epistemological elucidation.* The task of an explanatory account of the law/accident contrast is to locate the distinction within a wider context which somehow gives rise to it. We have seen (section 2) the failure of attempts like Ramsey's to achieve this *via* a truth-functional characterisation of the class of statements that we call 'laws of nature'. Equally (section 3) the modal resources of possible-worlds logic are incapable of achieving the required elucidation. But we should not be too disappointed by these failures. It would really be quite surprising if there were indeed some equivalent locution that was not rather trivially synonymous. We learn a lot in philosophy by seeking such a solution and discovering why this or that proposed analysis is inadequate. But human language is rarely so rich in unexpected equivalences that a reductive analysis can be both correct and interesting. After all there are very many fields of humdrum, everyday vocabulary that cannot be wholly taught by means of standardly equivalent locutions. The names for the days of the week are a good example. An ostensive definition – 'To-day is a Monday' – will give you an entry into the charmed circle, or even a generalisation like 'Friday is the day that the rubbish is collected.' But neither definition would suffice at all times and places. Equally perhaps the interconnected vocabulary of 'physical possibility', 'causal explanation', 'non-accidental truth', 'law of nature', 'must', *etc.* has to be picked up initially *via* examples and plausible extrapolation therefrom. But this does not imply that the difference between natural laws and accidentally true generalisations is incapable of any elucidation, only that we shall probably not achieve such an elucidation by analysis, reduction or any other procedure sanctioned by the philosophy of *meaning*. We have here one of the many problems for which epistemological considerations are more important than semantical ones. We can gain a better understanding of how the difference between natural laws and accidentally true generalisations is possible if we attend to the difference between two obviously different methods of cognitive inquiry than if we seek some indirect and non-obvious characterisations for the different kinds of propositions that constitute the conclusions of such inquiry.

More specifically, what has to be noticed is that natural laws stand to eliminative or variative induction in very much the same way as accidentally true generalisations stand to enumerative induction. Belief in a particular generalisation's being nomologically, or accidentally, true – as the case may be – is the ideal outcome of the appropriate mode of inductive reasoning.

In eliminative induction we test the capacity of a low-grade generalisation to resist falsification by varying the experimental circumstances in which it is tested, and we test a high-grade scientific theory by its capacity to explain a variety of accepted lower-grade uniformities and predict some new ones. The better the results, the higher the grade of reliability that we attribute to the generalisation or theory. If a generalisation resists falsification under every relevant variation of circumstance that we know of, or if a theory explains every already known uniformity in its field and predicts some new ones, we have as good a reason as we ever have for calling it a law. But, of course, we may well turn out to have been mistaken. Our list of relevant factors to control, or of uniformities to explain, may turn out to have been incomplete. So if we are looking for absolutely conclusive proof that such-or-such a proposition is a law of nature we shall never get it. A real law of nature is, as it were, the crock of gold at the end of the inductivist rainbow. We can never be sure we have reached it because we can never be absolutely sure that our list of relevant variations or uniformities is complete. Assessments by eliminative induction are thus always empirically corrigible. Nevertheless, to the extent that we are entitled to assume this completeness for a particular domain we are also in a position to determine what is or is not a law for that domain. Indeed we can tailor the wording or meaning of a generalisation, where we need to, so as to preserve its lawhood for the domain.[1] And because our mode of reasoning here is always to infer from our observations that a generalisation applies to such-and-such combinations of circumstances, not to such-and-such individuals, we take ourselves to have obtained a generalisation from which ampliative counterfactuals are derivable. So far as the relevant surrounding circumstances of the counterfactual instance are appropriate (*i.e.* are among those to which the covering generalisation applies), the conditional must be true. The experimental results

<hr />

[1] Though lawhood is maintainable by precisification, of which the amount required varies inversely with the eliminative–inductive reliability of the imprecise formulation (Cohen 1970: 142ff), I should not now wish to uphold the thesis (Cohen 1966: 316ff) that lawhood is reducible to the empirical precisifiability of *a priori* truths. One fault of that analysis was its failure to preserve an adequate distinction between epistemic and alethic modalities. Another fault was its failure to show that accidental uniformities are incapable of description in the same way – by hypotheses that are held to be *a priori* true but empirically precisifiable.

that testify to the reliability of the generalisation should in principle be replicable again and again, whether or not the experiment is actually repeated.

In enumerative induction, however, we look only to the number of instances in which a generalisation has been favourably satisfied and to the absence of counter-instances. We are trying to establish a relationship, not between one property or natural kind and another, but between instances of one kind and instances of another. So here the ideal outcome is reached, not when we have run through all the relevant types of situation that might affect a relationship between the properties or natural kinds in question, but rather when we have run through all the relevant individual instances. That is, an exhaustive enumeration of all the actual instances, if favourable, establishes the truth of the generalisation. Here too it is, of course, logically possible that our enumeration is incomplete, and very often we know it to be so. Such assessments by enumerative induction are always empirically corrigible insofar as it is an empirical matter whether or not the instances listed as evidence constitute the whole of the class involved. But even to the extent that we are entitled to assume completeness we are still not in a position to assert that the resultant generalisation is a law in the sense that ampliative counterfactuals are derivable from it. Our mode of reasoning has been to infer from our observations that the generalisation applies to such-and-such individuals, not to such-and-such combinations of circumstances. Hence the only counterfactuals we can derive from the generalisation are non-ampliative ones, like (5) and (7) – on their most natural readings – and, so far as we know, the generalisation can be accounted only an accidental truth.

At least three factors have contributed to obscuring this close correlation between the nomological–accidental distinction, in regard to the deductive content of the generalisation, and the eliminative–enumerative distinction, in regard to the inductive method by which the generalisation is characteristically established.

First, modern writers on induction – for example, Johnson (1922: 197ff.), Stebbing (1930: 244), Kneale (1949: 25ff.) – have customarily treated the method of exhaustive enumeration as a distinct and inferior species of induction, sometimes called 'summary induction' or 'summative induction', which is contrasted with allegedly more interesting species, such as enumerative and eliminative, and the latter are regarded as being essentially ampliative in character.

The interesting forms of induction, it has been held, extrapolate beyond the actual evidence: induction that merely summarises the evidence is degenerate and uninteresting. Mill (1856: bk III, ch. II, §3) even thought it improper to use the term 'induction' at all in respect of the latter mode of reasoning. It is as if modern writers on induction had been so mesmerised by the problem that Hume's discussion of causation poses them – the problem of how to argue from the observed to the unobserved – that they have taken the critical divide, in the taxonomy of induction, to be the distinction between summative and ampliative reasoning. Yet in both eliminative and enumerative induction summation is merely the limiting-case. Up to that point we say that the evidence (weakly or strongly) supports taking the generalisation to be true. But, if all relevant variations, or all relevant instances, have been observed, the truth of the generalisation is fully established. So the older terminology of 'perfect' and 'imperfect' induction is more appropriate than the newer one of 'summative' and 'ampliative'. What is called 'summative induction' is best understood as the final, or perfect, stage – very often unreached – in a process of accumulating evidence that may be either enumerative or eliminative. The logically and methodologically interesting differences are not between perfect (summative) and imperfect (ampliative), but between eliminative and enumerative induction.

The details of these differences are explored at length in Cohen (1970: 106ff) and (1977: 121ff). But the bare bones of the matter are very simple. Eliminative induction builds on the variety of the evidential instances, and relations between its assessments of evidential support are constrained by a generalised modal logic. Enumerative induction builds on sheer numbers of favourable and unfavourable instances, and relations between its assessments of evidential support are constrained instead by the mathematical calculus of chance. And if you accept that this eliminative/enumerative distinction is the fundamental one, you can see just how the difference emerges between our concept of a law of nature and our concept of an accidentally true generalisation. An accidentally true generalisation is a generalisation that can be fully established – given ideal knowledge of the evidence – by enumerative induction but not be eliminative induction. For, since an accidentally true generalisation does not entail ampliative counterfactuals, we can never say that the results of a test on it could in principle have been replicated but weren't – which we want to be able to say about an eliminative induction. A law of nature, on the other hand, is correspondingly a generalisation that can be fully established – given ideal knowledge of the evidence – by eliminative induction alone. Or we can regard the status of being a law of nature as a defeasible one: this spectrum of strength, culminating in full law-hood, is the ascending scale of reliability-grades that eliminative induction entitles us to assign to generalisations on the basis of favourable results from more and more thorough experimental tests or from more and more wide-ranging explanatory enterprise. Counterfactual conditionals are then to be regarded as being no more and no less reliable than the generalisations from which they derive (unless we happen to know also that their surrounding circumstances are among those to which the generalisation definitely does apply, or definitely does not).

Secondly, philosophers have very commonly supposed that enumerative induction can afford a basis for belief in the existence of a law. Hume is archetypal here, but he saw the necessity of a law as an attitude of mind among those who accept it rather than as a feature of its content that licenses the derivation of ampliative counterfactuals.[2] So he had some excuse for not discerning the impotence of enumerative induction with regard to providing support for belief in the existence of a law. But later writers who have been interested in the derivability of ampliative counterfactuals, like Goodman (1954), have less excuse for failing to note the inappropriateness of enumerative induction as a method of establishing laws. Suppose that we know of an enormous number of As which are Bs and of no As which are not Bs. Perhaps you will suggest that we surely ought then to be inclined to accept it as a law that all As are Bs. But what if every one of those As is also a C, or a D, and we know of no Cs or Ds that are not B, whereas As could also be Es or Fs and we do know of some Es or Fs that are not B? The strength of our title to hold it a law that all As are Bs is going to depend, in the end, not on the sheer number of observed As that are Bs, but on their relevant variety.

[2] On the only occasion on which Hume mentions a counterfactual in defining 'cause', he asserts an incorrect equivalence. He says (1748: section VII, pt II) – with his own italics – 'we may define a cause to be *an object, followed by another, and where all the objects similar to the first are followed by objects similar to the second. Or in other words where, if the first object had not been, the second had never existed.*' The second sentence in this passage would only be a counterfactual of the type discussed in the present paper if the generalisation from which it was supposed to derive was that all objects of the second kind are preceded by objects of the first kind.

Thirdly, it may well be pointed out that anyone who uses eliminative induction to establish that a generalisation is a law, or even to determine some lower level of reliability for it, has to assume that the results of each of his experimental tests are replicable. So he has to assume that the circumstances which he is varying, or the factors which he is controlling, in such a test are all the relevant ones which are present in that particular experimental situation. But how else can this assumption be supported, it may be asked, except by belief in appropriate causal laws governing the operation of just those factors in regard to generalisations of the kind in question? Our knowledge of what has been learned from previous tests is thus vital to us in interpreting the results of new ones. So isn't there a circle here, or a regress, because the concept of a law of nature is being elucidated by reference to eliminative induction, but we cannot engage in eliminative induction unless we already assume the validity of certain such laws? The answer is that there is indeed a circle or regress here, but this is an objection only if your ambition is to achieve some kind of analytic reduction of laws to truth-functional discourse. If you believe that problems about meaning and reduction are central to philosophy, you will find – as I have already argued – that philosophical puzzlement about laws of nature looks like being irresoluble. But, if you accept that some concepts are best elucidated in terms of their role in cognitive inquiry, then it does not matter if a person is said to be incapable of establishing one law without assuming others.[3] When we recognise this incapacity we have recognised something important about the role that is played in cognitive inquiry by the concept of a law of nature.

The Queen's College, Oxford

REFERENCES

Braithwaite, Richard Bevan. 1953. *Scientific Explanation*. Cambridge.
Carnap, R. 1936. Testability and meaning, *Philosophy of Science* **3**, 419ff.
Cohen, L. Jonathan. 1966. *The Diversity of Meaning*. London.
Cohen, L. Jonathan. 1970. *The Implications of Induction*. London.

[3] This position still leaves open at least two different ways of conceiving natural necessity, which are called quasi-nominalism and realism in Cohen (1977: 331ff), according to whether or not every facet of a generalisation's reliability, or domain of valid application, has to be manifested by appropriate coinstantiations of its antecedent and consequent.

Cohen, L. Jonathan. 1977. *The Probable and the Provable*. Oxford.

Goodman, Nelson. 1954. *Fact, Fiction and Forecast*. London.

Hume, David. 1748. *An Enquiry Concerning Human Understanding*.

Johnson, W. E. 1922. *Logic*, Part II. Cambridge.

Kneale, W. C. 1949. *Probability and Induction*. Oxford.

Kripke, Saul A. 1972. Naming and necessity, *Semantics of Natural Language*, ed. Donald Davidson and Gilbert Harman, pp. 253–355. Dordrecht.

Lewis, David. 1973. *Counterfactuals*. Oxford.

Margalit, Avishai. 1979. Sense and science, *Essays in Honour of Jaakko Hintikka*, ed. E. Saarinen *et al.*, pp. 17–47. Dordrecht.

Mellor, D. H. 1977. Natural kinds, *The British Journal for the Philosophy of Science* **28**, 299–312.

Mill, J. S. 1856. *A System of Logic*, 4th. edn. London.

Popper, Karl R. 1959. *The Logic of Scientific Discovery*. London.

Putnam Hilary. 1962. It ain't necessarily so. Reprinted in his 1975 *Mathematics, Matter, and Method*, pp. 237–49. Cambridge.

Putnam, Hilary. 1973. Meaning and reference, *The Journal of Philosophy* **70**, 690–711.

Quine, W. V. 1969. *Ontological Relativity and Other Essays*. New York & London.

Ramsey, Frank Plumpton. 1978. *Foundations: Essays in Philosophy, Logic, Mathematics and Economics*, ed. D. H. Mellor. London.

Rescher, Nicholas. 1964. *Hypothetical Reasoning*. Amsterdam.

Stalnaker, Robert C. 1968. A theory of conditionals, *Studies in Logical Theory*, ed. N. Rescher, Oxford.

Stebbing, L. Susan. 1930. *A Modern Introduction to Logic*. London.

Zemach, Eddy M. 1976. Putnam's theory on the reference of substance terms, *The Journal of Philosophy* **73**, 116–27.

11 Hamilton's method in geometrical optics and Ramsey's view of theories

JERZY GIEDYMIN

In an essay entitled 'Theories', written in 1929 (1978), Frank P. Ramsey set out "to describe a theory as simply a language for discussing the facts a theory is said to explain". Though sketchy, Ramsey's essay is believed by many to contain important insights into the structure and functioning of scientific theories. The most interesting of these appears to be Ramsey's proposal to cast the whole empirical content of a theory in the form of a single sentence (in second order language) – known ever since as 'the Ramsey sentence of a theory' – which, in a sense, eliminates all the theory's theoretical (non-observational) terms and has, therefore, been claimed to be relevant to the instrumentalism *versus* realism issue. For this reason Ramsey's name is now often linked with Pierre Duhem's, who is believed (at least on one interpretation of his philosophy) to have maintained that the descriptive or empirical content of a theory is reducible to its observational consequences whereas the so-called abstract or theoretical terms of a theory have no empirical meaning whatever but are merely formal or mathematical symbols.

The aim of this article is to argue that two closely related views of theories may be distinguished and each of them may be claimed to be implicit in the writings of many scientists and philosophers. One of these views – usually opposed to realism and hence referred to as instrumentalism (formalism) – is the view just mentioned in connection with Duhem. The other, which will be labelled here *conventionalist structuralism* or *conventionalism* for short, differs from the former mainly with respect to its conception of the empirical (descriptive) content of a theory, with respect to the role played by theoretical terms and postulates and in its emphasis on the relational or structural nature of theories and of our knowledge in general. Hamilton's theory of geometrical optics will be briefly discussed as an example of a theory which could have been – logically and historically speaking – a model of Ramsey's description of theories and which seems – judging by Hamilton's own remarks – to have been conceived in the spirit of the conventionalist–structuralist philosophy. Not surprisingly, Hamilton's results – including his method used in geometrical optics (later generalised to dynamics) – had an impact on Henri Poincaré's philosophy of physics. It is impossible to say now with confidence whether Duhem's and Ramsey's actual views of theories were in fact distinct (in respects mentioned before) from conventionalist structuralism or whether the differences are only apparent and due to different linguistic presentation.

Ramsey on theories. In 'Theories' Ramsey constructed a simple example of a theory with two "universes of discourse", one called the primary and the other the secondary system. Propositions of the primary system, which represent facts to be explained, are truth-functions of quantifier-free expressions formed from predicate or function symbols A, B, C, D, *etc.* and a suitable number of individual constants as names of the individuals of the primary system. These individuals might be, for example, instants of time, in which case their names would be integers (or rationals) and the propositions would be one-valued numerical functions, *e.g.* $g(3) = 1$. Such atomic propositions and at least some of the truth-functions of such atomic propositions are empirical in nature.

The secondary system is obtained by a single expansion of the primary system. New predicate or function symbols α, β, γ, *etc.* are introduced (which can be thought of as the theoretical or abstract terms of the theory) to form truth-functional propositions with the individual constants of the primary system, $\alpha(n), \beta(n), \gamma(m, n)$ *etc.* These are constrained by a finite number of axioms, *i.e.* formulae whose predicate or function terms belong exclusively to the vocabulary of the secondary system and whose quantifiers range over the universe of discourse of the primary system, *e.g.* $(n). \alpha(n). \beta(n)$. Whatever formulae of the secondary system are deducible from these axioms (presumably on the basis of first order classical logic) are called theorems. The two systems are then linked by a "dictionary", *i.e.* a set of equivalence definitions of the predicate or function symbols of the primary system in terms of the symbols of the secondary system. General propositions in *A, B, C, D, etc.* deducible from the conjunction of the axioms and the dictionary are called 'laws' and represent empirical generalisations. Singular propositions in *A, B, C, D, etc.* deducible from that conjunction are called 'consequences'. The totality of laws and consequences, *i.e.* of universal and singular propositions in which no extra-logical symbols of the secondary system occur and which are deducible from the axioms in conjunction with the dictionary form the "eliminant" and it is only this eliminant-totality that the theory asserts as true (1978: 104).

Having made the above distinctions, Ramsey considers six questions about theories, the first four of which seem to be most important for the understanding of his views on theories. The four questions are as follows: (1) Can we say anything in the language of a theory (*i.e.* of the secondary system) that we could not say without it? (2) Can we reproduce the structure of a theory (*i.e.* the secondary system) by means of explicit definitions within the primary system? (3) Is this necessary for the legitimate use of the theory (as Russell, Nicod and Carnap insisted)? (4) If not, how are we to explain the functioning of a theory without such definitions? (Ramsey 1978: 108–9, 112). He answered these four questions in this way: (1') Obviously not, since we can easily eliminate all the specific terms of the secondary system and so say in the primary system "all that the theory gives us"; (2') There is no simple way of inverting the dictionary, *i.e.* of defining the non-logical terms of the secondary system using only the expressions of the primary system; nor is it possible to express each proposition of the secondary system in terms of the necessary and sufficient conditions formulated in the language of the primary system; however, it *is* always possible to define explicitly non-logical terms of the secondary system in terms of the primary system provided that definitions of any complexity are allowed *or* the universe of discourse is finite; (3') Although specific terms of the secondary system are explicitly definable in terms of the primary system (with the proviso given in (2')), it is not necessary for the legitimate use of a theory actually to provide such definitions; (4') The functioning of a theory without such definitions may be best explained if the original theory, which we assume to be given as a (finite) conjunction of the axioms and the "dictionary" both in first order language, is written in the form of a sentence obtained by second order existential generalisation on all extra-logical terms occurring in the axioms and in the dictionary. To use Ramsey's informal abbreviations (slightly modified), we rewrite the original theory in the form of the sentence (the "Ramsey-sentence", RS):

$$(\text{RS}) \qquad (\exists \alpha', \beta', \gamma'): \text{dictionary. axioms}$$

where α', β', γ' are (second order) variables replacing corresponding extralogical constants (α, β, γ) of the secondary system; 'dictionary' and 'axioms' are sentential forms obtained, respectively, from the dictionary and the axioms by writing suitable variables in place of corresponding extra-logical constants (1978: 120). A theory so reformulated is to be understood in such a way that, firstly, what it asserts is only the conjunction of its "laws and consequences" (both in the language of the primary system), secondly, the expressions of the secondary system are "simply a language" in terms of which the laws and consequences may be "clothed"; otherwise sentences in which the terms of the secondary system occur are not "strictly propositions by themselves", *i.e.* when isolated from the context of the theory just as the sentences in a story beginning 'Once upon a time' have no complete meanings and so are not propositions by themselves (1978: 120). This does not affect at all our *reasoning* but may affect our *disputes* (1978: 121–2). In other words, the deductive elaboration of a theory is not affected by the incomplete nature of isolated sentences of the secondary system; moreover, two theories which differ with respect to their secondary systems need not contradict one another (1978: 122), though they may appear to do so. Finally the RS formulation of a theory makes it clear that questions about the meaning and truth of sentences of the secondary system may only be answered in the context of the whole theory and not in isolation from it (1978: 120–1).

Apart from the four questions (1) through (4), Ramsey raises the problem of intertheory relations, *viz.* the problem of the clarification of the meaning of 'two contradictory theories', 'two equivalent theories', 'one theory contained in (reducible to) another'. He sketched definitions of these phrases in terms of the "content of a theory", which – as we have seen – he identified with "the totality of laws and consequences of a theory". So, for example, for two theories to be equivalent it is necessary and sufficient that their content, *i.e.* sets of laws and consequences be equivalent (1978:

121–2). Although he did distinguish between the content of a theory (what the theory asserts) and its symbolic form and pointed out that given two equivalent theories "there may be more or less resemblance between their symbolic form", he concluded that this type of resemblance is difficult if not impossible to define precisely (1978: 122).

It will be useful at this point to summarise and characterise briefly those of Ramsey's views on scientific theories which will be relevant to our further discussion:

(a) Assuming a theory to be in two-sorted language (primary and secondary system, or observational and theoretical language, *etc.*) and axiomatised by a finite set of axioms on the basis of first order logic, Ramsey claimed that the properties of the theory may be best seen if it is re-formulated as one single sentence (The Ramsey-sentence) obtained from the original theory by second order existential generalisation on all terms of the secondary system (theoretical terms).

(b) The RS reformulation of a theory replaces terms of the secondary system (theoretical terms) by existentially bound (second order) variables. In this sense the RS of a theory may be said to eliminate terms of the secondary system (theoretical terms) from the theory in question.

(c) The (empirical) content of a theory, *i.e.* what a theory asserts as true, is identified with the set of all "laws and consequences" which are formulated exclusively in terms of the primary system (observational terms) and form what Ramsey called the 'eliminant'. Since all laws and consequences derivable from the original theory are also derivable from its RS, the content of the RS is identical with the content of the original theory; in other words, the RS reformulation leaves the content of a theory unchanged and the RS expresses the content of the theory.

(d) Relations between two (or more) theories, such as equivalence, contradiction, reduction, *etc.* are defined in terms of corresponding relations between their empirical contents, *i.e.* eliminants.

(e) In so far as in the Ramsey view the sentences of the secondary system of a theory, its theoretical sentences, are not asserted as true, do not enter into its content (although they may be used as a secondary language in which to clothe the theory's content and also as formal inferential devices) and may be regarded as empirically uninterpreted, in contradistinction to the extra-logical expressions of the primary system, the Ramsey view appears to be a variety of the instrumentalist (or formalist) view of scientific theories. Since the content of the theory on the Ramsey view is identified with the theory's observational consequences (laws and consequences in this sense) and two observationally equivalent theories are regarded as equivalent, the Ramsey view may also be classified as a variety of pragmatism in the sense of Peirce's pragmatist maxim. Finally, the proposal to express the content of a theory in one single sentence (however complex) and the insistence that questions of the meaning, truth and testing can only be answered within the context of the whole theory, are features characteristic of what nowadays is called the *holistic* view of theories.

Duhem's instrumentalist interpretation of "saving the phenomena". Whether Ramsey was aware of it or not, views concerning the structure and functioning of scientific theories similar to his in some important respects at least had a long tradition in science and its philosophy. While this fact may moderate somewhat our appreciation of his originality, it may also indicate that his account of scientific theories is not descriptively vacuous.

Pierre Duhem is often mentioned today as one of those who anticipated the view that a scientific theory consists of two integrated systems: the primary system expressing experimental facts and laws and the secondary system which is a mathematical, uninterpreted calculus (Abraham & Marsden 1967: 231). He is also credited as one of the fathers of the holistic view of theories since he insisted, first, that experimental laws take different meaning depending on the theory into which they have been absorbed; secondly, that only whole theoretical systems can be tested against facts but not isolated hypotheses (Duhem 1906: Part II, chaps V, VI; 1969). For these reasons his name is sometimes explicitly linked with Ramsey's (Sneed 1971: IX).

We know, however, that Duhem's philosophy of science was based on his research into the history of astronomy and physics "from Plato to Galileo", the results of which he summarised in (Duhem 1906, 1969). According to Duhem, an adequate, critical account of the structure and functioning of scientific theories emerged gradually from the writings of Greek astronomers and cosmologists. Plato, who on *a priori* grounds believed that the motion of the heavenly bodies is circular, uniform and regular (in the same direction), set mathematical astronomers the task of finding hypotheses which would "save the phenomena presented by the planets" in terms of circular, uniform and perfectly regular motions. Henceforth ancient astronomy was concerned with geometrical constructions (mathematical models in modern terminology) which would assign each planet a path conformable to its visible path. Hipparchus appears to be one of the first to have discovered and proved that the same phenomena, for example the observed course of the sun, may be equally well accounted for by two apparently quite different hypotheses, *viz*, that of eccentric circles and that of concentric circles bearing epicycles. The two hypotheses were subsequently shown to be observationally equivalent, which fact persuaded Theon to claim that astronomy is not able ever to discover *the true* hypothesis and that the disputes among astronomers concerning apparently different but observationally equivalent hypotheses may be dismissed as idle. Some authors, Geminus for example (as reported by Simplicius), drew from these circumstances the conclusion, which appeared to conform to Aristotle's teaching, that the aims and methods of mathematical astronomy were different from those of physics (which was concerned with the discovery of the nature and causes of things) and that astronomers needed the help of physical principles to choose the true hypotheses from the totality of all observationally adequate ones. Others (Adrastus, Theon, Dercyllides) proclaimed that an astronomical hypothesis cannot be true to the nature of things unless craftsmen are able to construct its representation in hardware (wood or metal). These suggestions were rejected by Claudius Ptolemy who – according to Duhem – concluded that, first, an adequate astronomical theory is a geometrical contrivance which saves all observed astronomical phenomena; secondly, astronomers are unable and do not have to discriminate between observationally equivalent hypotheses (which save all the phenomena equally well); thirdly, they therefore do not and must not attribute physical reality to the conceptual elements in their models (Duhem 1969: 5–20). These views were adopted subsequently by Proclus who, moreover, gave the following logical analysis of the method of astronomy:

[astronomers] do not arrive at conclusions by starting from hypotheses, as is done in the other sciences; rather, taking the conclusions as their point of departure, they strive to construct hypotheses from which effects conformable to the original conclusions follow with necessity (Duhem 1969: 20).

Proclus' account of the method of astronomy is equivalent to Charles Peirce's description of the method of "abduction" ("inverse induction") to which other authors give the name 'reduction' or 'reductive inference' (Łukasiewicz 1912, 1970: 6–7) or 'the method of hypotheses' (Popper 1963). Taken in itself, Proclus' description of the method of astronomy is ambiguous with respect to the role of "secondary" (abstract, theoretical) system and therefore may and has been used by both instrumentalists and realists (in one of the senses of these words), *viz.* by those who see in the secondary system an empirically uninterpreted calculus (as Ramsey did) and those who attribute to it a descriptive function. But even in conjunction with the reported three theses of Ptolemy (who, by the way, did not consistently hold them) it would only amount to a "formalist" or "instrumentalist" view of the aims and method of astronomy, not of all science. According to Duhem, *the generalisation of the instrumentalist view* of the aim and nature of astronomical theories to all theories of physics occurred later in the writings of mediaeval and Rennaissance philosopher–scientists to be confronted by the similarly general realism of Kepler and Galileo. It is worth noting, however, that Duhem's reading of the history of science tended to emphasise the importance of the two extreme doctrines of (generalised) instrumentalism and realism, as if either were the limit of one of two rival, convergent series of historically evolving doctrines. An alternative reading would rather stress the existence and legitimacy of a variety of intermediate views, with varying amounts of "instrumentalist" and "realist" elements. One class of these intermediate doctrines may be called 'restricted instrumentalism', and one specific doctrine in this class would be the view that the theoretical postulates of a certain scientific discipline practised in isolation from others and, therefore, in abstraction from some relevant factors, may only be accorded the status of empirically uninterpreted sentences. Such restricted instrumentalism was seen as advantageous by many ancient astronomers who preferred to carry on their research as "mathematical astronomers" independently of (Aristotelian) physics.

Hamilton's method in geometrical optics. The theory of mathematical (geometrical) optics developed between 1827 and 1832 by Sir William Rowan Hamilton (1805–65) is an example of a theory on which Ramsey's description of theories could have been modelled except that Hamilton's starting-point – unlike Ramsey's – were *two* apparently rival physical theories, *viz.* the emission and the wave theory of light restricted to a common area of application (provided that the interference phenomena are disregarded) and the mathematics sufficient to systematise known experimental results in that area. Hamilton's method seems to have achieved for the overlapping parts of two rival theories what the Ramsey sentence does for one theory. It must be emphasised that far from being a trivial and sterile exercise, Hamilton's approach to geometrical optics proved to be very fruitful. It led to the theoretical prediction of a new, previously unknown phenomenon, *viz.* conical refraction, subsequently verified by Humphrey Lloyd's experiments (Hamilton 1833a; 1931: 302–3), and to the discovery of a new form of equations of dynamics (Hamilton's wave mechanics) (Hamilton 1833b; 1834a,b).[1]

From Hamilton's own accounts we know that he was prompted to undertake his theoretical research in optics by the following considerations. In spite of an abundance of experimental laws concerning optical phenomena accumulated over the centuries by ancient and modern physicists, there did not exist a mathematical theory which could systematise them and which would be comparable in precision, practical usefulness and formal beauty with other well-developed branches of science such as Lagrangean mechanics (Hamilton 1833b, 1931: 315). Two rival theories of light, Newton's emission theory and Huyghens's wave theory, competed for the attention of scientists and each of them in turn appeared for a time to win the upper hand. Two rival general principles, that of least action (Maupertuis law) and that of least time (Fermat's law), each associated with one of the two rival theories, were moreover originally understood in metaphysical terms as expressing teleology (goal-directedness), simplicity or economy of Nature. Yet whether one adopts the Newtonian (emission) or the Huyghenian (wave)

---

[1] Original dates of publication of Hamilton's papers are given. Page references are to *The Mathematical Papers of Sir William Rowan Hamilton*, Vol. I, 1931, Vol. II, 1940, Vol. III, 1967. Generally, where references contain two dates, the first is the date of original publication, the second the date of the later republication or translation to which the page numbers refer.

theory of light to explain the experimental laws of optics, one may regard the linear paths of light, their properties and relations between them, *i.e.* systems of rays and experimental laws concerning them as the object of an important separate science, *viz.* mathematical optics (Hamilton 1833b, 1931: 314).[2] The general problem which Hamilton proposed to himself in that area was to investigate the mathematical consequences of the (optical) law of least action as a possible general principle on which to base mathematical optics, "without adopting either the metaphysical or (in optics) the physical opinions that first suggested the name ('action' and 'the law of least action')" (Hamilton 1833b, 1931: 318). The method which he decided to use for that purpose was suggested to him by René Descartes' algebraic (analytic) geometry. A system of optical rays, *i.e.* a combination of straight or curved paths along which light is supposed to be propagated according to the law of least action, is characterised in this new approach by one single "characteristic relation". All the mathematical properties of the given system of optical rays are deducible from this characteristic relation in the same manner as the properties of a curve or of a surface are deducible in Cartesian analytic geometry from appropriate functions (Hamilton 1831, 1931: 295). Whereas in Cartesian geometry two or three elements are involved in a characteristic relation, *viz.* the elements of position of a variable point which has for its *locus* a curve or a surface, the elements involved in a characteristic relation of a system of optical rays are eight in number: six elements of position of two variable points in space visually connected, *i.e.* final and initial co-ordinates, an index of colour and *action* (or time) between the two variable points. The last one, *viz.* action, reflects through its dependence on the preceding seven all the geometric properties of the given system of rays, hence it is referred to as the *characteristic function* of the system. Denoted by V, the characteristic function is the integral given by the formula:

$$(V) \qquad V = \int v ds$$

where v is the medium function (refractive index of the medium) and ds is the element of the path (ray).

The method based on the characteristic function V of studying

---

[2] It is possible to treat geometrical optics as a limiting case of physical optics (the wave-length of light tending to zero). Hamilton, however, developed geometrical optics as an independent discipline.

optical phenomena was described by Hamilton (1837, 1931: 168–9) in the following way.

Assume that light is propagated according to the optical law of least action (or of swiftest propagation) along any curved or polygon ray, describing each element of the ray $ds = (dx^2 + dy^2 + dz^2)^{\frac{1}{2}}$ with a molecular velocity or undulatory slowness v. The latter (the medium function) depends in general on the nature of the medium, the position and direction of the element and the colour of the light, in other words v is a function of the three rectangular coordinates x,y,z, the three cosines of direction (cosines of the angles which the element of the ray makes with the axes of coordinates) α, β, γ:

$$\alpha = \frac{dx}{ds}, \beta = \frac{dy}{ds}, \gamma = \frac{dz}{ds}$$

and a chromatic index χ. Let us denote as follows the variation of v:[3]

$$\delta v = \frac{\delta v}{\delta x} \delta x + \frac{\delta v}{\delta y} \delta y + \frac{\delta v}{\delta z} \delta z + \frac{\delta v}{\delta \alpha} \delta \alpha + \frac{\delta v}{\delta \beta} \delta \beta + \frac{\delta v}{\delta \gamma} \delta \gamma$$
$$+ \frac{\delta v}{\delta \chi} \delta \chi$$

and, further, in view of $\alpha^2 + \beta^2 + \gamma^2 = 1$, let us determine

$$\frac{\delta v}{\delta \alpha}, \frac{\delta v}{\delta \beta}, \frac{\delta v}{\delta \gamma}$$

i.e. the partial differential coefficients of v, so as to satisfy the condition

$$\alpha \frac{\delta v}{\delta \alpha} + \beta \frac{\delta v}{\delta \beta} + \gamma \frac{\delta v}{\delta \gamma} = v$$

by making v homogeneous of the first degree with respect to α, β, γ.

On these assumptions it has been shown (Hamilton 1830, 1931: 107–44) that the variation of the definite integral $V = \int v ds$ considered as a function (the characteristic function) of the final and initial co-ordinates, *i.e. the variation of action or the time* expended by

---

[3] Hamilton's original symbolism is retained here. It must be noted that he used the symbol δ also for partial differential coefficients.

light of any colour in going from one variable point to another is given by the following formula (variational principle):

(A) $\delta V \ (=\delta \int v ds)$

$$= \frac{\delta v}{\delta \alpha} \delta x - \frac{\delta v'}{\delta \alpha'} \delta x' + \frac{\delta v}{\delta \beta} \delta y - \frac{\delta v'}{\delta \beta'} \delta y' + \frac{\delta v}{\delta \gamma} \delta z - \frac{\delta v'}{\delta \gamma'} \delta z'$$

where the primed quantities are the initial ones.

Formula (A) may be resolved into the following six equations:

(B) $\begin{cases} \dfrac{\delta V}{\delta x} = \dfrac{\delta v}{\delta \alpha}; \ \dfrac{\delta V}{\delta y} = \dfrac{\delta v}{\delta \beta}; \ \dfrac{\delta V}{\delta z} = \dfrac{\delta v}{\delta \gamma}; \\[3mm] -\dfrac{\delta V}{\delta x'} = \dfrac{\delta v'}{\delta \alpha'}; \ -\dfrac{\delta V}{\delta y'} = \dfrac{\delta v'}{\delta \beta'}; \ -\dfrac{\delta V}{\delta z'} = \dfrac{\delta v'}{\delta \gamma'}. \end{cases}$

If we eliminate from (B) the ratios

$$\frac{\alpha}{\gamma}, \frac{\beta}{\gamma}, \frac{\alpha'}{\gamma}, \frac{\beta'}{\gamma}$$

of which the partial derivatives of v are functions, then we obtain two partial differential equations of the first order between the characteristic function V, the co-ordinates and the chromatic index (colour):

(C) $\begin{cases} 0 = \Omega \left(\dfrac{\delta V}{\delta x}, \dfrac{\delta V}{\delta y}, \dfrac{\delta V}{\delta z}, x, y, z, \chi \right) \\[4mm] 0 = \Omega' \left(-\dfrac{\delta V}{\delta x'}, -\dfrac{\delta V}{\delta y'}, -\dfrac{\delta V}{\delta z'}, x', y', z', \chi \right). \end{cases}$

Let us now recapitulate in words the significance which Hamilton associated with his method in optics.

All the problems of mathematical optics are reducible to the study of the characteristic function V with the help of the variational principle (A) (Hamilton 1831, 1837, 1931: 295, 169).

Hamilton referred to the principle (A) variously as 'the principle of least (constant) action' or 'the principle of swiftest propagation', *etc.*, but sometimes he designated it "by the less hypothetical name of the Equation of the Characteristic Function" (Hamilton 1828, 1830, 1833a,b, 1837; 1931: 10, 107–9, 297, 311–18, 168). The last phrase was used by him to emphasise that mathematical optics is logically independent either of the wave (undulatory) or of the particle (emission) theory of light. In fact, as indicated before, formula (A) may be transformed either into the principle of least (stationary) action of the emission theory (the Maupertuis principle) or into the principle of least time (the Fermat principle) of the wave theory by suitable interpretation of 'v' in terms of the velocity of the ray element on the emission theory or in terms of the "undulatory slowness" on the wave theory. Accordingly V will be either the action integral or the time integral.

Assuming the emission theory of light we see from equations (B) that

the coefficients of the variations of the final coordinates in the variation of the integral called action are equal to the coefficients of the variations of the cosines of the angles which the element of the ray makes with the axes of coordinates in the variation of a certain homogeneous function of those cosines this . . . function . . . being equal . . . to the velocity of the element . . . estimated on the hypothesis of emission (Hamilton 1830: 1931: 107).

However, formula (A) "gives immediately the differential equation of that important class of surfaces, which on the hypothesis of undulation are called *waves,* and which on the hypothesis of molecular emission may be named *surfaces of constant action* " (1830; 1931: 107).

Assuming the wave theory of light, the partial derivatives of V with respect to final coordinates in equations (B) represent the components of "normal slowness of propagation of a wave", the function V represents the time of the propagation of light from the initial to the final point and waves are represented by the general equation

(C) $V = \text{const.}$

On this understanding equations (B) state that partial derivatives of V with respect to final coordinates, *i.e.* the components of "normal slowness of propagation of a wave" are proportional to the direction-cosines of the normal to the wave for which the time V is constant (Hamilton 1837; 1931: 277; 1833b; 1931: 329).

In view of the mentioned correspondence or duality between the two interpretations one may say that "in geometrical optics it is possible to regard the two theories (the corpuscular and wave theory) as different aspects of a single theory" (Sygne 1937: 12). Put another way, the ray theory and the wave theory are reconciled in geometrical optics at least so far as ordinary media are concerned (Sygne 1937: 16). This fact had a great heuristic value since it suggested to Hamilton the idea of wave mechanics (for Hamilton's own account see Hamilton 1834, 1940: 212–16):

The basic feature of Hamilton's method in optics is the reconciliation of a minimal principle (Least Action, or Fermat Principle) with a contact transformation (construction of Huyghens) and this fundamental duality is carried over into dynamics, in which field Hamilton, starting from the well-known principle of Least Action, reduced the equations of motion to an infinitesimal contact transformation (Conway & Sygne, in Hamilton. 1931: 487).[4]

Instead of 'reconciliation' and 'duality' we may prefer to use the terminology of 'observational equivalence' and 'translation', especially if we want to link Hamilton's method in optics with the Ramsey view of theories. Since from the variational principle (A) all the experimental laws of geometrical optics (laws of reflection, refraction, the theorem of Malus, *etc.*) are derivable and since these laws form the common empirical content of the two theories of light, the latter two theories (the wave and particle theories of light) are observationally equivalent within geometrical optics. We can say, therefore, that the particle and the wave theories of light are merely two different but intertranslatable languages so far as geometrical optics is concerned, or that they are two different but equivalent ways of talking about the same things. Systems of optical rays in Hamilton's terminology (Hamilton 1828; 1931: 1–106) as combinations of visual lines of light are models (realisations) of the theory of geometrical optics and thus models of the common observational part of the particle and wave theories of light (when certain phenomena such as interference are disregarded). These models can be extended to the models of either the particle or the wave theories of light and a correspondence established between these extended models. The variational principle (A), understood in Hamilton's neutral or "less hypothetical" way, asserts that *there exists* a quantity, *viz.* the characteristic function V, which has a stationary property and which is such that all the properties of systems of optical rays – in effect all experimental laws of geometrical optics – are derivable from it. The principle can,

---

[4] See also Conway and Synge Note 20, On group velocity and wave mechanics, pp. 500–2 of (Hamilton 1931). On the genesis of Schrödinger's wave mechanics from the ideas of Hamilton's optics see *Annalen der Physik* **79** (1926), 489 *et seq.*

therefore, be regarded as the Ramsey sentence formulation of either the particle or of the wave theory of light restricted to geometrical optics. It can be said to *replace* either of these theories within geometrical optics and, in this sense, to eliminate from geometrical optics the theoretical terms 'particle of light', 'light wave' and others associated with them. Alternatively, one may say that the two sets of theoretical terms and corresponding principles have been shown by Hamilton's method to be *interchangeable* within geometrical optics: the characteristic function V whose existence is asserted by the principle (A) is identified with the action integral on the particle interpretation and with the time integral on the wave interpretation. One is thus left to choose whichever theory one prefers and finds heuristically more valuable.

Having argued that there is a close affinity, logically speaking, between Hamilton's principle in geometrical optics and the Ramsey-sentence formulation of a theory as well as between Ramsey's view of the functions of a theory on the one hand and the motives guiding Hamilton in devising his method in geometrical optics on the other hand, are we to conclude that Hamilton's views on the epistemological status of theories were the same as Duhem's and Ramsey's?

In order to answer this question we ought to consider the following facts. First of all, there is no clear indication in Hamilton's writings that he subscribed to a view equivalent to Ramsey's claim that theoretical terms (*i.e.* terms of the secondary system) are best seen within the context of a scientific theory as empirically uninterpreted symbols or that these terms should be in principle eliminable on the basis of explicit definitions or otherwise. In geometrical optics he believed that a mathematical theory neutral with respect to the wave–particle controversy would be beneficial at the time, especially if one utilised heuristic suggestions associated with the images, analogies, *etc.,* implicit in either of these two theories. But he *did* consider and advance arguments in favour of Fresnel's theory in physical optics. Was it then a case of what we have labelled 'restricted instrumentalism'? Before we commit ourselves to this solution, one further point should be mentioned. Like many of his great contemporaries among mathematicians Hamilton *did* have philosophical views concerning science and mathematics and he *did* write about them, however briefly and parenthetically. For our present purposes his views which concern the epistemological status of algebra and analysis are relevant because they appear to be in contradiction with an instrumentalist or formalist epistemology. Hamilton's philosophy of algebra and analysis may be found in his paper on algebraic couples, which also includes an essay on "algebra as the science of pure time" conceived in the spirit of Kantian philosophy (Hamilton 1833c, 1967: 3–7). In the introductory remarks to that paper Hamilton explained the philosophical motivation behind his research in algebra and analysis which eventually led him to the invention and development of the theory of quaternions. Algebra – by which Hamilton meant both algebra and analysis in our sense (Hamilton 1833c; 1967: 6 footnote) – may be studied in three different ways, *viz.* as a practical art, as a symbolic language and as a science. Accordingly, there emerged three schools of thought, the practical, the philological and the theoretical, each favouring a corresponding approach. However, although algebra (*cum* analysis) proved to be a very useful art and a beautiful language, the state of its theoretical principles – unlike the state of the principles of Euclidean geometry – left much to be desired:

No candid and intelligent person can doubt the truth of the chief properties of *Parallel Lines,* as set forth by Euclid in his *Elements,* two thousand years ago . . . But it requires no peculiar scepticism to doubt, or even to disbelieve, the doctrine of Negatives and Imaginaries, when set forth [on principles used in Hamilton's time] (Hamilton 1833c, 1967: 4).

This is why a tendency could be perceived to the rejection of that view which regarded algebra "as a science, in some sense analogous to geometry" and to the adoption of the view of algebra as an art or as a language, as a system of rules or else as a system of expressions, but not as a system of truths. One tends thus to substitute for the theoretical question 'Is a theorem of algebra true?', the practical question 'Can it be applied as an instrument, to do or to discover something else in some research which is not algebraical?' or else the philological question 'Does its expression harmonise, according to the laws of language, with other algebraical expressions?' (Hamilton 1833c, 1967: 4–5). Hamilton mentions George Peacock as the leading representative of the philological view of algebra (in the narrow sense) in Britain and Martin Ohm in Germany. Lagrange is mentioned by him as representing the philological view of the calculus. It was in order to counter that "philological" or formalist tendency that Hamilton undertook the task of laying down the theoretical principles of algebra and analysis as *the science of variation and progression*, hence – in his Kantian view – as the science based on the *pure intuition of time*. The theory of algebraic couples (intended to replace the then current theory of negatives and imaginaries), of algebraic triplets and, finally, of quaternions, were the result of his research. Within the theory of quaternions Hamilton developed and used the idea of a four-space, one dimension of which represented time (one real axis represented time, three imaginary axes represented space) (Hamilton 1853, 1967: 152).

Now, if Hamilton rejected a purely "philological" and a purely instrumentalist view of algebra and analysis and insisted on developing the latter as a *science* of pure time in the Kantian sense, *i.e.* presumably as based on synthetic *a priori* truths derived from pure intuition of time, is it likely that he would have an instrumentalist view of physical theories?

In so far as Kant's philosophy affirms that science is concerned with the study of the phenomenal world and is unable to provide us with knowledge of the "nature of things" or of "things in themselves", whether it is matter, light, or forces, *etc.*, it favours a view of scientific theories which is close to Ramsey's (and Duhem's). Close but not identical, for there is another element in Kant's epistemology which separates it sharply from phenomenalism, *viz.* its emphasis on the formal or structural nature of scientific knowledge and which naturally had a very strong appeal to those Kantians who – like Hamilton and later Poincaré – were creative mathematicians. According to the doctrine in question, the content of scientific knowledge is not reducible to the "raw" phenomena given to our senses but consists of various types of relations between the phenomena which are perceived in terms of *a priori* forms of "sensibility" and are systematised by our mind in terms of *a priori* categories of understanding. Whatever the original meaning of this doctrine may have been it was interpreted by nineteenth-century Kantians (and neo-Kantians) in the following way: the theories of mathematical physics do not merely systematise experimental results and enable one to derive observable predictions from suitable premises; they also reveal through the form of mathematical equations a deeper reality, *viz.* the relational structure of the directly unobservable world the nature of which will otherwise remain unknown to us. Accordingly, for Hamilton – as for other nineteenth-century Kantians – the cognitive or descriptive content of a scientific theory was not exhausted in terms of all the theory's observational consequences but was co-determined by the formal structure of the theory, which excludes some "possible worlds" or models. Unlike the instrumentalist doctrine attributed to Duhem and Ramsey, the view which we want now to attribute to Hamilton (as a Kantian), and even more emphatically to Poincaré, does not imply that theoretical terms are uninterpreted symbols or merely formal instruments. Rather it stresses that the cognitive role of the abstract (theoretical) part of a theory consists in postulating a structure which reflects the structure of the domain(s) of application of the theory, or – in another terminology – which imposes relational restrictions on admissible interpretations of theoretical terms and thus reduces the class of possible models of the theory. Two rival theories are distinguishable one from another only up to the similarity of their formal structure, unless they also yield different observational predictions. Otherwise theoretical terms are conventional (which does *not* mean absolutely arbitrary) and are more expressive of the habits and preferences of their users than descriptive of physical reality. The epistemological implications of this doctrine, which we have labelled *conventionalist structuralism* or *conventionalism* for short, were elaborated by Poincaré and amount to the claim that reality is knowable only up to the observational equivalence and up to the isomorphism of the abstract postulates of apparently rival theories. Alternatively, in ontological (semantical) terminology: any two *similar worlds*, *i.e.* such that one can pass from one to another either by changing the co-ordinate axes, or by changing the scale of lengths, or by any point transformation, are *indistinguishable* (Poincaré, 1905, 1958: 39).

The following mathematical concepts proved especially important for the evolution of conventionalist structuralism between Hamilton's and Poincaré's time. The concept of a *higher space* is implicit in Hamilton's optics (8-space). Later on he used a 4-space to define the multiplication of quaternions but claimed "no originality as respects the paradox of the fourth dimension of space" and conceded priority to Cayley in constructing a geometry of four dimensions (Hamilton 1967: 108; letter to H. Lloyd dated 1844). It was J. Plücker who pointed out that the dimensionality of space depends on our *choice* of the elements (points, lines, planes, *etc.*) from which space is constructed. He also pointed out that a right line may be construed in two different ways and that, accordingly, there are two constructions of space: in one, space is traversed by lines themselves consisting of points, in the other it is traversed by lines determined by planes passing through them. The first is used in optics when luminous points are assumed to send rays in all directions, the second when instead of rays one considers wave-fronts and their consecutive intersections (Plücker, 1865: 725–6).

Essential to Hamilton's optics and wave dynamics were *contact-transformations* (as mathematical representations of advancing wave-fronts). One property of these transformations is that they preserve the order of contact of surfaces (hence the name invented by Sophus Lie); another that they may establish correspondence between different categories of space elements, *e.g.* they may transform a point (and directions issuing from it) into a surface and all the normals to the surface; or a line into a surface or into a point. Lie's theory of groups of continuous transformations, in which properties of a group were studied indirectly by investigating the properties of a system of equations independent of the choice of coordinates, exerted considerable influence on Poincaré's conventionalist philosophy of geometry and physics (Giedymin 1977).

Hamilton and Poincaré. There are undoubtedly close links, logically and historically speaking, between several of Hamilton's ideas and Henri Poincaré's philosophy of mathematics and physics, though the extent of those links and the manner in which they came about is largely a matter of conjecture.

It is easy to establish that Poincaré was familiar with Hamilton's main contributions to algebra, especially with Hamilton's theory of quaternions, the discovery of which he compared to that of non-Euclidean geometry. There is, however, no direct evidence that he was familiar with Hamilton's paper on algebraic couples with the philosophical remarks in its introduction or with the essay on algebra as the science of pure time which forms part of that paper. The hypothesis that Poincaré knew Hamilton's philosophy of geometry, algebra and analysis would have to be based on the following general arguments: (a) Hamilton's main contributions to pure and applied mathematics were in the areas in which Poincaré took special interest either in his own research or in his university lectures; (b) Hamilton had close personal relations with leading French mathematicians, the French Academy and the mathematical journals in the second quarter of the nineteenth century; (c) we know that throughout his life Poincaré used extensively to read original writings of many British mathematicians and physicists, among them Arthur Cayley (1821–95) and James Clerk Maxwell (1831–79) both of whom made use of and wrote about Hamilton's results in optics, dynamics and algebra, and both of whom considerably influenced Poincaré's views on mathematics and science; (d) Hamilton was a Kantian and Poincaré's own philosophy of mathematics resulted from the rejection of the Kantian philosophy of geometry and the retention of the Kantian philosophy of analysis; (e) the main ideas of Hamilton's philosophy of analysis with references to Kant's original texts may be found in some of Hamilton's writings on quaternions (especially Hamilton 1853). At any rate, it is tempting to *conjecture* that Poincaré's philosophy of mathematics was, at least, in some measure, a response to Hamilton's, and especially that (1) when Poincaré criticised and rejected the Kantian view of geometry as based on pure intuition of space he had in mind as much Hamilton as Kant; (2) when he developed his conventionalist doctrine of metric geometries as alternative languages associated with three different types of isometries (Cayley, Lie), and denied that geometrical axioms were either true or false, he was embracing consciously what Hamilton referred to as the "philological view"; (3) when he retained the Kantian view of analysis, he was aware of Hamilton's idea of analysis as the science of pure time (progression, change).[5] If these hypotheses are true, there was a direct historical link between Poincaré's and Hamilton's philosophy of mathematics (Gergonne's essay on definitions which represented the "philological view" of mathematics in general was in all probability known to both Hamilton and Poincaré).

There is no need to be purely hypothetical about the influence of

---

[5] Discussing the transition from Fresnel's to Maxwell's theory (1902, 1952: 160–1) Poincaré argued that Fresnel's work was not in vain for his "object was not to know whether there really is an ether, if it is or is not formed of atoms, if these atoms really move in this way or that; his object was to predict optical phenomena. Thus Fresnel's theory enables us to do to-day as well as it did before Maxwell's time." Then he goes on to claim that this view does *not* reduce physical theories to simple practical recipes for it implies that "equations express relations": 'They teach us now, as they did then, that there is such and such a relation between this thing and that; only the something which we then called *motion*, we now call *electric current*. But these are merely names of the images we substituted for real objects which Nature will hide for ever from our eyes' (1952: 161).

The rejection of instrumentalism at the beginning of the passage reported here (the passage having been written for the 1900 Paris International Congress of Physics) may have been in response to LeRoy or some other contemporaries, but it is in the same spirit or tradition as Hamilton's epistemology.

Hamilton's method in geometrical optics and dynamics upon Poincaré's philosophical views concerning the role, structure and evolution of theories in physics, indeed upon his main epistemological concern, which was: to show how objective scientific knowledge was possible in spite of frequent changes ("the ephemeral nature") of theories in theoretical physics (Poincaré 1902, 1952: 160). Poincaré's argument in defence of objectivity is based on a view of physical theories with which Ramsey's view shares main features and it refers explicitly to the role played in scientific change by the general principles such as Hamilton's principles in optics and in dynamics and the principle of conservation of energy (Poincaré 1902, 1952: 123–4, 162, 166–7, 220–3). In outline the argument is as follows.

A physical theory, properly analysed and understood, consists of three components: a set of empirical (experimental) laws based on measurements, a set of equations (a calculus) and a set of hypotheses formulated in a metaphorical language (of particles, waves, ether, *etc.*). Any of these components is susceptible to change, correction and improvement. However, rapid, fashion-like experimentally unmotivated changes, to which sceptics and relativists refer when they doubt the objectivity of science, in fact occur only in the third of the mentioned components, *viz.* in "indifferent hypotheses" clothed in the language of images and metaphors. The first two components are usually not affected by these upheavals and may be regarded as *invariants* under theoretical change (Poincaré 1905, 1958: last part). The cognitive content of a scientific theory is, however, exhaustively given by its empirical laws and by its formal structure. The former represents observable phenomena, the latter the relationships corresponding to "a profound reality" (Poincaré 1902, 1952: 161–2). Both represent "the truth which will ever remain the same in whatever garb we may see fit to clothe it" (Poincaré 1902, 1952: 162). What a theory asserts as true is that there exist definite relations between abstract objects to which we give different names at different times and which account for the observed phenomena. Two apparently rival theories which do not differ with respect to these two components are in fact equivalent.[6]

---

[6] Hans Reichenbach's account of Lande's interpretation of the duality of waves and particles within quantum theory (Reichenbach 1944; 1965: 17–23) in terms of what Reichenbach claims to be *his* "theory of equivalent descriptions" and in terms of the distinction between the phenomena and 'interphenomena' is very similar to Poincaré's view of theories which can be found in Poincaré's *Science and Hypothesis* (1902, 1952: especially in chapter X) as well

The growth of objective knowledge in science (physics) is possible because, and to the extent, that empirical laws and the formal structure of theories remain unaltered (the latter up to isomorphism) when one conceptual–theoretical (metaphorical or metaphysical) frame is replaced by another (Poincaré 1902, 1952: 160–5, 211–13). This claim, central to Poincaré's conventionalist philosophy of physics, may be given the name of the epistemological principle of relativity.[7]

Now, according to Poincaré, general principles such as Hamilton's principle of least action (in optics and in dynamics) or the principle of conservation of energy or of conservation of angular momentum have to be distinguished from ordinary laws of physics for several reasons. One of these is the fact that "they were obtained in the search for what there was in common in the enunciation of numerous physical laws", another being that on account of their generality they are no longer capable of verification or falsification in a direct fashion and in isolation, but are rather revoked on pragmatic grounds (*viz.* when they are no longer useful in predictions within a theory or branch of science). Since we cannot give a general definition of, or a unique empirical interpretation to, the term 'energy', "the principle of conservation of energy simply signifies that *there is something which remains constant*". Whatever future results of experiments may be we are certain beforehand that there is something which remains constant and which may be called energy. This does not mean that the principle of conservation of energy is a tautology, *i.e.* devoid of any empirical content unless we apply it (in conjunction with the determinist hypothesis) to the whole universe. What it means (when applied to limited, isolated systems) is that the term 'energy' has no unique empirical interpretation and that the principle of conservation of energy imposes only a structural, relational restriction on admissible interpretations of 'energy' when it is combined with different empirical laws in

as in (Poincaré 1905, 1958: last part; *cf.* Giedymin 1977). Here, as in his other writings, Reichenbach failed to give credit to Poincaré.

[7] One of the concerns of nineteenth-century mathematicians was to search for formulations of equations which would be independent of the choice of the type of co-ordinates (perpendicular, polar, *etc.*) or invariant under translation and rotation of a co-ordinate system in space. This concern was very much in evidence in Hamilton's papers on geometrical optics but, of course, especially in the papers in which he later applied the language of quaternions to optics and dynamics (Hamilton 1862, 1967: 465–7; 1847, 1967: 441–8). Poincaré frequently compared the choice of (the language of) a metric geometry to the choice of a co-ordinate system with respect to translatability (descriptive equivalence) and simplification of problems.

different applications of the theory or on different stages of the evolution of the theory (Poincaré 1902, 1952: 138–9, 166). The same applies to other principles: they serve to express the formal structure of the theory, *i.e.* the second of a theory's components distinguished in our account of Poincaré's views of the structure of a theory. They do it often in close connection with the metaphorical (or metaphysical) components. For example, from the molecular hypothesis within the undulatory theory "we borrow . . . two things – the principle of the conservation of energy and the linear form of the equations which is the general law of small movements as of all small variations" (Poincaré 1902; 1952: 212). The structure of the abstract part of a theory implicit in general principles, or in the form (order, degree) of a set of equations to which they are equivalent, enriches the empirical content of the theory as determined by the set of its directly testable laws. This seems to be the main point on which Poincaré's view of theories differs from Ramsey's, for Ramsey identified the empirical content of a theory with the totality of its empirical laws and despaired of the possibility of ever finding a definition of a theory's "form" or "structure" and of 'identity of form or structure'. Poincaré's idea of making the "mathematical form" of a theory – by which he meant the type of equations (ordinary or partial differential equations, their order, degree, *etc.*) – part of the concept of a theory's descriptive content was a vague anticipation of certain recent attempts to improve on the Ramsey view of theories (Sneed 1971). Poincaré emphasised one further function of general principles within physics. Their satisfaction in a given domain guarantees the existence of indefinitely many explanations of a certain type (defined in terms of relevant principles). In his account of Maxwell's method in the electromagnetic theory, which according to some commentators is one of the sources of Poincaré's physical conventionalism (or of his 'instrumentalism' as Duhem referred to it in this context), Poincaré pointed out that, for example, the necessary and sufficient condition for a *mechanical* explanation to be possible is that "we may choose the functions T and U (the kinetic and potential energy, respectively) so as to satisfy the principle of least action, and of the conservation of energy" (Poincaré 1902, 1952: 220–1). But whenever one explanation is possible an unlimited number is also possible, and no positive method can help us choose one of them rather than another. Poincaré saw the main feature of Maxwell's method in that "he throws into relief the essential – *i.e.* what is common to all theories; everything that suits only a particular theory is passed over almost in silence" (Poincaré 1902, 1952: 224). It seems that this feature of Maxwell's method was the continuation of the spirit we find in Hamilton's method in optics and dynamics, and that Poincaré in his philosophy of physics became the spokesman for both.

Poincaré had not only a synchronic but also a diachronic view of theories. In the evolution of mathematical physics he distinguished three stages each characterised by a different type of theory as paradigmatic. The first was "the physics of central forces", which originated from celestial mechanics and was modelled on the mechanics of point-masses. After a crisis a second stage followed, dominated by "the physics of the principles". No longer concerned mainly with uncovering hidden "ultimate elements" and their laws, physicists were satisfied with understanding the universe's mechanism in terms of abstract principles like the principle of conservation of mass, of energy, the principles of entropy, of least action, of relativity, *etc.* which yielded the desired predictions and left alternative explanations possible. Maxwell's electromagnetic theory was "the most remarkable example". A second crisis set in at the turn of the century with the critique of some of the principles mentioned. The characteristic features of the new physics to emerge were not quite clear but they would include "an entirely new mechanics" (with the velocity of light as the limiting velocity) and possibly the domination of all theoretical physics by statistical laws (Poincaré 1904, 1905, 1952: 91–5, 104, 110–11).

Presumably echoing Poincaré's typology of theories, though without its historical implications, Albert Einstein distinguished in 1919 among physical theories between "constructive theories" and "principle-theories"; he characterised the relativity theory as one of the latter type (Einstein 1954: 228).

We have claimed in this article that Poincaré had a different conception of the empirical content of a theory from Ramsey's, since the latter was identified with the set of all the observational consequences of the theory. The following should be noted, however. According to more recent research (Sneed 1971, for example) the Ramsey sentence of a theory T although observationally equivalent with T is, in a sense, stronger than the set of all the observational consequences of T: of all the models of the observational language of T only those are admitted by the Ramsey sentence of T which are extendable to the full models of T.

University of Sussex

REFERENCES

Abraham, R. & Marsden, J. E. 1967. *Foundations of Mechanics.* New York–Amsterdam

Duhem, D. 1906. *La Théorie Physique: Son Objet-Sa Structure.* Paris.

Duhem, P. 1969. *To Save The Phenomena,* trans. E. Doland and C. Maschler. Chicago–London.

Einstein, A. 1954. What is Relativity Theory? *Ideas and Opinions.* New York.

Giedymin, J. 1977. On the origin and significance of Poincaré's conventionalism, *Studies in History and Philosophy of Science,* **8**, No. 4.

Hamilton, W. R. (all references are to *The Mathematical Papers of Sir William Rowan Hamilton,* Cambridge.) 1931. Vol. I: *Geometrical Optics,* edited by A. W. Conway, J. L. Synge: 1828. Theory of Systems of Rays, 1–106; 1830. First supplement to an essay on the theory of systems of rays, 107–44; 1837. Third supplement to an essay on the theory of systems of rays, 164–293; 1831. On a view of mathematical optics, 295–6; 1833a. On some results of the view of a characteristic function in optics, 297–303; 1833b. On a general method of expressing the paths of light and of the planets, by the coefficients of a characteristic function, 311–32; Editors' Appendix Note 14. On the relation of Hamilton's optical method to dynamics, 484–7; Note 19 On the transition from the emission theory to the wave theory, 479–9; Note 20 On group velocity and wave mechanics, 500–2.

Hamilton, W. R. 1940. Vol. II: *Dynamics,* edited by A. W. Conway, A. J. McConnell: 1834a. On a general method in dynamics; by which the study of the motions of all free systems of attracting or repelling points is reduced to the search and differentiation of one central relation, or Characteristic Function, 103–60; 1834b. On the application to dynamics of a general mathematical method previously applied to optics, 212–16.

Hamilton, W. R. 1967. Vol. III: *Algebra,* edited by H. Halberstam, R. E. Ingram: 1833c. Theory of conjugate functions, or algebraic couples; with a preliminary and elementary essay on algebra as the science of pure time, 3–100; 1853. Preface to 'Lectures on Quaternions', 117–55.

Łukasiewicz, J., 1970. *Selected Works.* Amsterdam–London–Warsaw.

Peirce, Ch. 1958–60. *Collected Papers.* Cambridge, Mass.

Plücker, J., 1865. On a new geometry of space, *Philosophical Transactions of the Royal Society,* London, 725–91.

Poincaré, H., 1952. *Science and Hypothesis.* New York.

Poincaré, H., 1958. *The Value of Science*. New York.

Popper, K., 1963. *Conjectures and Refutations*. London.

Ramsey, F. P., 1978. Theories, *Foundations*. Essays in Philosophy, Logic, Mathematics and Economics, edited by D. H. Mellor. London.

Reichenbach, H., 1965. *Philosophical Foundations of Quantum Mechanics*. Berkeley.

Sneed, J., 1971. *The Logical Structure of Mathematical Physics*. Dordrecht.

Synge, J. L., 1937. *Geometrical Optics. Introduction to Hamilton's Method*. Cambridge.

Index of subjects

Index of names